S0-BYS-396

ANTHEMS

AND

ANTHEM COMPOSERS

Da Capo Press Music Reprint Series

GENERAL EDITOR

FREDERICK FREEDMAN

VASSAR COLLEGE

ANTHEMS

AND

ANTHEM COMPOSERS

AN ESSAY UPON THE DEVELOPMENT OF
THE ANTHEM FROM THE TIME OF THE
REFORMATION TO THE END OF THE
NINETEENTH CENTURY

BY MYLES BIRKET FOSTER

𝄐 DA CAPO PRESS · NEW YORK · 1970

A Da Capo Press Reprint Edition

This Da Capo Press edition of *Anthems and Anthem Composers*
is an unabridged republication of the first edition
published in London and New York in 1901.

Library of Congress Catalog Card Number 76-125047

SBN 306-70012-3

Published by Da Capo Press
A Division of Plenum Publishing Corporation
227 West 17th Street, New York, N. Y. 10011

ANTHEMS

AND

ANTHEM COMPOSERS

Henry Purcell,
from the painting by Clostermann.

ANTHEMS

AND

ANTHEM COMPOSERS

AN ESSAY UPON THE DEVELOPMENT
OF THE ANTHEM

*FROM THE TIME OF THE REFORMATION TO THE END
OF THE NINETEENTH CENTURY*

WITH A COMPLETE LIST OF ANTHEMS (IN ALPHABETICAL
ORDER) BELONGING TO EACH OF THE FOUR
CENTURIES, A FRONTISPIECE, AND
SEVERAL RARE PORTRAITS, &c.

BY

MYLES BIRKET FOSTER,

FELLOW OF THE ROYAL ACADEMY OF MUSIC; FELLOW OF THE ROYAL COLLEGE OF ORGANISTS;
FELLOW OF TRINITY COLLEGE, LONDON, &c.

LONDON : NOVELLO AND COMPANY, LIMITED
AND
NOVELLO, EWER AND CO., NEW YORK.
1901.

TO

SIR JOHN STAINER,

M.A., OXON.; D.C.L., DUNELM.; MUS.D., OXON. ET DUNELM.

A STRONG LINK IN THE GREAT CHAIN OF

ANTHEM COMPOSERS,

THIS WORK

IS RESPECTFULLY AND AFFECTIONATELY

DEDICATED.

Having received a much prized letter from the late Sir John Stainer last year, in which he accepted the above dedication in terms of well-nigh flattering kindness, I venture to retain the original inscription, in memory of a great and good man, and a true, faithful friend.

M. B. F.

PREFACE.

THE following short and, in many respects, imperfect essay on one of the most interesting sections of the music of the Church Service, is the extension of two lectures delivered by me a few years ago at Hampstead, on the invitation of Mr. J. D. Macey and others. I have been asked several times to amplify my original lectures upon the Anthem, and here is the result.

Whatever strength may be discovered in the work is not due to myself, but to the unfailing courtesy and assistance of the greatest living authorities on this subject.

To Dr. A. H. Mann (of Cambridge) and to Mr. J. S. Bumpus (of London), whose names alone carry conviction in any question dealing with the Church music of the past, I owe so great a debt that I can but feebly acknowledge here their invaluable guidance and help so courteously and freely given.

Without Dr. Mann's marvellous collection of Words of Anthems, my important list of these works would never have reached its present size, and failing a knowledge of Mr. Bumpus's superb library (many of the works being in the original MSS.) it would have been impossible to verify numbers of these anthems, the names of which I present to my readers. Mr. Bumpus has also revised the whole work.

Yet another good friend (Mr. C. T. Johnson) has rendered invaluable help to me in supplying most of the rare and interesting portraits which grace the book. I wish also to thank Mr. Barclay Squire and Mr. Hughes-Hughes (of the British Museum) for their generous assistance; Mr. Julian Marshall, for his courteous permission to use his rare portraits and works, and for all his kind help; Dr. W. H. Cummings, and the Royal Society of Musicians, for generously allowing me to reproduce their portrait of Henry Purcell as the frontispiece of this book; Dr. Philip Armes, Mr. Henry King (who most kindly read and revised the proofs), Dr. D. J. Wood (of Exeter); Mr. F. G. Edwards, Editor of the Musical Times ; Mr. David Baptie (of Glasgow) ; and other kind friends all over the United Kingdom, for their helpful suggestions and useful information.

To name the various books, periodicals, MSS., and catalogues which have been consulted for this work would involve a list of enormous length, starting from the Additional MSS. in the British Museum, and ending with Mr. Henry Davey's " History of English Music " and Mr. John E. West's admirable account of " Cathedral Organists " (1899).

As a proof of the interest at all times evinced in this style of sacred writing, it will be observed that the composers range from Archbishops, Princes, and Earls to the most humble of the Monarch's subjects.

Should my poor efforts kindle any fresh interest in the Anthem, or insure a stronger defence of its purity, or act as an incentive, however small, to a higher and more manly style of composition, my labour of love will not have been in vain.

MYLES B. FOSTER.

London, 1901.

CONTENTS.

LIST OF PORTRAITS.

ABBREVIATIONS EXPLAINED.

Add. MSS., Myriell MSS., &c., refer to the valuable Additional MSS. in the British Museum.

Arnold. = Samuel Arnold's "Collection of Cathedral Music," 4 vols., 1790.

Attwood. = Thomas Attwood's "Cathedral Music," edited by Dr. T. A. Walmisley, 1850.

Barnard. = Rev. J. Barnard's "Church Music," 1641.

Boyce. = William Boyce's "Cathedral Music," 1760.

Bumpus. = John S. Bumpus's unique collection, mostly MSS., in the composers' autograph.

Cath. Mag. = "The Cathedral Magazine." A Collection of Anthems, in 3 vols., 4to, c. 1780.

Canterbury, Carlisle, &c. = Books of Words of Anthems used in the Cathedrals named.

Choir. = Music published in "The Choir," a journal now defunct.

Chorister's Handbook. = A Collection of Anthems, edited by Joseph Warren, 2 vols., 1845.

Clifford. = Rev. James Clifford's Two Collections, 1661 and 1663.

Cope. = "Anthems by Composers of the English Church," by the Rev. Sir William Henry Cope, Bart. 8vo, 1846-50.

Corfe. = Joseph Corfe's "Cathedral Music," edited by Josiah Pittman.

Day. = Thomas Day's "Service Book," 1565.

Div. Har. = William Croft's "Divine Harmony," published in 1712; except in the case of Benjamin Cuzens, when the latter's "Divine Harmony" is intended.

Dublin. = MS. Scores in the Cathedrals of Christ Church and St. Patrick's, Dublin.

Ely. = The Collection of rare MS. Church Music in the Library of Ely Cathedral, a catalogue of which was printed by James Hawkins, Senr., Organist there from 1682 to 1729. A later edition, greatly enlarged, by Rev. W. E. Dickson, Precentor of Ely, was brought out in 1858.

Europ. Psal. = S. S. Wesley's "European Psalmist," 2 vols., 1872.

Fitzw. = Richard, the seventh Viscount Fitzwilliam's Collection (no date).

Fowle. = Thomas Lloyd Fowle's Collection of Anthems, 1873.

Hawes. = A Collection of Anthems and other Sacred Music, as sung at the Chapel Royal; folio, 1833, edited and published by W. Hawes.

Haycraft. = Henry Haycraft's two Collections of Sacred Music, folio, 1837 and 1851.

Husk. = W. H. Husk's Catalogues of the Library of the Sacred Harmonic Society, 1853, 1862, and 1872.

Joule. = B. St. John Baptist Joule's Collection of Words of 2,270 Anthems, 1859.

Langdon. = Richard Langdon's "Divine Harmony," 1774.

Mann. = Dr. A. H. Mann's unique Collection of Anthems, both in autograph and in print.

Marshall. = William Marshall's "Anthems used in the Cathedral and Collegiate Churches," 1840.

Mus. Antiq. = The Musical Antiquarian Society's Publications, edited 1845, &c., by Dr. E. F. Rimbault.

Nat. Psal. = Charles Danvers Hackett's "National Psalmist," 1839 and 1842.

Page. = John Page's "Harmonica Sacra," 1800.

Parish Choir. = Music published in "The Parish Choir," 1846-51.

Peterh. = The Collection of rare MS. Church Music in the Library of St. Peter's College, Cambridge; a catalogue of which was printed by Dr. Jebb, 1859.

Playford. = John Playford's "Divine Companion," 1701.

Publishers of Anthems include the names of *Addison, Boosey, Cramer, Gall and Inglis, Hime and Addison, Longman and Broderip, Lonsdale, Metzler, Novello, Parker, Patey and Willis, Ransford,* and *Weekes.*

Tenbury. = Anthems in the Library of the late Rev. Sir F. A. Gore Ouseley, at St. Michael's College, Tenbury.

Tudway. = Thomas Tudway's MS. "Collection of Anthems," 6 vols., 1715-20, in the Harleian Collection, British Museum.

Turle and Taylor. = "The People's Music Book," by these Editors, 1894.

Warren. = Preface to Joseph Warren's Edition of Boyce's Collection, 1849.

Weldon. = John Weldon's "Divine Harmony" (no date).

CHAPTER I.

INTRODUCTORY.—THE DERIVATION OF THE TERM ANTHEM.

THE subject of the following little essay is so extensive, and so closely connected with the chronicles of the Reformed Church of England and the very History of England itself, that, in venturing to present it to my readers, in however poor and incomplete a form, I have thought it a good plan to divide the matter into centuries and, as far as compatible with undisputed facts, to make each century the repository of a particular style or form of anthem.

Considering our history broadly, this will be found to be correct, although the styles overlap one another and finally are all more or less in use at the same time ; however, I venture to speak of the first period, or from the Reformation until the forty-third year of Queen Elizabeth's reign—*roughly*, the sixteenth century—as the " Motet " Period ; of the second period—the seventeenth century, or from the end of Queen Elizabeth's reign to the tenth year of King William III., as the " Verse " Period ; of the third period— the eighteenth century, or from King William III. to the thirty-ninth year of King George III.'s reign, as the " Mixed " or " Degenerate " Period ; and finally of the fourth period—up to the end of the nineteenth century, as the " Modern," one might fairly say " Victorian," era.

Of the composers living and working throughout these four centuries, from the commencement of the anthem to its latest and fullest development, it is my purpose to treat, giving you a short account of each of the leaders of his period ; but the true history of the Anthem will be found in the (as far as possible) complete list of works from King Henry VIII.'s day to the present year of grace, the record of which has survived the wrath of the bigot and the fire of the ignorant Revolutionists ; many are still in MS., but many notable examples are in print, some in separate voice parts, some in score.

These lists are also arranged in centuries, according to the date of each writer's birth, and, both as regards the anthems and their composers, are in alphabetical order.

Concerning the derivation of the term of this peculiar heritage of the Church of England, the " Anthem," there is to this day much doubt and considerable diversity of opinion.

It is supposed by many that *Anthem* is a corruption of *Antiphon.* 'Aντίφωνοι were originally intended to mean sounds in octaves, responsive to, or over against one another ; but in later times the term was applied to the alternate singing of choirs.   In the early Christian services at Antioch, Flavian introduced a system of Antiphonal singing, in which a choir of women and boys was responded to by men's voices.   But even in the Old Testament there appears to be sufficient evidence that the Jews knew of this mode of singing, and that David, "the sweet singer of Israel," designed many of his Psalms with this object in view.

The dividing of our choirs into Decani and Cantoris is but a continuation of the same idea, and when Chaucer alludes, in the Canterbury Tales, to the Antym, we presume that he means the Anti-hymnus, or singing of a hymn from side to side of the choir.

Another derivation, supported by many earnest students, is from ἄνθος, *a flower,* and it is worthy of remark that certain very old Anthem or Antiphon books are named Antho-logia, which might be translated " Nosegays ! "   Not to weary the reader too much in what must of necessity be the driest part of this essay, I will briefly add my own suggestion that "Anthem" *might be* derived from part of ἀνατίθημι, a verb meaning to set up or dedicate as an offering. Thus " Anthem " could mean "A votive offering," and, as such, I hope and pray it may ever be regarded; as such alone is it possible for us to introduce it worthily into man's service of praise and prayer to the Maker of " all things bright and beautiful."   Whatever the proper derivation of the term may be, the modern definition of an anthem is " A composition for voices, with or without accompaniment, to be sung as part of the service of God's House."   This definition is sufficiently broad to include *any music* set to sacred words ; but in this little work I have endeavoured to eliminate all movements originally composed with some other object in view, such as excerpts from larger works, Cantatas or Oratorios, and, above all, movements torn from Masses and Services, and adapted to words which are foreign to their original connection ; and I desire to present to your notice those complete works *only,* which were written *as Anthems,* and intended to be introduced in those positions in which, " in Quires and Places where they sing," the Anthem followed.

I am convinced that, however fine these adaptations may be, and however appropriate to God's worship, they are not strictly and in the first place to be regarded as Anthems.

CHAPTER II.

ORIGIN OF THE ANTHEM.

THERE exists no such mystery in regard to the origin of the Anthem as pertains to the derivation of the term.

The Anthem is simply the successor to the Motet, from which form it has been developed.

Some of the earliest anthems *were* motets, with their Latin words translated into English. The anthem dates from the Reformation, and has continued to thrive more or less vigorously up to the present day, only excepting the cruel years of the Civil War.

Had Luther resembled Calvin and certain other reformers, we might never have had any anthems at all; but his belief in the power of music as a means of worship is evident in both his writings and his speeches. "I am not of opinion," he says, "that through the Gospel all arts should be banished and driven away as some zealots want us to believe, but I wish to see all arts, principally music, in the service of Him who gave and created them."

He calls music one of the greatest gifts of the Creator, and gives it the first place next to divinity.

From about the sixteenth century, an anthem was permitted as part of the Church Service, and early in Queen Elizabeth's reign were issued the "Queen's Injunctions," granting permission for the use of a "Hymn or *such like song* in churches"; but it was not until the final revision of our Prayer Book, in King Charles II.'s reign, that the rubric stood as it does nowadays, after the third Collect in morning and evening service—viz., "In Quires and Places where they sing, here followeth the Anthem."

As already stated, the anthem grew out of the motet, a simple form, not unlike an extended hymn tune in some cases, and not until the seventeenth century did this "Motet" form give place to the solo and verse anthem, no longer independent, as the earlier form was, of accompaniment upon an instrument.

Later still, we find no *new* forms, but combinations of solo, verse, and full anthems, and, finally, the Modern Period, in which both vocal and instrumental resources find their most advanced development.

Whether this evolution has always been for the better, and whether improvements in instruments have led to similar advances in reverent and intelligent singing is a matter of opinion, upon which some light may be thrown in the pages of this short, and, I fear, very incomplete little history.

CHAPTER III.

THE FIRST PERIOD.

The first period, already alluded to as the "Motet" Period, extended (roughly speaking) from 1520 to 1625; in other words, from the eleventh year of King Henry VIII.'s reign until the death of King James I.

The early motet must have been a fairly gay, lively composition as compared with the plain-song, for Morley, in his well-known "Introduction to Musicke," speaks of a motet as a " Song made for the Church, either upon some Hymn or Anthem or such-like," and considers that the name is given " in opposition to the other, which they called canto-fermo, and which we do commonlie call plain-song " ; and he adds that the " name of *moving* (moto) was given because it is in a manner quight contrarie to the other, which after some sorte, and in respect of the other, standeth stille."

Just as from Dufay's time in 1400 secular melodies and popular ballad airs of the period were often used for the *Cantus-fermus*, so, on the other hand, the motet, solemn enough as far as the music was concerned, was at first set to words of a decidedly profane character ; to such an extent was this the case that the Church, corrupt as it was, issued decrees forbidding the use of the motet in the service.

By degrees the growth of musical study and knowledge enabled composers to rely more upon their own conceptions and to discard the use of these secular tunes, whilst a keener sense of what was decent and reverent led them towards the use of words either from the Psalms or other parts of Holy Scripture, of course in Latin.

This was the kind of motet which the Reformation was shortly to convert into a full anthem, the nature of which was contrapuntal, reverent, strong, and, by certain modern ears, would be considered somewhat heavy.

Try to realise the troublous and ever-changing times in which our earliest anthem composers had to work.

King Henry VIII., brought up a strict Roman Catholic, would be alternately alarmed and attracted by that great movement of which Luther was the head. One day he was receiving from the Pope the title of " Defender of the Faith " (a title still retained by our monarchs) as a reward for his pamphlet denouncing Luther and his reforms, and another day he would be disgracing Wolsey, and sacking and demolishing monastic institutions ; at one moment professing to maintain the Catholic doctrines and guard the imagined purity of his tenets; at another, sanctioning the publication of the complete Bible *in English*, and ordering it to be placed in every Parish Church in the Kingdom!

Can we not picture the puzzled state of these poor composers, never knowing whether, by setting their music to the new English words, they would be burned alive, or, by using the old Latin ones, they would be hanged!

CHAPTER IV.

THE EARLIEST ANTHEM WRITERS.

The man who must be regarded as the leader amongst the first composers of anthems is undoubtedly John Redford, born in 1491, and an organist of S. Paul's, the *old* Cathedral, early in the sixteenth century. Of his work, we possess one anthem, " Rejoice in the Lord alway," a fine, broad, contrapuntal work, which compares favourably with any composition of that day, whether English or Continental, and is sufficient proof that music in England stood at this period on a high level, fully equal to the writings of the schools of Italy and the Netherlands. Redford died in 1547.

He was one of a school of men who were at work when the first flicker of the Reformation fires began to show itself, and several of these scholarly composers suffered in consequence from that uncertainty to which allusion was made in the last chapter. Amongst these pioneers was John Taverner, organist of Boston Church in Lincolnshire, and of Christ Church College, Oxford, who narrowly escaped a martyr's end ; his Anthems exist in MS.

Then there were Mark Smeaton, executed in 1536, and Thomas Abel, who suffered the same death in 1540; George Etheridge, born at Thame, in Oxfordshire, and Robert Parsons, who was born at Exeter, and was drowned in the Trent at Newark in 1569, and several others, whose anthems, if extant, are in MS. still. The works of these early writers, which escaped the destruction and dismantling of the monasteries, did eventually perish in large numbers during the wanton spoliation by the followers of Cromwell.

King Henry VIII. should be introduced at this point, not only in the character of patron of the school whose members we have named above, but also as a reputed anthem composer.

He was, without doubt, a well-educated musician in many branches of the art.   In those days it was part of every gentle-born person's education to play an instrument and take part in reading a madrigal at sight.   Even more marked were these accomplishments in Shakespeare's time, when the English Madri-galian School was at its zenith.

But in King Henry's case there was the additional reason for being duly instructed in music, that it was originally intended that he should enter the Church.   In those days music was an essential subject in the education of the clergy.   Would that such were the case nowadays!   What discomforts and heartburnings would be removed if organists and choirmen had to deal with educated musicians, when either vicar or curate asserted his rights in matters of Church service.   The anthem " O Lord, the Maker of all thing " is attributed to the king, although Barnard and others say that William Mundy wrote it.   More recently, Dr. Armes, of Durham, has discovered that neither the king nor Mundy wrote the anthem, but that it was the work of John Sheparde, or Shepherd, organist of Magdalen College, 1542-1547.

CHAPTER V.

TYE, TALLIS, AND FARRANT.

WITH the music of Tye, the old vagueness of tonality is fast disappearing ; and, in fact, we are approaching that powerful period in English music in which contrapuntal skill reaches its highest position and the writing is, in the best sense, polyphonic ; an equal melodic interest being given to each part, from the highest to the lowest.

Christopher Tye, the date of whose birth is not known, took his musical degrees at Cambridge, and became Mus. Doc., Oxon. (*ad eundem*), in 1548.   He was a chorister and Gentleman of the Chapel Royal, and, from 1541 to 1562, was organist of Ely Cathedral.   Tye was also in Orders.

In 1553, a month or two before Edward VI.'s death, he published an extraordinary work ; the first fourteen chapters of the Acts of the Apostles, translated by him into English metre, and set to his music, " with notes to eche to synge and also to play upon the Lute."

THOMAS TALLIS.

WILLIAM BIRD

The music is wonderfully melodious and free from the stilted manner of the earlier schools, its contrapuntal intricacies being so gracefully clothed as to be forgotten ; but the words are very funny and rather of the Sternhold and Hopkins order. Let me give a specimen :—

> It chanced at Iconium,
> As they oft times did use,
> Together they into dyd cum
> The Sinagoge of Jues.

He advertises his work in an amusing way on the title-page, as " very necessarye for studentes, after theyre studye, to file theyre wittes, and also for all Christians that cannot synge to read the goode and godlye storyes of the lives of Christ hys Apostles."

Dr. Tye taught King Edward VI. music, and he died about 1580, in Queen Elizabeth's reign. But few of his anthems are published. He composed many, of which Christ Church (Oxford) Library has seven, besides motets. No doubt the anthems were, most of them written to the Latin, and then adapted to the English words. Amongst published ones we find " O come, ye servants of the Lord," * " I will exalt Thee," " Sing unto the Lord," " Mock not God's Name," " Let Thy loving mercy come also unto me," and " O Lord, Thy word endureth."

Thomas Tallis (or Tallys), the exact date of whose birth is, like Tye's, uncertain, though it must have been very early in the sixteenth century, is better known, perhaps, than any of his *confrères* to the English churchman, not so much through the medium of his anthems as of his celebrated Preces, Responses, and Litany, used (in a four-part arrangement) to this day. These were composed in Edward VI.'s reign, shortly after the Prayer Book was authorised in its new form by the young king, but they were not *printed* until 1641.

He has been dubbed the " Father of English Cathedral Music," and it is marvellous what an amount of work he accomplished during a very long life.

Beginning as a chorister of old St. Paul's, he seems to have been transferred to the Chapel Royal Choir, to have been a Gentleman of that Chapel during four reigns, and organist of it in the time of Queen Elizabeth.

Until King Henry broke up Waltham Abbey in 1540, Tallis had been organist there also, having been appointed when quite a youth. When, as a result of the dissolution of the monastery, he was dismissed, he received " twenty shillings for wages and twenty shillings for reward."

In those days a pound was of greater specific value than at present.

---

* Originally set to " It chanced," &c., referred to above.

Tallis and his pupil Byrd, whose acquaintance we shall make in Chapter VII., composed, the former sixteen, the latter eighteen of the first set of *Cantiones Sacræ*, a collection of motets, especially celebrated, as they were *printed* under Letters Patent in 1575. The two patentees obtained sole right to print music and ruled music paper for twenty-one years.

The printing of notes from movable types, in place of the old wooden blocks, was the invention of Petrucci, in 1502. At this time Tallis composed his wonderful Song of Forty Parts: " Spem in alium non habui," written for eight choirs of five voices each. This *tour de force* was recently revived.

It seems extraordinary that he should have remained a Gentleman of the Chapel during the reigns of King Henry VIII., King Edward VI., Queen Mary, and Queen Elizabeth, but, to quote from Grove's admirable Dictionary, " like his contemporary, the Vicar of Bray, he outwardly conformed to whatever form of worship was the safest and most fashionable," and by this time-serving he managed to retain his post until his death.

One is inclined to think that he died in the older faith, from his evident predilection for Latin words up to nine years before his death, which occurred on November 23, 1585.

He was buried in the chancel of the Parish Church of Greenwich, where a brass quaintly records the chief events of his active life ; the original having been removed, a new one was placed there by admirers of Tallis's genius in 1876.

A blending of dignity and power with great grace and expression is the chief feature in Tallis's writings. Of his anthems the following are published: " All people that on earth do dwell," " Come, Holy Ghost," " Hear the voice and prayer," " I call and cry," in addition to Motets, such as " Salvator mundi " and " Caro mea vera est cibus," appearing also as " If ye love Me."

A great number of MS. anthems in English, as well as Latin motets, are preserved in the British Museum, Christ Church, the Music School, and St. John's College, Oxford, Peterhouse College, and the Fitzwilliam Museum, Cambridge, and other libraries, including that of the Sacred Harmonic Society, now the property of the Royal College of Music, London.

Richard Farrant, of the same school of writers, shows, in his humbler way, an even more delicate, graceful feeling than the great Tallis himself. His style was almost Italian, and bore some resemblance to the compositions of Giovanni della Croce, the Maestro di Capello of St. Mark's, Venice, in 1560. The date of his birth is unknown; he was, as all good musicians appear to have been, a Gentleman of the Chapel Royal, only resigning this post in order to take up the position of Master of the Children, Lay Vicar, and Organist of St. George's Chapel, Windsor. He was reinstated in the Chapel Royal in 1569, and remained there until his death, on November 30, 1580.

The published anthems of his, so well known and beloved by Church singers, "Call to remembrance," "Hide not Thou Thy face," and "Lord, for Thy tender mercies' sake,"* make one regret that a greater number are not preserved to us.

That English art at this time was fully acknowledged by visitors from the continental courts is evident from an interesting correspondence, quoted by Mr. W. S. Rockstro, between the Venetian Ambassador at the Court of King Henry VIII. and his friend in Italy. Amongst other laudatory remarks, the former writes: "The Mass was sung by His Majesty's choristers, whose voices were more divine than human. They did not chaunt like men, but gave praise like Angels."

CHAPTER VI.

OTHER SIXTEENTH CENTURY ANTHEM COMPOSERS.

I WILL devote this chapter, by way of relief, to lesser lights of the sixteenth century—that is, lesser in connection with the subject under consideration—before approaching Byrd and the great Gibbons family.

It is satisfactory to note that many of the men, whose genius in madrigal writing placed England in the forefront of the musical nations of Europe, were contributors to sacred music; amongst those to be found in my list being Dowland, Ford, Richard Edwardes, Benet, Bateson, Michael Este, Morley, Mundy, and

---

* I extract the following remarks from a letter addressed by the Rev. John Hanson Sperling to the Editor of the *Parish Choir*, Dec. 3, 1850, on the subject of "Lord, for Thy tender mercies' sake": "It seems very doubtful whether he (Farrant) was its real author, none of its cadences bearing any resemblance to the extant writings of Richard Farrant. Dr. Rimbault is of opinion that it is unquestionably the production of a later age."

"Besides the anthem bearing a remarkable resemblance to Hilton's other known compositions, there is strong external evidence of his being its real author."

The reverend gentleman points out the fact that Dr. Blow, Dr. Tudway, and James Hawkins attribute the work to John Hilton, as do the old MS. part-books in Ely Cathedral Library; whilst, on the other hand, we know that it did not publicly appear under Farrant's name until about 1770, in *The Cathedral Magazine*. He further suggests that "it was, in the hurry and great demand for MS. music at the Restoration, copied out anonymously, and afterwards ignorantly attributed to Farrant."

Weelkes, including most of the contributors to the " Triumphs of Oriana," Thomas Morley's great collection of madrigals in praise of the Virgin Queen Elizabeth.

Most of the organists and gentlemen of the Chapels Royal and the Cathedrals were also composers of anthems, one of the most prolific being Adrian Batten, who was vicar-choral and organist of St. Paul's about 1624. His works contain all the solemnity of style and the purity of part-writing that one finds in Tallis, and his anthems have lived until the present time and may still be heard in Westminster Abbey, of which he was a lay-vicar. He wrote over fifty anthems to our knowledge. The Tomkins family were also composers of a large number, the Reverend Thomas Tomkins having written 104, nearly all of which are forgotten! The style of these writers was contrapuntal, grave, and dignified, although a certain delicate grace was occasionally discernible, possessing all that dignity which is imparted to the gentle smile that may at rare moments be seen to light up the rugged visage of an old, hardened warrior.

Glorious beyond description is this period of breadth in idea, sublimity in motive, with the nobility and discipline of artistic restraint, applied with but little distinction to sacred and secular works alike. For at this time, as I mention in writing of Orlando Gibbons, there was the greatest similarity between the music of the madrigal and that of the anthem, and not so much " by their works" as by their *words* could you tell them.

Dr. John Bull, whose typical English name, in its supposed connection with " God save the King," has caused so much controversy and discussion, wrote about a dozen anthems. He was organist of Hereford Cathedral from 1582 and died in 1628.

It is very difficult to find records of the birth and death of many of these early writers, nor, in the majority of cases, is the history of their lives known. But, so far as it has been possible, I have preceded the list of their anthems with all the available dates and data that might prove interesting to my readers.

We have, preserved to us, the words of over twelve anthems apiece (and the music of several in Ely, Oxford, Cambridge, &c.) composed by Edward Holmes, organist of the Abbey; Nathaniel Giles, of the Chapel Royal; Michael Este, of Lichfield; Henry Lawes, of whom Milton wrote,* stripped of all his appointments in the Chapel Royal by the Commonwealth; and Thomas Morley, organist of St. Paul's. William Mundy and Thomas Weelkes have to their credit fully twenty each.

---

* " Whose tuneful and well-measured song
    First taught our English music how to span
    Words with just note and accent, not to scan
    With Midas' ears, committing short and long."   SONNET XIII.

One thing is difficult for us, in these over-populated, ultra-competitive times, to clearly comprehend—viz., how these men, living in much less peaceful years than ours, and having, instead of the stable rule of one good and virtuous sovereign, frequent changes in both monarch and creed, composed anthems only as the spirit and the occasion inspired them, copied out all the parts in MS., and had no thought for either public or publisher, writing simply for art's sake and for the glory of God.

In our times of comparative security, some, thank God, are writing from the highest motives, but others disfigure their compositions with the limitations consequent upon such questions as " Will they pay " ? or " Am I making them sufficiently popular to insure the necessary sale of so many copies " ?

CHAPTER VII.

BYRD AND THE GIBBONS FAMILY.

WILLIAM BYRD, the pupil of Tallis, is best remembered by his celebrated Canon " Non nobis, Domine." As an anthem writer he is not so generally recognised nowadays. His Libri I., II., Cantionum sacrarum, were published under the patent already alluded to in connection with Tallis, his master. He also wrote four anthems as a contribution towards Sir William Leighton's " Teares and Lamentacions of a Sorrowfull Soule," in 1614. Amongst his published anthems are " O Lord, turn Thy wrath," " Bow Thine ear," and " Sing joyfully."

About his birthday and parentage there appear to be several theories; it is conjectured that he was a son of Thomas Byrd, a Gentleman of the Chapel Royal in the reigns of King Edward VI. and Queen Mary; then there was a theory that he sang in old St. Paul's as senior chorister in 1554, which would fix his birth at about 1540; and a third idea is that he was the son of a former Mayor of Newcastle, who died, 1512, in Lincoln. As William Byrd died in 1623 this would make him 112 years old ! According to all accounts he *was* a very old man when he died, and was held in the greatest veneration. In the " Cheque Book " of the Chapel Royal he is styled " A Father of Musicke," and his pupil, Morley, writes of him as " My loving maister, never without reverence to be named of the Musicians." He is, perhaps, the most curious illustration of the confusion and instability existing in regard to religious matters. As he was not a very amiable person, it can only be due (Mr. Barclay Squire reasonably suggests) to his powerful and influential friends, and to the veneration in which he was held as a musician, that he, a Roman Catholic, should still be holding office in the Chapel Royal far into Queen Elizabeth's reign. It is distinctly curious, because, whilst actually in possession of a house and lands confiscated from a Catholic recusant, and holding his position in the Protestant service, both he and his family were undoubtedly Roman Catholics, and, as such, had been excommunicated by the Archidiaconal Court of Essex!

The last, but by no means the least, of those to whom I shall refer as belonging to the "Motet" period of anthem writers is Orlando Gibbons. The family of Gibbons was noted for its musicians. They lived in Cambridge, of which town the father, William Gibbons, was a Wait. Waits, in those days, were the licensed musical watchmen, attached either to corporations or to the households of nobles,* and they played upon a kind of hautboy, called a *wait;* hence their name.

Let us hope that they did not make night so hideous as certain bodies of peripatetic musicians have a habit of doing nowadays for three weeks before Christmas!

The eldest son, Rev. Edward Gibbons, born 1570, graduated at Cambridge as Bachelor of Music, and in 1592 was incorporated at Oxford. At this time he received the appointment of organist, priest-vicar, sub-chanter, and master of the choristers to Bristol Cathedral. These he resigned in 1611, on being appointed organist and custos of the College of Priest-Vicars to Exeter Cathedral, where he remained until the organ and choir were silenced, most likely during Fairfax's campaign in the West in 1645.

It must have been in these sad days that he wrote his anthem "How hath the city sate desolate," which had a prelude for the organ and an accompaniment for viols.

It is reported that he "lent" King Charles £1,000 for war expenses, and that, in consequence, his estate was confiscated, and he, when over eighty years old, was turned out of house and home.

Matthew Locke, the supposed writer of the music to "Macbeth," was a pupil of his in Exeter.

The next brother, Ellis Gibbons, was organist of Salisbury Cathedral until the commencement of the seventeenth century.

The youngest son, the greatest of them all, Orlando Gibbons, was born in 1583, and was, perhaps, the finest composer and organist of his period; nay, one of the best musicians England has produced.

---

* Until quite recently the Waits of the City of Westminster were sworn in before the Court of Burgesses!

About the commencement of King James I.'s reign he was appointed organist of the Chapel Royal. In 1622 he was permitted to "accumulate" the degrees of Mus. Bac. and Mus. Doc. at Oxford, a distinction conferred at the request of Camden, the noted historian.

For his degree exercise he wrote the eight-part anthem " O clap your hands."

In 1623 he succeeded John Parsons as organist of Westminster Abbey, and, just two years later, whilst in Canterbury, preparing for the performance of his wedding-music at the marriage of the new king, Charles I., with Princess Henrietta of France, he died of apoplexy, only a month or so after the death of King James I.

Great as are the madrigals of Orlando Gibbons, it is his grand, solemn church music which has gained for him the title of " The English Palestrina."

In 1614 he contributed two compositions to Leighton's "Teares." There are also several anthems in Barnard's and Boyce's collections and others in Ouseley's. Such fine examples as "Hosanna," "Lift up your heads," and " Almighty and everlasting God " are likely to live for ever.

Up to this period it is remarkable how similar is the style of both madrigal and anthem, the latter, excepting in the character of the words, being almost identical with the secular music of the age.

You need only to compare Gibbons's beautiful madrigal " The Silver Swan" with one of his anthems, in order to prove this. Notice another point, that nearly all the anthems written before this same period could be sung without any accompaniment; the reason being that, although (as Dr. Ritter of Vassar College wisely observes) a great number of instruments were known and in use in the sixteenth century, instrumental music made but slow progress, as compared with the high degree of perfection reached by vocal music. Composers directed their chief attention to the latter form of art.

Whether William Byrd's quaint appeal in favour of learning to sing helped on this state of things, I know not; but his reasons are so amusing, that I extract them from his Preface to " Songs of Sadness "—

1. It is a knowledge easily taught and quickly learned, where there is a good master and an apt scoller.
2. The exercise of singing is delightful to nature, and good to preserve the health of man.
3. It doth strengthen all parts of the breast and doth open the pipes.
4. It is a singular good remedie for a stutting and stammering in the speech.
5. It is the best means to procure a perfect pronounciation and to make a good orator.
6. It is the only way to find out where nature hath bestowed the benefit of a good voice.

7. Because there is no music of instruments whatever to be compared to the voyces of men, when they are good, well-sorted and ordered.

8. The better the voyce, the meeter it is to honour and serve God therewith, and the voyce of man is chiefly to be employed to that end.

Since singing is so good a thing
I wish all men would learn to sing.

The eighth reason for learning to sing, in order to worthily join in the music of the Church service, may be commended to every earnest and intelligent churchman ; for the anthem, the subject proper of this little book, is the *only* portion of all the service music which the congregation are *not* to join in.

In concluding the first period, let us look back over the history and experiences of the early years through which we have just passed.

Starting in the reign of that regal musician, Bluff King Hal, we found the old form of worship extant, and in its service was included the motet. Then came the great Reformation, and Luther, musician as well as reformer, was appearing on the horizon. We have already observed his remarks about Music. With the Reformation came the anthem, in the guise of a motet with *English* words, which continued into King Edward VI.'s short reign ; then came the five years of Queen Mary's cruelty, and with them the return of the old Latin forms. It was fortunate for the anthem, as for many other things, that her reign was so short.

Finally, under the rule of Queen Elizabeth, the "Oriana" of the madrigal writers, the Protestant form was re-established. One cannot but feel proud of the nation's talent, and of the countless stores of noble contrapuntal works, whether sacred or secular, produced at a time in which neither oratorio nor opera had been heard of, or even invented.

ORLANDO GIBBONS.

LIST OF ANTHEMS AND COMPOSERS OF THE SIXTEENTH CENTURY.

ALLISON, RICHARD. B. latter half of 16th century; D. *c.* 1610.
Composed "The Psalms of David in Meter," 1599; "An Hour's Recreation in Musick," 1606.

1. Have mercy upon me   *Durham* | 2. O Lord, bow down   *King's*

AMNER, Rev. JOHN, Mus.B., Oxon., 1613; Cantab., 1640. D. 1641.
Org. Ely Cath.,1610-41.

1. A stranger here	*Ely*	11. Lord, I am not high-minded	*Ely*
2. Blessed are those	*Bumpus*	12. Lord, in Thy wrath	,,
3. Blessed be the Lord	*Ely*	13. O come hither	,,
4. Christ rising	,,	14. O God my King	,,
5. Glory be to God	,,	15. O Lord, of Whom I do depend	,,
(*For Easter Communion.*)		16. O sing unto the Lord	*Peterh.*
6. Hear, O Lord	,,	17. Out of the deep	,,
7. How doth the city remain		18. O ye little flock	,,
solitary	*Peterh.*	19. Rejoice, rejoice	*Ely*
8. I will sing unto the Lord	*Ely*	20. Remember not, Lord	,,
9. Lift up your heads	*Peterh.*	21. Sing, O heavens	,,
10. Like as the hart	*Clifford*	22. Woe is me	*Peterh.*

AYLEWARD, RICHARD. B. —; D. 1669.
Org. Norwich Cath., 1660-69.

1. Almighty and everlasting God
2. Blow the trumpet in Zion
3. Gently, Father, doe not bruise
4. Great God, with all the world made flesh
5. Hark! methinks I hear the trumpet
6. Have pity upon me
7. Holy, Holy, Holy
8. I charge you, O ye daughters of Jerusalem
9. I was glad
10. O how amiable are Thy tabernacles
11. O Jerusalem, thou that killest
12. O Jesus sweet
13. O that I were as in months past
14. Praise bee unto our God
15. Sweet Saviour
16. The King shall rejoice
17. Who could bring down this high and lofty one?
18. Why should this world be pleasing to us?

All in Dr. Mann's library.

BARCROFT (BACROFTE), Rev. GEORGE, B.A. D. 1609.
Org. Ely Cath., 1579.

1.*O Almighty God   *Ely* | 2. O Lord, we beseech Thee   *Ely*

---

* Attributed to *Thomas* Barcroft, by Tudway.

BATESON, THOMAS, Mus.B., Dublin. B. late in 16th century.

Org. Chester Cath., 1599; Christ Church Cath., Dublin, 1608. The *first* Dublin Bachelor of Music. A writer of Madrigals and contributor to the "Triumphes of Oriana."

1. Holy, Lord God Almighty
   Mus. Antiq. |

BATTEN, ADRIAN. B. c. 1590; D. probably 1637.

Pupil of John Holmes at St. Paul's; Lay-Vicar of Westminster Abbey, 1614, and Vicar-Choral and Org. St. Paul's Cath., 1624.

1. Almighty God, Which madest　*Clifford*
2. Almighty God, who in Thy wrath　,,
   (*Composed during the Plague,* 1625.)
3. Almighty God, Whose praise　,,
4. Behold, I bring you.
5. Behold, now praise　*Clifford*
6. Blessed are all they　*Peterh.*
7. Bow down Thine ear　*Clifford*
8. But let all those.
9. Christ, our paschal Lamb　*Clifford*
10. *Christ rising　,,
11. Deliver us, O Lord our God　,,
12. Godliness is great riches　,,
13. God so (so God) loved the world　,,
14. Haste Thee, O God　*Barnard*
15. Have mercy upon me　*Clifford*
16. Hear my prayer, O God, and hide not　*Peterh.*
17. Hear my prayer, and with Thine ears consider　,,
18. Hear the prayers, O our God　*Clifford*
19. Hide not Thou Thy face　*Barnard*
20. Holy, Holy, Holy　*Clifford*
    (*For Trinity Sunday.*)
21. I am the Resurrection　,,
22. If ye love Me　,,
23. I heard a voice from Heaven　,,
    (*For Michaelmas.*)
24. In Bethlehem town　,,
    (*For "Twelfth Eve."*)
25. Jesus said unto Peter　*Peterh.*
    (*St. Peter's Day.*)

26. Let my complaint　*King's*
27. Lord, I am not high-minded *Husk*
28. Lord, we beseech Thee　*Barnard*
29. Lord, who shall dwell?　*Clifford*
30. My soul truly waiteth　*King's*
31. Not unto us, O Lord　*Clifford*
32. O clap your hands　,,
33. O God, my heart is ready　,,
34. O God, the King of Glory.
35. O God, Thou art my righteousness　*Boyce*
36. O how happy a thing it is　*Clifford*
37. O Lord, let me know mine end　*Peterh.*
38. O Lord our Governour　*Clifford*
39. O Lord, Thou hast searched me out　,,
40. O praise God in His holiness　,,
41. O praise the Lord, all ye heathen　,,
42. O praise the Lord, laud ye *Barnard*
43. O sing joyfully.
44. O sing unto the Lord　*Clifford*
45. Out of the deep　*Barnard*
46. Ponder my words　*Clifford*
47. Praise the Lord, O my soul　,,
48. Save us, { Good Lord, } { O God, while } waking　,,
49. Shew us Thy mercy　*Chester*
50. Sing we merrily　*Clifford*
    (*Composed* 1623.)
51. The Lord is my Shepherd　,,
52. Turn Thou us, O good Lord　,,
    (*For Ash Wednesday.*)
53. We beseech Thee　,,
54. When the Lord turned　*Barnard*

BECK, ANTHONY.

Precentor of Norwich Cathedral.

1. Who can tell how oft　*Bumpus* |

---

* Easter Anthems as entered in the earlier Prayer Book.

BENET (BENNETT), JOHN. B. c. 1570 ; D. c. 1615.

Contributor to " Triumphes of Oriana."

1. O God of gods   Clifford | Pt. 2. To the Almighty

BEVIN, ELWAY. B. c. 1570 ; D. c. 1650.

Pupil of Tallis; Master of W. Child; Org. Bristol Cath. and Gent. Extraordinary of the Chapel Royal, 1589-1637.

1. Bow down Thine ear   Fitzw. | 4. O praise the Lord of Heaven Fitzw.
   (MS. organ part only.) | (MS. Organ part only.)
2. Hear my crying. | 5. Praise the Lord   Barnard
3. My God, my God   Fitzw. | 6. Turn us, O God.
   (MS. Organ part only.) |

BLACKWELL, ISAAC. B. late in the 16th century.

Composer of " Choice Ayres, Songs, and Dialogues to the Theorbo-lute and bass-violo," 1657.

1. O Lord our Governor   Ely |

BULL, JOHN, MUS. DOC., OXON. B. 1562 ; D. (at Antwerp) 1628.

Pupil of Wm. Blitheman ; Org. Hereford Cath., 1582; Org. and Gent. of the Chapel Royal, 1585 ; First Gresham Professor, 1596-1617; Musician to Prince Henry, 1611 ; Org. Notre Dame, Antwerp, 1617-28.

1. Almighty God   Fitzw. | 7. In Thee, O Lord   Clifford
   (Differing from No. 2.) | 8. Let me tread in the
2. Almighty God, Which by | right path   Myriell MSS.
   the leading   Clifford| 9. O God, best Guide.
   (" Star " Anthem.) | 10. O God, Who by the leading.
3. Attend unto my tears. | (Same as No. 2.)
4. Deliver me, O Lord   Barnard | 11. O Lord my God   Boyce
5. How joyful and how glad. | 12. Praise we the Lord.
6. In the departure of | 13. Preserve, most mighty God.
   the Lord   Myriell MSS.|

BULLMAN, BARUCH.

1. I beseech Thee to give | 3. Lord, Thou hast com-
   me grace   Add. MSS. | manded   Add. MSS.
2. I will give thanks   " |

BYRD (BYRDE or BIRD), WILLIAM. B. c. 1538 ; D. 1623.

Senior Chorister of St. Paul's Cath., 1554; Org. Lincoln Cath., 1563-69 ; Gent. of the Chapel Royal, 1659; Joint Org. with Tallis, his master, 1585.

1. Alack! when I look back Clifford | 9. Bow Thine ear   Boyce
2. Arise, O Lord   Fitzw. | (2nd part of No. 44.)
3. Behold, I bring you   Peterh. | 10. Christ being raised   Barnard
4. Behold, O God. | 11. Christ is risen again   Clifford
5. Be not wroth very sore   Novello | (2nd part of No. 12.)
   Ne Irascaris (Peterh.). | 12. Christ rising   Barnard
6. Be unto me, O Lord   Clifford | 13. Come, helpe   Myriell MSS.
7. Bless the Lord, ye | 14. Deliver me from mine
   His Angels   Motet Society | enemies   King's
8. Blow up the trumpet   Fitzw. | 15. Even from the depths   Clifford

BYRD (BYRDE or BIRD), WILLIAM (*continued*).

16. Exalt Thyself   *Clifford*
17. From depth of sin   *Add. MSS.*
18. Glory to God on high   *Clifford*
19. Hear my prayer   *Barnard*
20. How long, O Lord   *Peterh.*
21. How long shall mine
     enemies   *Clifford*
22. I laid me down to
     rest   *Myriell MSS.*
23. I will not leave you   *Cope*
24. Lead me, O Lord   *Clifford*
25. Let not Thy wrath   ,,
26. Lift up your heads   ,,
27. Look down, O Lord   ,,
28. Lord, hear my prayer   *Add. MSS.*
29. Lord, in Thine anger   ,,
30. Mine eyes with
     fervency   *Myriell MSS.*
31. My soul oppressed   ,,
32. Not unto us   *Marshall*
33. O Absolom   *Ely*
34. O be joyful   *Chap. Roy.*
35. O God, the proud   *Clifford*
36. O God, Whom our offences *Fitzw.*

37. O how glorious art Thou.
38. O Lord give ear   *King's*
39. O Lord God of Hosts   ,,
     (*Same as Nos. 5 and 36.*)
40. O Lord, make Thy
     servant Charles   *Lincoln.*
41. O Lord, my God   *Add. MSS.*
42. O Lord, rebuke me not   *Barnard*
43. O Lord, turn not away   *Clifford*
44. O Lord, turn Thy wrath
     away   *Boyce*
45. O praise the Lord, ye
     saints above   *Add. MSS.*
46. Prevent us, O Lord   *Motet Society*
47. Rejoice with heart   *Add. MSS.*
48. Retire, my soul   *Fitzw.*
49. Save me, O God   *Motet Society*
50. Sing joyfully   *Boyce*
51. Sing unto God   *Bumpus*
52. Sing we merrily   *Chap. Roy.*
53. Teach me, O Lord   *Clifford*
54. Thou God that guidest   *Barnard*
     (*A Prayer for the King.*)

N.B.—Several of these are his Latin Motets, with English words by Dr. Aldrich and others.

CARLTON, Rev. RICHARD, MUS. BAC.
     Contributor to the "Triumphes of Oriana." Published "Twenty-one Madrigals for Five Voyces," 1601.

1. Let God arise. |

CAUSTON, THOMAS. D. 1569.
     Gent. Chapel Royal during the reigns of King Edward VI., Queen Mary, and Queen Elizabeth.

1. Exaudiat te Dominus   *Day* | 3. Turn Thou us, O good Lord   *Day*
2. Rejoice in the Lord   ,, |

COBBOLD, WILLIAM. B. 1559 or 1560; D. 1639.
     Org. Norwich Cath., 1598-1608. He contributed to Este's "Whole Book of Psalms" and to "The Triumphes of Oriana."

1. In Bethlehem towne   *Husk* |
     (*For Twelfth Eve.*) |

COPERARIO (COOPER), GIOVANNI. D. 1626.
     Published works in 1606 and 1613. Taught King Charles I. and the brothers Lawes.

1. I'll lie me down to sleep, | 2. Lord, how do my woes increase,
            Add. MSS. | *Myriell MSS.*

COSTE, THOMAS.

1. He that hath My commandments | 2. Save me, O God   *Myriell MSS.*
            Clifford |

CRANFORD, THOMAS.

One of the Vicars-Choral of St. Paul's.

1. I will love Thee, O Lord
    Durham MSS.
2. O Lord, make Thy Servant,
 Charles   *Bumpus*

3. The King shall rejoice *Bumpus*
 (*Identical with No.* 1.)

These are also attributed to *William* Cranford (17th century).

DAVY (DAVYS), RICHARD. B. in the 15th century.

Org. Magdalen College, Oxon., 1490. First composer of Passion Music (St. Matthew).

1. Have mercy on me *Husk*

DAY, THOMAS. D. *c.* 1654.

Musician to Prince Henry, 1612, and, later, to King Charles 1.; Org. Westminster Abbey, 1625-32; Master of Chapel Royal children, 1637.

1. By the waters of Babylon *Mann*

DERING (DEERING), RICHARD, Mus.B., Oxon., 1610. B. *c.* 1580; D. 1657.

Org. to Queen Henrietta Maria, Consort of King Charles I. Died a Roman Catholic.

1. Almighty God, Who through
 (*Collect for Easter Day.*) *Peterh.*
2. And the King was moved
    Myriell MSS.

3. Lord, Thou art worthy
    Myriell MSS.
4. Therefore with Angels *Peterh.*
5. Unto Thee, O Lord *Husk*

DOWLAND (DOULAND), JOHN, Mus.B., Oxon. et Cantab. B. 1562; D. 1626.

Lutenist to King Charles IV. of Denmark. Resided in England and Denmark. Shakespeare sings his praises in " The Passionate Pilgrim."

1. Bow Thine ear *Hawes*
2. Come, Holy Ghost *Novello*

3. Help me, Lord

EDWARDES, RICHARD, M.A. B. 1523; D. 1566.

Poet and Composer. Member of Lincoln's Inn and Gent. Chapel Royal.

1. Deliver me, O God *Durham*

ESTE (EAST), MICHAEL, Mus. Bac. Cantab. D. 1638.

Master of Choristers at Lichfield. Contributor to the " Triumphes of Oriana."

1. As they departed *Mus. Antiq.*
 Pt. 2. But what went ye out?
 Pt. 3. For this is He.
2. Awake and stand up ,,
3. Blow out the trumpet ,,
 Pt. 2. Let all the inhabitants
4. God is gone up *Myriell MSS.*
5. How shall a young man *Mus. Antiq.*
 Pt. 2. Thy words have I hid
6. I have roared for the very ,,
 Pt. 2. I am brought into so great
 Pt. 3. My joints are filled

7. O clap your hands *Peterh.*
8. Rise, O my soul *Myriell MSS.*
9. Sing we merrily *Mus. Antiq.*
 Pt. 2. Take the psalm
 Pt. 3. Blow up the trumpet
10. Turn Thy face *Mus. Antiq.*
 Pt. 2. O give me the comfort
11. When Israel came out ,,
 Pt. 2. What aileth thee, thou sea ?
12. Wherewithal shall a
 young man *Joule*

FARRANT, JOHN.   Living in the 16th century.

Son of Richard Farrant. Org. Ely Cath., 1567-72, and Salisbury Cath., 1598 ; also Christ Church, Newgate Street.

1. God, be merciful	*Bumpus*	2. O Lord Almighty *Ely*

FARRANT, RICHARD.   B. *c.* 1530 ; D. 1580.

Master of Choristers, St. George's Chapel, Windsor, 1564-69 ; Gent. Chapel Royal, 1564-80.

1. Call to remembrance *Boyce*	4. Lord, remember David *Calvert*
2. Hide not Thou Thy face ,,	5. O Lord, Almighty God *Brit. Mus.*
3. Lord, for Thy tender	6. Unto Thee, O Lord *Motet Soc.*
mercies' sake *Page*	(*No. 3, to other words.*)
(*Ascribed to John Hilton.*)	

FERABOSCO, ALFONSO, Jun.   B. 1580 ; D. 1652.

Taught Prince Henry (son of King James I.).

1. Be Thou exalted *Bumpus*	4. In Thee, O Lord *Ely*
2. Have ye no regard? *Peterh.*	5. The King shall rejoice *Bumpus*
3. Hear me, O God *Myriell MSS.*	6. The Lord hear Thee ,,

FERINGE ——

1. Christ is risen again   *Add. MSS.* | 2. O merciful Father   *Add. MSS.*

FIDOW (FIDO), JOHN.

Org. Hereford Cath., 1593-94.

1. Hear me, O Lord   *Peterh.* |

FORD, THOMAS.   B. *c.* 1580.   D. 1648.

Musician to Prince Henry (son of King James I.) and to King Charles I. Composed " Since first I saw your face." Buried in St. Margaret's, Westminster.

1. Almighty God, Who	3. Look, shepherds, look *Clifford*
hast me brought *Chichester*	4. Not unto us, O Lord *Myriell MSS.*
2. Let God arise *Mus. Antiq.*	

FOX, WILLIAM.   D. 1579.

Org. Ely Cath., 1572-79.

1. Teach me Thy way   *Ely* |

GEERES, JOHN.

1. Merciful Lord, we beseech *Peterh.*	2. O praise the Lord *Durham*
(*Collect, St. John Evangelist.*)	3. The eyes of all wait ,,

GIBBONS, Rev. EDWARD, Mus. Bac., Cantab. (et Oxon.)   B. *c.* 1565 ; D. *c.* 1650.

Org. King's College, Cambridge, 1592 ; Org. Bristol Cath. ; Org. College of Priest Vicars, Exeter, 1609-44.

1. How hath the city sate solitary   *Tudway*   (*For Viols and Organ.*)

GIBBONS, ORLANDO, Mus. Bac., Cantab.; Mus.D., Oxon. B. 1583 ;
D. 1625.

Gent. of Chapel Royal, 1604 ; Org. Westminster Abbey, 1623.

1. Almighty and everlasting *Clifford*
2. Almighty God   *Durham*
    (*St. Peter's Day.*)
3.†Almighty God (*Christmas Day*)
4. Arise, O Lord (O God)   „
5. Awake up, my glory   „
6. Behold, I bring you   *Ouseley*
    (*Christmas Day.*)
7. Behold the hour cometh *Durham*
8. Behold, Thou hast
    been   *Chap. Roy.*
9. Behold, Thou hast made
    my days   *Ouseley*
10. Blessed are all they   *Clifford*
11. Blessed be the Lord God   „
    (*2nd part of No. 9.*)
12. Deliver us, O Lord our God „
13. Glorious and powerful God „
14. God is gone up   *Boyce*
    (*2nd part of No. 29.*)
15.†God so loved (*Whitsun Day*).
16. God Who from time to
    time   *Durham*
17. Grant, Holy Trinity   „
18.†Grant, O Holy Trinity.
19. Great {King of Gods / Lord of Lords}   *Ouseley*
    (*With Viols.*)
20. Have mercy   *Durham*
21. Hosanna to the Son of
    David   *Clifford*
22. How long wilt Thou forget ?
23. If ye be risen again   *Clifford*
    (*Easter Day.*)
24. Lift up your heads   „
25. Lord, grant grace   *Ouseley*
26. Lord, how long !   *Calvert*
27. Lord, let me know   *Chap. Roy.*

28. O clap your hands   *Boyce*
    (*Degree Exercise.*)
29. O glorious God   *Clifford*
30.*O God, the King of glory.
31. O God, Thou art my
    God   *Chap. Roy.*
32. O Lord, how do my woes   *Ouseley*
    (*Hymn.*)
33. O Lord, I lift my heart   „
    (*Hymn.*)
34. O Lord, increase my
    faith   *Motet Soc.*
35. O Lord, in Thee is all   *Ouseley*
36. O Lord, in Thy wrath   „
37.*O Lord, rebuke me not.
38. O sing unto God   *Chap. Roy.*
39. O Thou, the Central Orb   *Ouseley*
    (O all true faithful hearts)
    (*With Viols.*)
40. Ponder my words   *Chester*
41.†Praise the Lord, O my soul.
42. See, see, the Word is
    Incarnate   *Ouseley*
43. Sing unto the Lord, O ye
    saints   „
    (*MS. Warren.*)
44. Teach me, O Lord   *Marshall*
45.*Teach us by His example.
46. The eyes of all wait   *Durham*
47. The secret sins   „
48.*This is the day.
49. This is the record of
    John   *Ouseley*
50.†Thou God of Wisdom.
51.†Unto Thee, O Lord.
52. We praise Thee, O
    Father   *Ouseley*
    (*Preface for Easter Day.*)
53. Why art thou so heavy? *Motet Soc.*

GILES (GYLES), NATHANIEL, Mus.D., Oxon. B. 1548; D. 1633.

Org. St. George's Chapel, Windsor, 1595; Gent. Extraordinary and Master of
Children of the Chapel Royal, 1597, and Org. 1623.

1.‡Christ rising   *Harl. MSS.*
2. Except the Lord   *Husk*
3. God, Which as on this day *Clifford*
    (*Collect for Whitsunday.*)
4. Have mercy upon me   *Peterh.*
    (*Psalm 51.*)
5. He that hath My command-
    ment   „

* Nos. 31, 38, 46, and 49 are in a folio volume, containing the words of the anthems as used in the King's Chapel, *temp.* Charles II. (Harl. MSS. Brit. Mus.)

† Nos. 3, 15, 18, 42, 51, and 52 are in an ancient MS. organ book, formerly in the possession of J. Warren, and there attributed to Gibbons.

‡ No. 1 is in a book of words, *temp.* Charles I. (Harl. MSS., 4,142), prefixed, M. Gyles et M. Gibbons.

GILES (GYLES) NATHANIEL (*continued*).

6. I will magnify	*Tudway*	13. O Lord, of Whom I do		
7. Lord, in Thy wrath	,,	depend	*Clifford*	
8. O come hither	*Bumpus*	14. O Lord, turn not away	*Husk*	
9. O give thanks	*Barnard*	15. O Lord, turn Thy wrath	*Peterh.*	
10. O hear my prayer, Lord.		16. Out of the deep	*Husk*	
11. O Lord, my God, in all		17. What Child was He ?	,,	
distresse	*Husk*			
12. O Lord of Hosts.				

GREAVES, THOMAS.   B. in the 16th century.

Lutenist.   Published " Songs of Sundrie Kindes," 1604.

1. How long wilt thou forget? *Chester* |

HASELTON (HASYLTON), ROBERT.

1. Praise we the Lord at all times *Day* |

" Hallelujah, for unto us a child is born," printed in " The Parish Choir " (1848), is an adaptation of this.)

HEATH, JOHN.   B. *c.* 1589 ; D. *c.* 1668.

Org. Rochester Cathedral. 1608-68 (?)

1. When Israel came out   *Clifford* |

HILTON, JOHN, Mus.B., Cantab.   B. *c.* 1569 ; D. 1657.

Deputy-Org. Lincoln Cathedral, 1593—94, and later on Org. Trinity College, Cambridge ; Org. and Parish Clerk, St. Margaret's, Westminster, 1628, and buried there.

1. Call to remembrance	*Peterh.*	3. Sweet Jesus	*Peterh.*
2. Hear my cry, O God	,,	4. Teach me, O Lord	*Clifford*

Hilton has been credited with Farrant's " Lord, for Thy tender mercies' sake," the copy with his name attached differing but slightly from Farrant's, and ending with four bars of florid counterpoint to the word " Amen."

HOLMES, JOHN.   B. 1570-80 ; D. 1638.

Org. Winchester Cath. and Salisbury, 1602-10.   Contributor to " The Triumphs of Oriana," and teacher of Batten and Lowe.

1. Hear my crying, O God	*Joule*	5. I will love Thee, O Lord	*Joule*
2. Hear my prayer	*Marshall*	6. Lord, in Thy wrath	
3. I am the Resurrection	,,	7. O Lord, of Whom	
4. I will give land	*Husk*	8. O Lord, I bow the knees	*Bumpus*

HOOPER, EDMUND. B. *c.* 1553; D. 1621.

Master of the Boys, Westminster, 1588; Gent. of Chapel Royal, 1604, and Org. Westminster Abbey, 1606.

1. Almighty God, Who hast given *Tudway* (*Christmas Day.*)
2. Almighty God, Who madest *Ely* (*Circumcision.*)
3. Behold, it is Christ *Barnard*
4. Hearken, ye nations *Clifford* (*For Gunpowder Treason Day.*)
5. I will magnify Thee ,,
6. O God of Gods ,, (*For the King's Day.*)

7. O how glorious art Thou *Clifford*
8. ⎧ O Lord, ⎫ in Thee is all ⎩ O God, ⎭ my trust ,,
9. O Lord, turn not away *Husk*
10. O Thou God Almighty *Barnard*
11. Teach me, O Lord ,,
12. Teach me Thy way *Clifford*
13. The Blessed Lamb *Peterh.* (*For Good Friday.*)

HORSLEY (HORSLEYE).

1. O Lord, on whome I doe depend *Durham MSS.*

HUNT, THOMAS. Flourished in 16th century.

Contributor to " The Triumphs of Oriana."

1. Put me not to rebuke *Husk*

HUTCHINSON, RICHARD. D. 1646.

Org. Durham Cath., 1614-44.

1. Hear my crying, O God *Clifford* (*Also attributed to Mudde.*)
2. I will magnify Thee ,,
3. Lord, I am not high-minded *Peterh.*
4. O God, wherefore art Thou absent? ,,

5. O God, my heart pre-parèd is *Clifford*
6. O sing unto the Lord ,,
7. Unto Thee, O Lord ,,
8. Ye that fear the Lord *MSS. Durham*

There is some confusion between Richard and John Hutchinson, of Southwell, who wrote at least three Anthems (*see* list of 17th century).

JEFFERIES (JEFFERYS), MATTHEW, Mus.B., Oxon, 1593.

Vicar-Choral of Wells Cathedral.

1. If the Lord Himself *Myriell MSS.*
2. In Thee, O Lord ,,
3. Lord, remember David ,,
4. My soul shall be alway *Husk*

5. O Lord, the very heavens *Husk*
6. Rejoice in the Lord *Joule*
7. Sing we merrily.

JENKINS, JOHN. B. 1592; D. 1678.

Musician to Kings Charles I. and II. Lived much in Norfolk.

1. And art thou grieved.
2. Awake, sad heart.
3. Bright spark.
4. Cease, my soule.
5. Glorie, honour, and praise.

6. Holy and blessed Spirit.
7. Mercie, dear Lord.
8. O Domine Deus.
9. O Nomen Jesus.
10. Turne me, O Lord.

All MSS. in the Library of Christ Church, Oxford.

JOHNSON, ROBERT.   B. late in the 16th century ; D. after 1625.
Known as "Johnson of Windsor." Composer and Lutenist. Musician to
Prince Henry.

1. Come, pale-faced Death *Add. MSS.*	4. This is My commandment
2. I will give thanks „	*Clifford*
3. O Eternal God Almighty ⎫	5. When shall my sorrowful
Pt. 2. Save Thy people, ⎬ *Clifford*	sighing? *Add. MSS.*
O Lord ⎪	
Pt. 3. We shall give ⎭	
thanks	

JONES (JONYS), ROBERT, Mus. Doc., Oxon.   Flourished late in the
16th century.
Contributor to the "Triumphs of Oriana," and one of the ten harmonisers
of Este's Psalms.

1. Let Thy Salvation   *Clifford* | 2. What shall I render   *Clifford*

JUXON, WILLIAM.   B. 1582 ; D. 1663.
As Bishop, he attended King Charles I. to the scaffold ; he became Archbishop of Canterbury after the Restoration.

1. Christ rising   *Peterh.* | 2. Come, Holy Ghost   *Husk*

KINDERSLEY, ROBERT.

1. Judge them, O Lord *Myriell MSS.* |

KIRBYE, GEORGE.   B. *c.* 1570 ; D. 1634.   Of Bury St. Edmunds.
Contributor to the "Triumphs of Oriana," and one of the harmonizers of
Este's Psalms.

1. O Jesu, look !   *Myriell MSS.* |

LAUD, WILLIAM.   B. 1573 ; beheaded 1645.
Archbishop of Canterbury.

1. Praise the Lord, O my soul   *Ely* |
     Tudway Harleian MSS. call him *Mr.* LAUD.

LAWES, HENRY.   B. 1596 ; D. 1662.
Pupil of Coperario ; Epistler and Gent. Chapel Royal, 1625 ; Member of King
Charles I.'s private band.   Stripped of appointments during Protectorate.

1. Blessed is everyone that		6. My soul the Great God's	
feareth	*Husk*	praises sings	*Clifford*
2. Happy sons of Israel	*Clifford*	7. Sitting by the streams	„
3. Hearken, O daughter	„	8. The Lord in thy adversity	„
4. Lord, aloft Thy triumphs	„	9. The Lord liveth	„
raise	„	10. They that put their trust	„
5. My song shall be of mercy	*Ely*	11. Zadock the priest	*Bumpus*

LAWES, WILLIAM. B. 1582; D. 1645 (killed at the siege of Chester).
Brother of Henry Lawes, Vicar-Choral of Chichester; Gent. Chapel Royal,
1602; and Musician in Ordinary to King Charles I.

1. Let God arise	*King's*	3.*The Lord is my Light	*Boyce*
(*Verses only ; Chorus by Ferabosco.*)		4. Who is this that cometh ?	,,
2. Not unto us	*Rochester*		

LEIGHTON, Sir WILLIAM (knight). Born in the 16th century.
Published "Teares or Lamentations of a sorrowful soule."

1. Thou art my God

LUGG, JOHN.
Vicar-Choral of Exeter, 1634.

1. Behold, how good and joyful	*Peterh.*	3. It is a good thing to give thanks	*Myriell MSS.*
2. I am the Resurrection	*Bumpus*	4. Let my complaint	*Bumpus*
		5. Lord, we beseech	,,

It is doubtful whether these were all by John Lugg, or whether some were
written by Robert Lugg, Mus.B., Org. St. John's College, Oxon.

LUPI, EDUARDI. B. *c.* 1530.
Of Portuguese extraction.

1. Now it is high time   *Peterh.*

LUPO, THOMAS.
Court musician to Kings James I. and Charles I.

1. O Lord, give ear	*Myriell MSS.*	4. Save me, O God	*Add MSS.*
2. Out of the deep	,,	5. Whither then shall I go ?	
3. Malorie "Maister"			*Myriell MSS.*

MARSON, GEORGE (*Mason,* in Clifford). Born in the 16th century.
Org. Trinity College, Cambridge, 1612-29.

1. Judge me, O God	*Clifford*	3. O Lord, Who still dost guide	*Husk*
2. O gracious God	*Husk*	4. O sing unto the Lord	,,

MASON, Sir JOHN, Mus.B., Oxon., 1508.

1. God is our hope	*Peterh.*	2. O clap your hands	*Peterh.*

There is some doubt as to which John Mason wrote these Anthems.

MILTON, JOHN. D. 1646.
Scrivener in Bread Street, Cheapside. Father of the poet (see the latter's
"Ad patrem"). Contributor to the "Triumphs of Oriana."

1. How doth the holy city	*Myriell MSS.*	†5. O had I wings	*Add. MSS.*
Pt. 2. She weepeth continually.		6. O Jonathan	*Myriell MSS.*
†2. I am the Resurrection		†7. O Lord, behold my miseries	,,
†3. If that a sinner's sighs	*Add. MSS.*	†8. Thou God of might	,,
4. O all ye nations	*Marshall*	†9. When David heard	,,

---

* Composed, according to an old part-book belonging to Mr. Bumpus, in conjunction
with Ferabosco. Set to the "King of Kings." Hullah's "Vocal Scores."
† Published in score by Joseph Williams, and edited by Mr. Arkwright.

MORLEY, THOMAS, Mus. Bac., Oxon. B. *c.* 1560 ; D. $\left\{\begin{array}{l}1602\\1604\end{array}\right\}$

Pupil of Byrd ; Org. St. Paul's until 1591 ; Gent. Chapel Royal, 1591-1602. Obtained Patent to print music books, 1598.

1. Blessed are all they	*Calv.*	10. O that men would therefore	
2. How long wilt Thou forget			*Tudway*
me ?	*Clifford*	11. Out of the deep	*Barnard*
3. I am so weary	*Husk, Tudway*	12. Out of the deep	*Durham*
4. I am the Resurrection	*Boyce*	(*Different setting.*)	
5. I heard a voice	,,	13. Ponder my words	*Div. Harm.*
6. Let my complaint	*Marshall*	14. Praise the Lord, ye	
7. Man that is born	*Boyce*	servants	,,
8. O give thanks (Ps. 105)	*Joule*	15. Teach me Thy ways	*Peterh.*
9. O Jesu meek	*Husk*		

MUDDE (MUDD), THOMAS. ? B. *c.* 1560 ; ? D. 1620.

Org. Peterborough Cath., 1580-1620.

1. Bow down Thine eare	*Ely*	5. Let Thy merciful ears	*Durham*
2. God, which hast prepared	,,	6. O clap your hands	*Peterh.*
3. I will always give thanks	,,	7. Out of the deep	
4. I will sing the mercies	*Clifford*	8. We beseech Thee	*Ely*

There was a dissipated Mr. Mudde at Lincoln about 1662, dismissed for misconduct.

MUNDY, JOHN, Mus. Doc., Oxon., 1624. B. Middle of the 16th century ; D. 1630.

Studied with his father, Wm. Munday. Org. Eton College and St. George's, Windsor. Contributor to the "Triumphs of Oriana."

1. Blessed art Thou	*Husk*	4. Praise the Lord, O my soul	
2. Blessed is God in all His			*Add. MSS.*
gifts	*Peterh.*	5. Sing joyfully	*Myriell MSS.*
3. Give laud unto the Lord	,,	6. This is My commandment	,,

MUNDY (MUNDAY), WILLIAM. D. (?) 1591.

Gent. Chapel Royal, 1563 ; Vicar-Choral of St. Paul's at the time of his death.

1. Ah, helpless wretch	*Clifford*	10. O give thanks	*Clifford*
2. Behold, it is Christ	*Warren*	11. O Lord, I bow the knees	*Fitzw.*
3. Blessed are all they	*Husk*	12. O Lord our Governour	*Clifford*
4. Bow down Thine ear	*Clifford*	13. O Lord, the world's Saviour	,,
5. Give laud unto the Lord	*Husk*	14. O Thou God Almighty	*Husk*
(*Attributed to John Mundy.*)		15. Prepare you, time weareth.	
6. God be merciful.		16. Teach me, O Lord.	
7. Increase my joy	*Clifford*	17. Teach me Thy way	*Joule*
8. Let us now laud	,,	18. The secret sins	*Clifford*
9. My song shall be	,,		

OKELAND (OCLANDE), CHRISTOPHER. Lived about Tallis's time.

1. Grant, we beseech Thee	*Husk*	3. The King shall rejoice	*Husk*
2. Praise the Lord, O my soul	*Day*		
(*In two Sections.*)			

OKEOVER (OKER), JOHN, Mus.B., Oxon., 1633.

Org. Wells Cath., 1619-39; Gloucester Cath., 1640. Described in Add. MSS. 17,791, as " Wellensis."

1. God shall send forth His mercy
   Bumpus
2. Grant, we beseech Thee   *Husk*

3. The King shall rejoice   *Husk*

PALMER, HENRY.   Dates unknown.

Contributor to Ravenscroft's Psalter.

1. Almighty and everlasting *Durham*
   (*Feast of the Purification.*)
2. Almighty and everlasting   ,,
   (*Ash Wednesday.*)
3. Almighty God, Who out
   of the mouths   ,,
4. Blow up the trumpet   ,,

5. Hear my prayer, O God   *Durham*
6. Lord, what is man ?   *Peterh.*
7. O God, Whose nature   *Durham*
8. The end of all things is at hand
   Durham
9. Thou, O God, art praised   ,,

PARSONS (PERSONS), JOHN.   B. 1563 ; D. 1623.

Org. St. Margaret's, Westminster, and Westminster Abbey, 1621-23 (after Hooper).

1. I am the Resurrection   *Mann*
2. I heard a voice   ,,

3. Man that is born   *Mann*

PARSONS (PERSONS), ROBERT.   B. *c.* 1535 ; D. 1569 or 1570 (drowned in the Trent).

Father of John Parsons, and known as " Mr. Parsons, of Exeter."

1. Ah, helpless wretch.
2. Deliver me.
3. Ever blessed Lord.

4. Holy Lord God.
5. Lord, comfort those.
6. O bone Jesu.

No. 6 was an Anthem for the seven days before Christmas (the seven O's).

PATRICK, NATHANIEL.

Org. Worcester Cath., 1597, composed " Songs of sundry natures," 1597.

1. Prepare to dye   *Add. MSS.* | 2. Send forth thy sighes *Add. MSS.*

PATRICK, RICHARD.

Lay-Vicar of Westminster Abbey, 1616-24.

1. I will lift up mine eyes   *King's* | 2. O clap your hands   *King's*

PHILIPPS, PETER (PETRUS PHILLIPPUS).   B. in the 16th century ; D. *c.* 1625, abroad.

Entered the Roman Church, lived in Rome, and was in 1610 Canon of Soignies.

1. Blessed art thou that
   fearest   *Add. MSS.*

2. O give thanks   *Durham*

PIERSON (PEARSON), MARTIN, Mus.B., Oxon., 1613.   B.   c.   1580;
    D. 1650.

Master of the Children of St. Paul's Cath. and Almoner, 1613.   Composed
    "Motects, or grave chamber musique," 1630.

1. Blow ye the trumpet	*Clifford*	8. O let me at Thy footstool	
2. Bow down Thine ear	*Peterh.*	fall	*Myriell MSS.*
3. Fly, ravished soul, to⎫		9. O that my ways ⎫	
Calvary	*Myriell*	Pt. 2. I will thank Thee⎭	,,
Pt. 2. Rest there awhile	*MSS.*	10. Plead Thou my cause	,,
Pt. 3. Muse still thereon⎭		11. Weep, soul, in tender	
4. Go not from me	,,	memory	,,
5. I am brought into so⎫		12. Who will rise up with me⎫	
great trouble	,,	Pt. 2. But when I said ⎭	,,
Pt. 2. My heart panteth⎭			
6. I will magnify Thee	*Clifford*		
7. Lord,Thou hast searched⎫			
me out			
Pt. 2. Thou art about	*Myriell*		
my bed	*MSS.*		
Pt. 3. Thou hast fash-⎭			
ioned me			

RANDALL (RANDOLL), WILLIAM.

Chorister of Exeter Cath. and Org. Chap. Royal, 1592 to (?) 1621.

1. Give sentence   *Brit. Mus.* |

RAVENSCROFT, THOMAS, Mus. Bac., Cantab., 1607.   B. 1593;   D. 1635.

Chorister of St. Paul's Cathedral under Martin Pierson.

1. Ah, helpless wretch	*Myriell MSS.*	4. O Jesu, meek	*Durham*
2. All laud and praise	,,	5. O Jesu, Saviour mine	
3. Let me hear	*Durham*		*Myriell MSS.*

READE, ——

1. God standeth   *Durham* |

REDFORD, JOHN.   D. 1546 or 1547.

Org., Almoner, and Master of Choristers at St. Paul's Cath., 1491, until his
    death.

1. Rejoice in the Lord alway   *Motet Soc.*   (*Attributed to Causton.*)

SHEPPARDE (SHEPHERD, &c.), JOHN, Mus. Doc., Oxon.   B. 1501;
    D. 1563 (? 1597).

Chorister in St. Paul's; Org. Magdalen College, Oxon., 1542-47; Gent.
    Chapel Royal in Edward VI.'s time.

1.*Haste Thee, O God ⎫	*Clifford*	4. O Lord, the Maker	*Durham*
Pt. 2. But let all those⎭		(*Formerly attributed to King*	
2. I give you a new		*Henry VIII. or J. Mundy.*)	
commandment	*Parish Choir*	5. Praise ye the Lord	*Add. MSS.*
3. Let my complaint	*Clifford*	6. Submit yourselves one	
		to another	*Clifford*

---

* Attributed to *Thomas* Shepherd by Tudway.

SMITH, EDWARD. D. 1611.
Org. Durham Cath., 1609-11.

1. If the Lord Himself.
2. Let my complaint.
3. O Lord, consider.
4. O Lord my God, to Thee I do complain.
5. O praise God in His holiness.

All in the Old Durham Organ Books.

SMITH, ELIAS.
Org. Gloucester Cath. until 1620.

1. How is the golde become dimme   *Durham*

SMITH, Rev. WILLIAM.
Priest-Org. of Durham, 1588-98.

1. Almighty and everlasting God.
2. Grant, we beseech Thee.
3. I will preach the law.
4. I will wash my hands.
5. O God, Who for our sakes.
6. O God, who through the preaching.

All in the Old Durham Organ Books.

STEVENSON, ROBERT, Mus.D., Oxon., 1596. B. *c.* 1542.
Org. Chester Cath., 1569-1602.

1. When the Lord turned   *Peterh.*

STONARD, WILLIAM, Mus. Doc., Oxon. B. 16th century ; D. 1630.
Org. Christ Church Cath., Oxford. His MSS. are in the Oxford Music School.

1. Almighty and merciful God   *Clifford*
2. Hearken, all ye people *Add. MSS.*
3. Hear, O My people   *Peterh.*
4. Lord of all power and might   ,,
5. My God, my God *Durham, Clifford*
6. Rejoice in the Lord, O ye righteous   ,,
7. Sing unto God   *Husk*
8. When the sorrows of hell *Clifford*

STUBBES, SIMON.

1. Father of love   *Myriell MSS.*
2. Have mercy upon me *Myriell MSS.* (*Ps.* 51.)

TALLIS, THOMAS. B. *c.* 1520 ; D. 1585.
Org. Waltham Abbey till 1540 ; Gent. Chapels Royal in reigns of King Henry VIII., King Edward VI., and Queen Mary ; Org. in Queen Elizabeth's reign.

1. All people that on earth   *Arnold*
2. A new commandment   *Clifford*
3. Arise, O Lord, and hear   *King's* (*Salvator mundi.*)
4. Blessed are those   *Motet Soc.*
5. Blessed be Thy Name   *Barnard* (*Mihi autem nimio.*)
6. Christ rising   *Bumpus*
7. Come, Holy Ghost   *Parish Choir*
8. Deliver me, O God   *Lichfield*
9. Discomfort them, O God   *Ely*
10. Forgive me, Lord.
11. Great and marvellous   *Motet Soc.*
12. Hear my prayer, O God   *Joule*

TALLIS, THOMAS (*continued*).

13. Hear the voice and
    prayer   *Motet Soc.*
14. Holy, Holy, Holy   *Clifford*
15. I call and cry   *Boyce*
    (*Adapted to these words by
    Dean Aldrich, from the
    motet "O Sacrum Con-
    vivium" in the "Can-
    tiones Sacræ," 1575.*)
16. If ye love Me   *Motet Soc.*
17. I give you a new command-
    ment.
18. I will cry.
19. I will give thanks unto
    Thee   *Joule*
20. Let the wicked   *Calvert*
21. Like as the doleful dove *Husk*
22. Lord, for Thy tender mercies
23. O give thanks unto the Lord.
24. O God, be merciful   *Peterh.*
25. O God, Whom our
    offences   *Barnard*

26. O Lord, give ear   *St. Paul's*
27. O Lord, give Thy Holy
    Spirit   *Barnard*
28. O Lord God of Hosts.
29. O Lord, in Thee is all my
    trust
30. O praise the Lord   *Husk*
31. Praise the Lord, O ye
    servants.
32. Remember not, O Lord *Clifford*
33. Save, Lord, and hear us *Marshall*
34. The Lord said unto my
    Lord.
35. Up, Lord, and help me   *Exeter*
36. Verily, verily   *Ely*
37. We be Thy people   *Fitzw.*
38. When Jesus went in to
    Simon   *Add. MSS.*
39.*Wipe away my tears   *Clifford*
40. With all our hearts and
    mouths   *Barnard*

Most of these originally set to Latin words.

TAVERNER, JOHN.

Org. Boston Parish Church and Christ Church Cath., Oxford, about 1530.
He narrowly escaped martyrdom.

1. O give thanks unto the Lord   *Add. MSS.*

TOMKINS, GYLES. D. 1668.

Org., King's College, Cambridge, 1624-26, and Salisbury Cath.

1. In Thee, O Lord |

TOMKINS, JOHN. B. 1586 ; D. 1638.

Son of Thomas Tomkins, Org. King's College, Cambridge, 1606 to 1619
or 1621; St. Paul's Cath., 1621-24.

1. Holy, Holy, Holy   *Husk* | 4. Ye people   *Husk*
2. The King shall rejoice   ,, | (*Attributed to Thomas Tomkins.*)
3. The Lord hear thee   ,, |

TOMKINS, Rev. THOMAS, Senr. D. 1675.

Minor Canon of Gloucester Cath. Contributed to " Triumphs of Oriana."

1. O Lord, I have loved   *Fitzw.* |

* " My sins " in Barnard.

TOMKINS, THOMAS, MUS. BAC., OXON., 1607.   B. 1586; D. 1656.

Org. Worcester Cath.   Pupil of Byrd.   Gent. of Chapel Royal.

1. Above the stars my Saviour
   dwells   *Clifford*
2. Almighty and everlasting
   God   *Mann*
3. Almighty and everlasting
   God   *Joule*
4. Almighty God, the fountain *Clifford*
5. Arise O Lord (God)   *Joule*
6. Behold, I bring you glad
   tidings   ,,
7. Behold, the hour cometh *Calvert*
8. Be strong and of a good
   courage   *Clifford*
9. Blessed be the Lord God   ,,
10. Come ye, and let us go up *Calvert*
11. Death is swallowed up   *Clifford*
12. Except the Lord build the
    house   *Joule*
13. From deepest horror *Myriell MSS.*
14. Give sentence with me   *Clifford*
15. Glory be to God   *Ely*
16. God, which as on this day *Joule*
    (*Collect for Whitsunday.*)
17. Great and marvellous   ,,
18. Have mercy upon me   ,,
19. Hear me, when I call   *Clifford*
20. He that hath pity   *Calvert*
21. I am the Resurrection   ,,
22. I will lift up   *Joule*
23. Jesus came   *Peterh.*
    (*For St. Thomas's Day.*)
24. Leave, O my soul   *Clifford*
25. Lord, enter not into judgment ,,
26. Lord, who shall dwell?   *Joule*
27. Merciful Lord   ,,
28. My beloved spake   *Clifford*
29. My help cometh   *Durham*
30. O Almighty God, Who hast
    instructed (*St. Mark*)   *Joule*
31. O Almighty God, Who hast
    knit (*All Saints*)   ,,

32. O be favourable   *Clifford*
33. O clap your hands   *Calvert*
34. O give thanks unto the Lord,
    and call   *Joule*
35. O God, the proud are risen *Ely*
36. O God, wonderful art Thou *Clifford*
37. O how amiable   *Joule*
38. O Israel   *Clifford*
39. O Lord God of Hosts   ,,
40. O Lord, graciously accept   ,,
41. O Lord, grant the King   *Joule*
42. O Lord, I have loved   *Clifford*
43. O Lord, I have sinned   *St. Paul's*
44. O Lord, let me know   *Husk*
45. O praise the Lord   *Ely*
46. O pray for the peace   ,,
47. O sing unto the Lord   *Clifford*
48. O that the salvation   ,,
49. Out of the deep   *Joule*
50. Praise the Lord   *Clifford*
51. Praise the Lord, ye servants ,,
52. Sing unto God   ,,
53. Steven, being full of the
    Holy Ghost   ,,
54. The King shall rejoice *St. Paul's*
55. The Lord, even the most
    mighty   *Clifford*
56. Then David mourned   *Tudway*
57. Thou art my King   *Clifford*
58. Turn Thou us   *Tudway*
    (*Canon.*)
59. Turn unto the Lord   *Peterh.*
60. When David heard that
    Absolom   *Calvert*
61. Who can tell how oft?   *Joule*
62. Who is this that cometh
    out?   *Clifford*
63. Why art thou so full of
    heaviness?   ,,

No. 35 is written for eight and No. 45 for twelve voices.

TYE, REV. CHRISTOPHER, MUS.D., Cantab. et Oxon. B. c. 1508;
   D. 1572.

Rector of Little Wilbraham, Newton, and Doddington-cum-March in the
diocese of Ely.   Chorister and Gent. Chapel Royal, and Org. Ely Cath.,
1541-62.   First composer of Passion Music according to St. John's Gospel.

1. Almighty and everlasting *Mann*
   (*Collect for 14th Sunday after Trinity.*)
2. Arise and help us   *Clifford*

3.*As sparks in close succession
                             Gloucester
   (*Adaptation by Oliphant.*)

TYE, Rev. CHRISTOPHER (*continued*).

4. Come, Holy Ghost.
5. *Come, let us join.
   (*Adaptation by Oliphant.*)
6. Father of all.
   (*Adaptation by Oliphant.*)
7. *Few are the days.
   (*Adaptation by Oliphant.*)
8. From the depths   *King's*
9. Give alms of thy goods   *Bumpus*
10. Happy is the man   *Wells*
11. Haste Thee, O God.
12. Have mercy upon me *Marshall*
13. *How still and peaceful   *Husk*
    (*Adaptation by Oliphant.*)
14. *Ho ! ye that thirst.
    (*Adaptation by Oliphant.*)
15. I have loved   *Clifford*
16. I lift my heart   *Barnard*
17. *In life's gay morn.
    (*Adaptation by Oliphant.*)
18. I will exalt Thee   *Barnard*
19. I will magnify Thee   *Joule*
20. Let the people rejoice.
21. Let Thy loving mercy *Lichfield*
    (*Adaptation by Philip Hayes*)
22. *Lift up the everlasting   *Joule*
    (*Adaptation by Oliphant.*)
23. *Mock not God's Name *Novello*
24. O come, ye servants   ,,
(*Adapted by Rev. Gilbert Heathcote
    to " Laudate nomen Domini," from
    Tye's " Acts of the Apostles."*)
25. O God, be merciful   *Barnard*

26. *O God of Bethel   *Novello*
    (*Adaptation by Oliphant.*)
27. O happy is the man   ,,
    (*Adaptation by Oliphant.*)
28. O let the people rejoice.
    (*Cf. No. 15.*)
29. O Lord, deliver me   *Tudway*
30. O Lord, how gracious *King's*
31. O Lord of Hosts   *Clifford*
32. O Lord, Thy word   *Rochester*
    (*Adaptation by Dr. P. Hayes.*)
33. *O may the grace.
    (*Adaptation by Oliphant.*)
34. Our God ascendeth *Jesus Coll.*
35. Praise the Lord, ye children
                   Peterh.
36. Save me, O God   *Clifford*
37. *Sing to the Lord in joyful *Novello*
(*Adaptation by Oliphant. Same music
    as No. 19.*)
38. Sing unto the Lord   *Novello*
    (*2nd part of No. 17.*)
39. Sing we merrily   *Calvert*
40. That we may know.
41. The Lord preserveth   *Boyce*
42. The proud have digged *Novello*
(*Adaptation by Dr. P. Hayes. Same
    music as Nos. 19 and 31.*)
43. This is the day   *Ely*
    (*Identical with No. 31.*)
44. *While others crowd.
    (*Adaptation by Oliphant.*)

Some of these were composed to Latin words.

Those marked * are from Tye's " Acts of the Apostles." The music to the newly-adapted words was published by Thos. Oliphant, for many years Secretary to the Madrigal Society.

WARDE, JOHN. B. *c.* 1580 ; D. before 1640.

Called a " Gentill Man " by Adrian Batten. Writer of Madrigals ; numbers in Leighton's " Teares " and a Morning Song for Prince Henry.

1. How long wilt thou
   forget   *Myriell MSS.*
2. I heard the voice of a
   great multitude   *Peterh.*
3. I will praise the Lord *Barnard*

4. Let God arise   *Barnard*
5. O Lord, consider
   my great moans *Myriell MSS.*
6. Praise the Lord   *Husk*
7. Unto Thee, O Lord *Clifford*

Weelkes (Wilkes), Thomas, Mus.B., Oxon., 1603. b. 1578 ;
d. (?) 1640.

Org. Winchester College, 1597, and Chichester Cath., 1608. Contributor to
the " Triumphs of Oriana."

1. Alleluia, salvation
     and glory   *Myriell MSS.*
2. All laud and praise   *Husk*
3. All people, clap your hands
                         Mus. Antiq.
4. Deliver us, O God   *Husk*
5. Give ear, O God   *Myriell MSS.*
6. Give the King thy
     judgments   *Clifford*
7. Hosanna to the Son
     of David   *Add. MSS.*
8. If King Manasses   *Husk*
9. I lift my heart   ,,
10. In Thee,O Lord   *Clifford*
11. Let us lift up   ,,
12. Lord, to Thee I make   ,,
13. Most mighty and All-
     knowing   ,,

14. O how amiable   *Clifford*
15. O Jonathan, woe is
     me   *Myriell MSS.*
16. O Lord, arise   *Husk*
17. O Lord God Almighty   *Clifford*
18. O Lord, grant the king   *Fitzw.*
19. O mortall man   *Husk*
20. Plead Thou my cause
                             ,,
21. Rejoice in the Lord   *Bumpus*
22. Sing, my soul, to
     God thy Lord   *Add. MSS.*
23. Sing unto the Lord   *Clifford*
24. Thy mercies great   ,,
25. What joy so true   *Husk*
26. When David heard   } *Myriell*
     Pt. 2. O my son, Absolom } *MSS.*
27. With all our hearts   *Bumpus*

Whitbroke, Rev. William.

Minor Canon of St. Paul's, 1566.

1. Let your light so shine   *Cope* |

It appears in Day's Service Book *unbarred*, and was so reproduced by Rev.
Sir W. H. Cope.

White, F.

1. The Lord bless us   *Add. MSS.* |

White, Matthew, accumulated Mus.B. and Mus.D., Oxon., 1629.

Bass in Wells Cath. ; Gent. Chapel Royal and Org. of Christ Church Cath.,
Oxon., 1611-13.

1. Behold now, praise   *Peterh.* | 3. O praise God in His holiness *Peterh.*
2. O how glorious art Thou   ,, | 4. Zacchæus stood forth   *Husk*
                No. 2 is also attributed to *Robert* White.

White (Whyte), Robert, B.A., Mus.B., Cantab., 1561. b. *c.* 1540 ;
d. 1574.

Org. Ely Cath., 1562-67, after Tye, whose daughter he married ; Org. Westminster Abbey, 1570.

1. Deliver me   *Joule* | 5. O praise God   *Ely*
2. Give alms of your goods *Add.MSS.* | 6. O sing unto the Lord   *Husk*
3. Lord, who shall dwell? *Clifford* | 7. Praise the Lord   ,,
     (*Burney refers to this.*) | 8. The Lord bless us   *Ely*
4. O Lord our Governour   *Husk* |

Nos. 6 to 8 are also attributed to *Matthew* White, and Aldrich's " O Lord,
rebuke me not," is a *fac-simile* of No. 7.

WHITE, WILLIAM. B. late in the 16th century.

Known as "Mr. Willm. White of Durham." Thomas Jenkins dedicated a piece to him.

1. Almighty God	*Myriell MSS.*	3. Bend down, O Lord,	
2. Behold now, praise	*Durham MSS.*	Thy gracious eyes	*Myriell MSS.*

WIGTHORPE, WILLIAM, Mus.B., Oxon., 1605. B. *c.* 1590.

1. My shepherd is the living God　*Clifford*

WILKINSON, THOMAS.

1. Behold, O Lord	*Peterh.*	8. O Lord, consider	*Durham*
2. Blessed, O Lord	,,	9. O Lord God of my salvation	*Ely*
3. Deliver me	*Durham*	10. O Lord my God	*Durham*
4. Hear my prayer	*Ely*	11. Praise the Lord, ye servants	,,
5. Help, Lord	*Peterh.*	12. Preserve me, O God	*Clifford*
6. I am the Resurrection	*Tudway*	13. Put me not to rebuke	,,
7. Lord, I am not high-minded	*Peterh.*	14. Unto Thee, O Lord	*Durham*

WILSON, JOHN, Mus.D., Oxon. B. 1594 ; D. 1673.

Professor of Music at Oxford. Supposed to be Shakespeare's "Jack" Wilson.

1. Blessed is he	*Calvert*	3. Hearken, O God, unto a wretch's cryes	*Clifford*
2. By the waters	*Durham*	4. Teach me, O Lord	,,

WOOD, JOHN.

1. O Lord, the world's Saviour　*Durham*

ANONYMOUS.

1. Let all the congregation　*Day's Book*, 1560
(? *By Mulliner.*)

SECOND PERIOD.

SEVENTEENTH CENTURY.

CHAPTER VIII.

THE SECOND PERIOD.

MANY of the great writers of the Madrigalian era were living and still composing in King James I.'s reign.

Passing through that, we come to King Charles I.'s unhappy period, followed by the terrible Civil War and subsequent Commonwealth, a time when organs and Cathedral churches were shut up, singers silenced (except for Psalm tunes), and our anthem at a standstill.

Anthem writers appear to have dropped the pen and taken up the sword, mostly in the service of the King's army. Orlando Gibbons's son, Christopher, who was organist at Winchester Cathedral, had to quit his instrument in 1644, and he joined the Royalist forces. The Chapel Royal was closed, and we find on that account one of its choristers, Henry Cooke, under the royal banner. He joined in 1642, when the war broke out, and at once obtained a captain's commission. These two soldier-musicians were destined to meet in 1660 under happier conditions.

Just as one extreme is likely to be met by another, so the innovations of the high church Bishop of London (Laud), and his alterations in the ritual, gave place to an absurd suspicion of everything connected with the service of the Church, and even the use of organs and choir-singers was felt to be a sore grievance. Laud's high church proclivities, while they encouraged the Court of Rome in the hopes of regaining its old authority in England, at the same time thoroughly disgusted the Puritan party.

Metrical psalms alone were tolerated, but deans and chapters did not then regard these as part of the regular service music, and it is only within the last thirty years that hymns and psalm tunes have been sung in these venerable buildings as an integral part of the ordinary service.

CHAPTER IX.

THE RESTORATION.

It was not until the Restoration of King Charles II. to the throne, in 1660, that anthems, and Cathedral services generally, were resumed, and, with their return, the anthem assumes a form which at once differs materially from its solemn, majestic predecessor.

The change was scarcely for the better, and this was partly due, with shame be it written, to the whim of a *blasé* monarch. During the king's exile in France he imbibed French tastes, and their effect is thus described by Thomas Tudway, who, in addition to making a fine MS. collection of "Anthems from the Reformation to the Restoration of King Charles II., composed by the best masters," a work of six volumes now in the British Museum, composed several anthems himself. Tudway, one of the first choristers after the Restoration, writes : "His Majesty was soon tired with the grave and solemn way which had been established by Byrd and others, and ordered the Composers of his chapel to add symphonies with instruments to their Anthems ; and established a select number of his private band to play the symphony and the ritornellos which he had appointed. The old masters of music such as Dr. Child and Dr. (Christopher) Gibbons hardly knew how to comport themselves with these new-fangled ways, but proceeded in their compositions according to the old style."

The Dr. Child (or Childe) named here was an old chorister of the Chapel, born in Bristol, 1606, Mus. Doc., Oxon., 1663. He was organist of St. George's Chapel, Windsor, in 1632, and died at Windsor, March 23, 1697. He wrote several anthems "without any great depth of science or elevation of genius," but they "possess a great degree of warmth and exhibit imagination."

Dr. Christopher Gibbons was the son of Orlando Gibbons, and was born 1615, and died October 28, 1676.

King Charles called upon these two musicians, together with Captain Cooke, Matthew Locke, and Henry Lawes, to form the new choir at Whitehall.

Captain Cooke became Master of the Boys, as soon as boys could be found for him to train ; his old fellow-soldier was appointed organist to the Chapel, and Dr. Child became a member of the King's band, in which he suffered, as I quoted above, from the new-fangled notions imported from France.

Hawkins tells us, in his "History of Music," of the difficulty there was to find boys capable of singing the service; so neglected had

JOHN BLOW.

the art become during the Commonwealth, that, for at least a year, the treble part had to be taken by men with *feigned* voices, and by cornets !

Both cornets and sackbuts had already been in use in King James's reign, but never as a substitute for boy's voices. The cornet was a reed instrument of the hautboy class, not its blatant namesake of modern times, and the sackbut was, very likely, a bass trumpet with a slide, like a trombone.

CHAPTER X.

PELHAM HUMFREY, WISE, AND BLOW.

Upon Captain Cooke devolved the anxious responsibility of finding boys and training them for the Chapel service. These difficulties were overcome in a far more successful manner than he ever anticipated. For not only was he training singers, but was introducing some of the finest composers of anthems that this country has ever possessed.

It seems the irony of fate that the most promising of that first set of choir-boys in 1660 should have been a nephew of Bradshaw's sword-bearer, Bradshaw, the president of the High Court which tried and impeached its sovereign. But so it was, and Pelham Humfrey (or Humphrey), the boy in question, sang as chorister until his voice broke.

He wrote at least six anthems whilst still a chorister, and showed such talent for composition that the king sent him abroad to acquire that style which the monarch so much affected.

Before leaving for the Continent, he composed, together with Blow and another fellow-chorister, William Turner, what is known as the Club Anthem, of which Humfrey composed the first movement, Blow the last, and Turner the intermediate bass solo. With the use of solos commences the "Verse" Anthem period, to the origin of which the next chapter will be devoted.

A few months before young Pelham started on his journey, when only sixteen years old, a setting of his of the Fifty-first Psalm is noticed thus by Pepys in his invaluable Diary : "Nov. 22, 1663. The Anthem was good after Sermon,* being the 51st psalm, made for five voices by one of Captain Cooke's boys, a pretty boy, and they say

---

* This unusual place for the Anthem is still in vogue at Westminster Abbey.

that there are four or five of them that can do as much." He adds,
"and here I first perceived that the King is a little musical, and
kept good time with his hand all along the Anthem." The Stuart
kings were evidently not such thorough musicians as the Tudors.
It is stated of King Charles II. that "he was altogether intolerant
of counterpuntal artifice."

Pelham Humfrey went to Paris, where he studied under Lulli.
He also visited Italy, where he would find Scarlatti founding the
Neapolitan school, Cavalli and Ferrari upholding the fame of
the Venetian school, and Carissimi, in Rome, endeavouring
to carry on the traditions of Palestrina. His trip and his lessons,
which cost £450 during his three years' absence, were paid for
out of the Secret Service Fund!

Whilst abroad, he was appointed a Gentleman of the Chapel
Royal, and on the 26th of the following October, having returned
safely, he was sworn in. His newest anthems were at once
introduced in the Royal Chapel, to ascertain, no doubt, whether
the French influence had been properly inoculated.

On the death of Captain Cooke, who, in addition to training boys,
found time to compose several anthems, Humfrey was appointed
Master of the Children. This was in 1672, in which year he
became Composer in Ordinary for the violins to His Majesty,
together with Henry Purcell's uncle, Thomas Purcell.

On July 14, 1674, when only twenty-seven years old, Humfrey
died at Windsor. He was buried in the cloisters of Westminster
Abbey, near the South-East door. Seven of his anthems are in
Boyce's Collection and six others in Tudway's, and there are others
in MS. in the libraries of Ely, Salisbury, and Windsor. He was
peculiarly fond of writing in the minor mode, and he was the first
to infuse into English Church music the light new style which he
had acquired from Lulli in Paris, and which was destined to supplant
altogether the grand old school of "Motet" writers. "Hear, O
Heavens," verse A.T.B., is a good specimen of his anthems.

Michael Wise was born at Salisbury in 1638, and was one of the
first set of Chapel Royal boys under Captain Cooke, becoming organist
and choirmaster of Salisbury Cathedral in 1668, Gentleman of the
Chapel Royal, 1675, and, in 1686, Master of the Choristers of St.
Paul's Cathedral. In August of the following year, during a visit to
his native city, he was killed in a midnight brawl with the watch.
Well known amongst his anthems are "Awake, awake, put on
Thy strength" and "The ways of Zion do mourn."

Another of the boys, one year younger than Pelham Humfrey,
was Dr. John Blow. He was born at Westminster, in 1648,
and was also one of the first set of "Children of the Chapel."
He began to compose while yet a chorister, being one of the
contributors to the Club Anthem. He quickly rose to eminence,

being appointed organist of Westminster Abbey, 1669, succeeding Humfrey as Master of the Children in 1674. He resigned his post at the Abbey (or was deposed) in favour of another Chapel Royal boy, who was but two years old when the king came "to enjoy his own again," and who was destined to become (short lived though he was) the greatest of them all. I need hardly say that the boy was Henry Purcell. When Purcell died, in 1695, Blow resumed his post at the Abbey. He was organist and composer to the king, and in 1687 succeeded Wise as Master of the Choristers at St. Paul's, resigning this also in 1693 in favour of his pupil, Jeremiah Clarke.

He seems to have been what one might call a thoroughly *retiring* man!

He died October 1, 1708, in the reign of Queen Anne, at sixty years of age, and was buried in the North Aisle of Westminster Abbey, where there is a monument to his memory.

Blow was both a versatile and voluminous composer. Besides fourteen services, many odes, including an ode by Dryden on the death of Purcell, numbers of songs, catches, and harpsichord lessons, he composed over 100 anthems; these he intended to publish, a purpose unfortunately never accomplished; only a limited number are obtainable. And this is the more to be regretted, as his fame chiefly rests upon that form of composition. His degree of Doctor was conferred by Sancroft, Archbishop of Canterbury.

Amongst "Verse" anthems his fine "I was in the Spirit" and "I beheld, and lo!" are best known. Several, such as "Save, Lord, and hear us," are short, full anthems.

CHAPTER XI.

THE VERSE ANTHEM AND ITS ACCOMPANIMENTS.

In Stainer and Barrett's Dictionary a "Verse" anthem is thus defined: "A Verse Anthem is one which begins with soli portions, as opposed to a Full Anthem which commences with a chorus."

I think we may add that a "Full" anthem continues to be "chorus" to the end.

Dr. Jebb* supports this view, saying: "Full Anthems, properly so-called, which consist of chorus alone." But he also speaks of

---

* "The Choral Service of the Church." By Dr. Jebb.

so-called Full Anthems, *with verses.* " These verses, however, which form a very subordinate part of the composition, do not consist of solos or duets, but, for the most part, of quartets, to be sung by one side of the choir."

A consequence of the change was novelty in design and construction, expressive illustration of the words, a more extended system of harmony, and much more fluent melody in the voice parts. Another result followed—namely, that instrumental music began to assert its independence and to exercise an important influence on the progress of the art, and the addition of interludes for strings, and so on, gradually led composers away from the purely vocal style of the Elizabethan era.

I have already referred to the use of cornets as " treble voice substitutes "; and now let me quote a passage or two from the old diaries of Pepys and Evelyn on the subject of the accompaniments, which were gradually being introduced into the King's Chapel, to elaborate the anthems.

Pepys writes on September 14, 1662 :—

" To Whitehall Chapel . . . and I heard Captain Cooke's new musique. This the first of having vialls and other instruments to play a symphony between every verse of the Anthems, but the music more full than it was last Sunday, and very fine it is."

Three months later Evelyn, who, I am afraid, was not such a good attendant at church, records : —

" One of his Majesty's chaplains preached, after which,* instead of the ancient, grave, and solemn wind musique accompanying the organ, was introduced a concert of twenty-four violins between every pause, after the French fantastical light way, better suiting a tavern or playhouse than a church. *This was the first time of change ;* and now we no more heard the cornet which gave life to the organ ; that instrument quite left off in which the English were so skilful."

The latter statement proves that, by this time, three years after the choir's formation, the boys were able to hold their own, and the choirmaster to dispense with their reedy substitutes.

The simple string parts, to which Evelyn took such exception, soon developed into a much fuller band.

In regard to the organ itself, Dr. Rimbault says that in the very earliest " Verse" anthems the " verses " were accompanied by viols, the organ being used only in the full parts.

At the time of the Restoration, the celebrated organ builder, Renatus Harris, returned with his father from France, following his rival Bernard Schmidt (known as Father Smith), and these

---

* There were two Anthems, the first in the usual place, the other after the sermon.

men introduced certain stops, until then unknown in English organs, adding also a new manual, called the " Echo " organ, which became so vulgarly popular that, in Dr. Boyce's time, special " Echo " voluntaries were written to show off this rather clap-trap effect.

Another point to notice is the way in which the "Verse" anthem affected the actual writing of the composition.

From Purcell's time onward, to the end of the eighteenth century, a system of musical shorthand was gradually developed, whereby only a figured bass was written down, and it was left to the performer to fill in this outline in any of the many ways possible. The short scores under the voice parts were discontinued, and this "shorthand" became known by the name of Thorough Bass. In committing to paper the accompaniments to solo, duet or trio in the "Verse" anthems of this period, "the figured bass (writes Mr. Hipkins*) was generally all that was associated with the voice part, but in the symphonies or ritornellos a treble part was not infrequently supplied, usually in single notes only, for the right hand, in addition to the figured bass. Occasionally also a direction was given for the use of a particular organ register, or a combination of them : as ' cornet stop,' ' bassoon stop,' ' trumpet or hautboy stop,' 'two diapasons, left hand,' ' stop diapason and flute,' and in a few instances the particular manual to be used, as ' Eccho,' ' swelling organ,' " &c.

We noticed in Chapter VII. that sacred music, in the time of Gibbons, was so similar in character to secular, that the words alone decided its intention for worldly or ecclesiastical use. But now, and most probably through the bad influence of King Charles II.'s Court, secular music had arrived at a condition totally unfitted for the decency or solemnity of Divine worship.

To meet this difficulty, as we saw, a compromise was effected, and that compromise was the " Verse" anthem. Perhaps the complete divorce of sacred from secular was scarcely fulfilled before the commencement of the eighteenth century, when dramatic music, now in its infancy, banished from the mind of the composer the tradition of a strict Church style, and nearly blotted out the image of those great models and prototypes, with whom, in the earlier pages, I have been dealing.

---

* Grove's Dictionary : " Accompaniment."

CHAPTER XII.

HENRY PURCELL.

In the limited space of this essay I will adhere carefully to my subject, and only notice this marvellous genius, Henry Purcell, as an anthem writer.

To whatever branch of the Divine Art we choose to direct ourselves, we find that Purcell stands, head and shoulders, above all other English musicians.

Consider for a moment the cramped conditions under which, in his short, too short, life, he produced all his mighty masterpieces. The Puritans had put down most of the organs and destroyed all the fine old music they could lay their hands on. Fortunately, some anthems by the great masters had been saved, and for nine years he had the advantage of singing them in the Chapel Royal.

But the boy was original in style and bold and inventive in harmonies and modulations from the first. He extended the existing melodic forms and largely developed the orchestral accompaniments, adding these to his anthems and services. As a mere child in the choir he began to compose anthems, in which he eventually distanced his predecessors, his contemporaries, and most of his successors.

To Dr. Blow he owed much of his early training; and Blow was so proud of his clever pupil that he requested that the statement "Master to the famous Mr. Henry Purcell" might be engraved on his tomb! But Purcell, to a vast extent, must have been self-taught.

Of anthems alone he composed 107. "It seems" (says Dr. E. G. Monk) "to have been reserved for Purcell, himself a most distinguished singer, to bring to perfection the airs and graces of the 'solo' Anthem." His bright and peculiar genius tired of gratifying the king's taste for *French* mannerisms, and he has declared himself "to lean towards a just imitation of the most famous *Italian* masters, principally to bring the seriousness and gravity of that sort of music into vogue and reputation amongst our countrymen, whose humours it is time now should begin to loathe the levity and balladry of our neighbours, the French."

There is no doubt that, at this period, Purcell was not only the greatest composer of his own country, but of all Europe; for you could not find, over the whole Continent at that day, a brighter genius, nor were there any works by contemporaries to compare with his vigour of ideas, his breadth of style and power of expression.

His anthems have a broad and dignified bearing, which we are very proud, every one of us, to designate "British." Placed beside these examples, full of reliance and strength, how artificial and stilted appear the arias of Lulli or Scarlatti!

It is difficult to speak of any of these fine works in particular, but we might name "O give thanks," "O Lord God of Hosts," "Remember not, Lord," "Thou knowest, Lord," and the Bell Anthem, "Rejoice in the Lord alway," as favourites. Purcell was born January 30, 1658, in Westminster, entered the Chapel Royal in 1664, became copyist in Westminster Abbey, and organist (in the place of Blow), 1680, organist of the Chapel Royal two years later, and then composer to the King in 1683. He died in Westminster on November 21, 1695, the eve of St. Cecilia's Day, and was buried by his brother musicians in the North Aisle of the Abbey, where there is a tablet, telling us, in pathetic language, that he is gone "to that Blessed Place, where only his harmony can be exceeded."

A folio volume, containing anthems with symphonies and instrumental parts, has recently come to light in the Royal Library at Buckingham Palace, and at York Minster several other volumes of sacred music have happily been discovered; but, alas, his glorious works are seldom heard, his name scarcely recognised, in these modern days.

It is a disgrace to Englishmen that the memory of this, their greatest composer, should be so slighted; it is a national reproach which the members of the recently formed Purcell Society (1876) desire to partially wipe out by the publication of all his great works.

It is to be hoped that the Society may receive the support of all lovers of their national music in their praiseworthy endeavours to bring all these treasures into print. The Purcell Festival in Westminster Abbey in 1895, the bi-centenary of his death, was another worthy and interesting effort to stir up the English people to a sense of the value of their greatest composer.

Several attempts have been made from time to time to bring his anthems and other compositions within the reach of musical people, and we owe Vincent Novello a debt of gratitude for carrying on, from 1828 to 1832, with such unselfish energy, the publication of much of the master's sacred music.

It should be a humiliating rebuke for English music-lovers to read a Frenchman's eloquent tribute to Purcell in such language as the following—I translate from M. Amadée Mereaux's writing: "We have here a name which is not anything like so well known as it deserves to be! It is that of a great musician, whose career in the world of music left traces of extraordinary progress. Nevertheless, the musical world, if it has not wholly forgotten him, has not paid the tribute justly due to his genius. Henry Purcell is one of the artistic glories of England; he is, without doubt, the most able and most fertile of all the English composers.'

CHAPTER XIII.

CROFT, WELDON, JEREMIAH CLARKE, AND ROGERS.

A LESS distinguished, but nevertheless a distinguished, pupil of Blow's was William Croft (or as he sometimes wrote his name, Crofts), born in Warwickshire in 1678. He studied under Blow as one of the Children of the Chapel Royal, became a Gentleman of the Chapel in 1700, and, four years later, joint-organist with his old fellow chorister, Jeremiah Clarke. When Dr. Blow died, in 1708, Croft succeeded him at the Abbey. He had also been organist of St. Anne's, Soho, from the time an organ was erected in that church; a church which to this day honours in an especial manner, by its admirable performance of Bach's Passion Music, that art of which Croft was so earnest and serious an exponent.

Hogarth, the Scottish musical historian (whose daughter was married to Charles Dickens), writes : " Dr. Croft's Anthems are very good and solemn ; their harmony is pure and their melody elegant and expressive."

Many of his noble anthems were composed in Queen Anne's reign to celebrate, by public thanksgiving, the victories of the Duke of Marlborough, culminating in the Peace of Utrecht, for which event Croft wrote two Odes, one being his doctor's exercise at Oxford.

In 1715 he was allowed an extra stipend of £80 by the new monarch, King George I., for teaching the Chapel children " to read, write, and cast accompts."

In 1724 he published, in two folio volumes, with a portrait finely engraved by Vertue, thirty anthems and that noble music to the Burial Service which accompanies our great ones to the tomb on so many solemn and sad occasions.

In his preface Croft states that his is the first attempt to print church music *in score* from pewter plates. Only separate *parts* had been issued previously.

Croft died in 1727, just after King George I.'s death, and was buried alongside the other great church musicians who preceded him, in the North Aisle of Westminster Abbey.

Among his finest anthems must be numbered " God is gone up," " Cry aloud and shout," and " Hear my prayer, O Lord." In his earlier days he also wrote for the stage, and composed Sonatas for both violin and flute.

One of the men who had the proud distinction to be a pupil of Henry Purcell claims our attention here—namely, John Weldon.

He was educated at Eton and received his earlier instruction there from John Walter. In 1694 he went to Oxford as organist of New College. Like most good musicians of the period, he was sworn in as Gentleman of the Chapel Royal, and, upon Dr. Blow's death, became organist and, nine years later, composer at Whitehall. He died in 1736. Although a composer of many songs, which were popular at the time, he will be best remembered by his church writings, beautiful in melody and strong in harmony. Six anthems with alto solos were written for the well-known alto of his period, Richard Elford. His beautiful " In Thee, O Lord, have I put my trust " is still a favourite anthem.

Jeremiah Clarke, familiarly known as " Jerry," was the first organist of the new St. Paul's Cathedral, which was opened with great ceremony and state on the 2nd December, 1697.* He was born in 1670, and was a pupil of Blow's, at the Chapel Royal. He then went to Winchester as organist of the College, but came to London again in 1693, in order to succeed his old master as Almoner of St. Paul's, being fully admitted as vicar-choral in 1705. He was joint-organist of " His Majesty's Chappell " with Croft in 1704. A curious foreboding of the tragic termination to his life seems to pervade Clarke's anthems. They appear to be the work of a highly sensitive and melancholy man, being pathetic in nature and with an elegiac tendency.

He is supposed to have aspired to the hand of a lady far above him in position, and to have taken the rejection of his suit so seriously that, in a fit of mad dejection, he shot himself, on December 1, 1707, in St. Paul's Churchyard.

An exception to the generally pathetic tone of such anthems as " Bow down Thine ear," &c., will be found in his powerful thanksgiving anthems for Marlborough's great victories against the French, and in his Coronation Anthem for Queen Anne, " Praise the Lord, O Jerusalem."

His reported jealousy of Charles King, his pupil and, later, his brother-in-law, was also supposed to prey upon his mind, but would scarcely have led to his suicide.

Dr. Benjamin Rogers, the last writer of this period to be mentioned, was not only born in Windsor but spent a large part of his life there. He was chorister and afterwards lay-clerk at St. George's Chapel, and about the time of the Restoration became organist of Eton College. Until the Rebellion in 1641 he was organist of Christ Church Cathedral, Dublin. During the English rebellion, when in 1644 the choir at St. George's Chapel was broken up, he still lived and taught music in Windsor.

---

* A complete and most interesting description of this is given by Mr. J. S. Bumpus, in his valuable work, " The Organists and Composers of St. Paul's Cathedral," p. 56.

His " Hymnus Eucharisticus " is sung at five o'clock on May-Day morning every year on Magdalen Tower, Oxford.   Several of his tuneful anthems—tuneful, but of no great strength—may still be heard in our Cathedrals.

Before considering the Third Period, let us take a short review of the Anthem of the seventeenth century.   For the remaining three years of Queen Elizabeth's reign and during that of James I., the old, strong, contrapuntal style was still in vogue, and some of the finest anthem writers still living.

The sacred and the secular, the anthem and the madrigal, were also so similar in treatment that the words more than the music denoted which was which.   Then in King Charles I.'s reign came the Civil War, the closing of organs, destruction of music, breaking up of Cathedral choirs, and the anthem almost at a standstill. Finally, in 1660, with the Restoration of King Charles II. came the re-opening of the Cathedral service, the reconstitution of the Chapel Royal, and fresh life put into Church music, but obtained partly at the cost of the former dignified, ecclesiastical strictness of form. In place of simple vocal counterpoint, of which the accompaniment, a scarcely necessary adjunct, was but the *fac-simile*, there were gradually introduced the verse and solo anthems, with their independent symphonies and ritornellos, often graced (as the King fancied), or more possibly disgraced, with twiddles and turns enough to upset the reverence of the music and mar the serious character of the words.

With brilliant exceptions, this state of things extended to the eighteenth century.

WILLIAM CROFT.

LIST OF ANTHEMS AND COMPOSERS OF THE SEVENTEENTH CENTURY.

AKEROYDE, SAMUEL.
Popular Composer of the latter part of the 17th Century. Wrote songs in the
" Theater of Musick," 1685-7, and " The Banquet of Musick," 1688, &c.

1. They that put their trust
   Congreg. Church Music

ALDRICH, Very Rev. HENRY, M.A., D.D. B. 1647 ; D. 1710.
Rector of Wem, Shropshire ; Dean of Christ Church, Oxon., 1689.

1. By the waters	*Calv.*	13. O God, Thou art my God	*Tudway*
2. Comfort ye My people	*Tudway*	14. O Lord, grant the King	,,
3. Give the King	,,	15. O Lord, I have heard	,,
4. God is our hope	*Page*	16. O Lord, our Governour	,,
5. Have mercy upon me	*Tudway*	17. O praise our God	*Chester*
6. Hear my prayer	*Husk*	18. O praise the Lord	*Tudway*
7. Hide not Thou Thy Face	*Mason*	19. Out of the deep	*Wells*
8. If the Lord Himself	*Tudway*	20. Save me, O God	*Joule*
9. I will love Thee	,,	21. Sing unto the Lord	*Tudway*
10. Like as the hart	*Husk*	22. The Lord is King	,,
11. Man that is born	*Joule*	23. Who is this that cometh ?	,,
12. O give thanks	*King's*		

And adaptations and arrangements from Italian and English masters.

ALLINSON (ALLANSON), THOMAS, D. 1704.
Org. Lincoln Cath. after Hecht, 1693-1704. MSS. in Lincoln Cath. Library.

1. Behold, God is my Helper	*Lincoln*	4. Have mercy upon me	*Lincoln*
2. Behold, God is my salvation	,,	5. I will bless the Lord at all	
3. Behold now, praise the Lord		times	,,
	Durham	(*Thanksgiving Anthem.*)	

ARBUTHNOT, JOHN, M.D. B. 1667 ; D. 1735.

As pants the hart   *Croft* |

BISHOP, JOHN. B. 1665 ; D. 1737.
Org. King's College, Cambridge (for three months) ; Org., Winchester College,
1695, and Cath., 1729, after Vaughan Richardson.

1. Blessed are all they	*Joule*	8. O give thanks	*Joule*
2. Blessed are the people	*Bumpus*	9. O how amiable	*Marshall*
3. Bow down Thine ear	*Weekes*	10. O Lord our Governour	*Cath. Mag.*
4. Call to remembrance	*The Choir*	11. Out of the deep	*Joule*
5. Holy, holy, holy	*Cope*		(*Adapted by Mason*)
6. I will magnify Thee	*Bumpus*	12. Thou art my King	*Bumpus*
7. O be joyful	*The Choir*	13. Withdraw not Thou	

BLOW, JOHN, MUS. DOC., Cantuar. B. 1648; D. 1708.

Chapel Royal boy, 1660; Org. St. Peter's, Westminster, 1669-80 and 1695-1708; Gent. and Master of Children of the Chapel Royal, 1674; Org. 1676; First *Composer* to the Chapel Royal, 1699; Almoner of St. Paul's, 1687-93.

1. And I heard a great voice   *King's*
   (*Nearly identical with* 38.)
2. Arise, O Lord   *Warren*
3. Ascribe unto the Lord   ,,
4. Awake, awake, utter a song   ,,
5. Behold, how good and joyful ,,
   (*with Croft and J. Clark*)
6. Behold, how good and joyful
   (3 *voices.*)   *Warren*
7. Behold, in heaven   *Husk*
8. Behold, now praise   *King's*
9. Behold, O God   *Warren*
   (*Coronation Anthem.*)
10. Be merciful   *Husk*
11. Blessed be the Lord   ,,
12. Blessed is he whose   *Warren*
13. Blessed is the man   ,,
   (2 *voices.*)
14. Blessed is the man   ,,
   (3 *voices.*)
15. Blessed is the man   ,,
   (4 *voices.*)
16. Bow down Thine ear   *Husk*
17. Bring unto the Lord   *Warren*
18. Christ being raised   *Ely MSS.*
19. Consider mine enemies   *Novello*
20. Cry aloud and spare not *Warren*
21. Glory be to the Father.
22. God is our hope   *King's*
   (*Full with verse, 8 voices.*)
23. God is our hope   *Boyce*
   (8 *voices.*)
24. God is our hope   *Warren*
   (2 *voices.*)
25. God spake sometime   *Ely*
   (*Coronation of James II.*)
26. Hear my prayer.
27. Hear my voice   *King's*
28. Holy, holy, holy   *Marsh*
29. How art thou fallen   *Warren*
30. How dear are Thy counsels *Calvert*
31. How doth the city   *Warren*
32. I beheld, and lo! a great *Boyce*
33. I beheld, and lo! in the *King's*
34. In the time of trouble   *Husk*
35. I said "In the cutting off" *Ely*
36. I waited patiently   *Warren*
37. I was glad, when they said *Ely*
(*Opening of St. Paul's Cathedral,* 1697.)
38. I was in the spirit   *Boyce*
   (*Nearly identical with No.* 1.)

39.*I will alway give thanks
             Club Anthem
   (*3rd part only by Blow.*)
40. I will call upon the Lord *King's*
41. I will cry unto Thee   ,,
42. I will hearken   ,,
43. I will magnify Thee   *Warren*
44. I will praise the Name   *Husk*
45. Jesus, seeing the multitude
             Warren
46. Let my prayer   *Husk*
47. Let the righteous be glad   ,,
48. Let Thy Hand be strengthened
             Warren
49. Let Thy merciful kindness   ,,
   (*3rd part of Club Anthem.*)
50. Lift up your heads   *King's*
51. Look upon mine adversity *Novello*
52. Lord, how are they increased
            Cath. Mag.
53. Lord, remember David   *Ely*
54. Lord, Thou art become   *Warren*
55. Lord, Thou art become   *Husk*
   (*Full, with verse.*)
56. Lord, Thou hast become   *Warren*
57. Lord, Thou hast been our
   refuge   ,,
58. Lord, Thou knowest   *Husk*
59. Lord, who shall dwell?   *King's*
60. Man that is born   *Warren*
61. My days are gone   *Husk*
62. My God, my God, look!   *Boyce*
63. My God, my soul is vexed
             Warren
64. O be joyful in God   *Husk*
65. O give thanks, and call   *King's*
66. O give thanks for His mercy.
67. O God, my heart is ready   *Ely*
68. O God, wherefore art Thou
   absent?   *Boyce*
69. O how amiable   *Tudway*
70. O Lord God of my
   Salvation.
71. O Lord God, to Whom
   vengeance   *Husk*
72. O Lord, I have sinned   *Boyce*
   (*Funeral of Gen. Monk.*)
73. O Lord, rebuke me not   *Warren*
74. O Lord, Thou art my God   *Ely*
75. O Lord, Thou hast searched *Boyce*
76. O praise the Lord   *Warren*

---

* The Club Anthem, composed by Humfrey, Turner, and Blow.

BLOW, JOHN (*continued*).

77. O pray for the peace	*Tudway*	97. The Kings of Tharsis	*Tudway*
78. O sing unto God	*Warren*	98. The Lord, even the most	
79. O sing unto the Lord	*King's*	mighty	*Warren*
80. Ponder my words	*Warren*	99. The Lord God is a sun	,,
81. Praise the Lord, O Jerusalem	,,	100. The Lord hear thee	,,
82. Praise the Lord, O my soul		101. The Lord is King	*Husk*
	Tudway	102. The Lord is King	*King's*
(*Psalm* 104.)		103. The Lord is my Shepherd	*Tudway*
83. Praise the Lord, O my soul	*Husk*	104. The voice of the Lord	*Novello*
(*Psalm* 146.)		105. Thy hands have made me	*Husk*
84. Praise the Lord, ye servants		106. Thy mercy, O Lord	*King's*
	Warren	107. Thy righteousness, O Lord	
85. Praise thou the Lord	*Novello*		*Tudway*
86. Put me not to rebuke	*Husk*	108. Thy way, O God	*Warren*
87. Salvator Mundi	*Novello*	109. Turn Thee unto me	*King's*
88. Save, Lord, and hear us	,,	110. Turn Thou us	*Warren*
89. Save me, O God	*Boyce*	111. Turn us again, O God	,,
90. Shew us Thy mercy	*Novello*	112. Up, Lord, and help me	*Novello*
91. Sing unto the Lord a new	*King's*	113. We will rejoice	*Ely*
92. Sing unto the Lord, O ye	,,	114. When Israel came out	*Bumpus*
93. Sing we merrily	*Page*	115. When the Lord turned	*Ely*
94. Teach me Thy ways	*Husk*	116. When the Son of Man	*Husk*
95. The days of man	,,	117. Wherefore art Thou absent?	
96. The King shall rejoice	*Warren*	118. Why do the heathen?	*Ely*

BOWMAN, JOHN.
Org. Trin. Coll., Cambridge, 1709-30.

1. Show yourselves joyful   *Tudway* |

BREWER, THOMAS. B. 1611.
Educated at Christ's Hospital.

1.*Eternal King.

BRIND, RICHARD. B. 16—; D. 1718.
Org. St. Paul's Cath., after Clarke, until 1718. Taught Greene as articled pupil.

1. Behold, God is my salvation		3. I will magnify Thee	*Div. Har.*
	Div. Har.	4. Let God arise	,,
2. I will give thanks	,,	5. O sing unto the Lord	,,

BRODERIP, WILLIAM. B. 1683; D. 1726.
Org. Wells Cath., 1713-26.

1. God is our hope and strength |
Tudway |

BROWNE (BROWN), RICHARD. D. 1664.
Org. Wells Cath., 1614; Worcester Cath., 1662-64.

1. Christ rising	*Husk*	4. O Lord, rebuke me not	*Husk*
2. I have declared	,,	5. To Thee, O Lord, I make	,,
3. My God, my God	,,	6. Unto Him that loved us	*Clifford*

---

* Printed at the end of Clifford's "Divine Services and Anthems," 1664, as "A Psalm of Thanksgiving to be sung by the Children of Christ's Hospital."

BRYAN (BRYNE), ALBERTUS. B. *c.* 1621 ; D. 1669.

Pupil of John Tomkins; Org. St. Paul's Cath., 1638. Deposed by Commonwealth, and replaced by Charles II. When the Great Fire destroyed St. Paul's, he became Org. of Westminster Abbey (succeeding Christ. Gibbons) and of Dulwich College.

1. Behold, how good	*Clifford*	3. I heard a voice	*Clifford*
2. How long wilt Thou forget me	*Bumpus*		

BULLIS, THOMAS, Senr.

Lay Clerk of Ely Cath., 1677-82.

1. Holy, Holy, Holy	*Ely*	4. O God, Thou hast cast	*Ely*
2. Lord, Thou hast been	,,	5. O Lord, Holy Father	,,
3. O clap your hands	,,		

BULLIS, THOMAS, Junr.

Org. Ely Cath., 1682, for six months prior to Hawkins' appointment.

1. Blessed is the man	*Ely*	4. O ye little flock	*Ely*
2. I will magnify	,,	5. The Lord is my strength	,,
3. O Lord, rebuke me not	,,	6. Why do the heathen ?	,,

CARRE, GEORGE.

Org. Llandaff Cath. in 1629.

1. I have lifted up mine eyes	*Clifford*	2. Let Thy loving mercy	*Clifford*

CHILD, WILLIAM, Mus. Doc., Oxon. B. 1606 ; D. 1696.

Pupil of Elway Bevin (at Bristol Cath.); Org. St. George's, Windsor (after J. Mundy), 1631 ; Org. Chapel Royal; Composer to the King, 1661.

1.*Almighty God.		22. O Lord, grant the King	*Boyce*
2.*And though I were.		23. O Lord, grant the King	*King's*
3. Awake, my soul	*Clifford*	(*Different from No.* 22.)	
4. Behold, how good	*Ely*	24. O Lord, rebuke me not.	
5. Blessed be the Lord	,,	25. O Lord, Thou hast searched	
6. Bow down Thine ear	*Peterh.*		*Peterh.*
7. Give the King Thy judgments *Ely*		26. O Lord, wherefore art Thou	
(*Attributed to Weelkes or Woodson.*)		absent ?	,,
8. Hear, O My people	*Peterh.*	27. O praise the Lord, laud ye *Tudway*	
9. Holy, holy, holy.		28. O pray for the peace	*Novello*
10. I am the Resurrection	*Peterh.*	29. O sing unto the Lord	*Ely*
(*Part of Burial Service.*)		30. O that the salvation.	
11. If the Lord Himself	*Arnold*	31. O worship the Lord.	
12. I will be glad.		32. Praise the Lord, O my soul *Boyce*	
13. Let God arise	*Ely*	33.*Praise ye the strength.	
14. Lord, how long.		34. Save me, O God.	
15. My heart is fixed.		35.*Sing unto God.	
16.*My soul truly waiteth.		36. Sing we merrily	*Boyce*
17. O Almighty God	*Peterh.*	37. The earth is the Lord's.	
(*Collect for All Saints.*)		38. The King shall rejoice.	
18. O clap your hands	*Cope*	39.*The Spirit of Grace.	
19. O how amiable.		40. Thou art my King, O God	*Ely*
20. O let my mouth	*Ely*	41. Turn Thou us.	*Peterh.*
21. O Lord God, the heathen	,,	42. What shall I render	,,

---

* The *words* of these are in a MS. volume, *temp.* Charles I., in the Harleian Collection, British Museum.

CHURCH, JOHN. B. 1675; D. 1741.

Gent. Chapel Royal, 1697, and Lay-Vicar and Master of Choristers, St. Peter's, Westminster, 1704. Composer and writer,

1. Blessed are those that are undefiled	*Tudway*	9. O sing unto the Lord a new song	*Calvert*
2. Blessed is he whose	*Div. Har.*	10. Out of the deep	,,
3. I will call upon the Lord	*Dolben*	11. Praise the Lord	*Tudway*
4. I will give thanks	*Chap. Roy.*	12. Righteous art Thou	,,
5. I will magnify Thee	*Bumpus*	13. Thou art my Portion	
6. Lord, Thou art become	*Tudway*		*Chap. Roy.*, 1749
7. O Lord, grant the Queen	,,	14. Turn Thy face	*Tudway*
8. O Lord my God	*Husk*	15. Unto Thee, O Lord	*Husk*

CLARKE (CLARK), JEREMIAH. B. 1670; D. (suicide) 1707.

Org. Winchester College, 1692-95; Almoner, St. Paul's, 1693; Gent. Chapel Royal, 1700; Org. Chapel Royal (with Croft), 1704; Org. and Vicar-Choral, 1705.

1. Behold, how good *(With Croft and Blow.)*	*Div. Har.*	13. O be joyful in God	*Walsh's Div. Har.*
2. Bow down Thine ear	*Page*	14. O Jerusalem	*Dublin*
3. Hear my crying, O God (MS.)	*Mann*	15. O Lord God of my salvation	*Boyce*
4. Holy, Holy, Holy	*Calvert*	16. O Lord, rebuke me not	*St. Paul's*
5. How long wilt Thou	*Boyce*	17. Praise the Lord, O Jerusalem *(Coronation of Queen Anne.)*	*Boyce*
6. I am the Resurrection	*Wells*		
7. I will give thanks	*Ely*	18. Praise the Lord, O my soul	*Playford's Div. Com.*
8.*I will love Thee, O Lord *(Thanksgiving for Marlborough's victories.)*	*Boyce*	19. Praise the Lord, O my soul *(Different to No. 18.)*	*Warren*
9. I will magnify Thee	*Ely*	20. The earth is the Lord's	*Tudway*
10. I will sing of the Lord *(Part of No. 5.)*	*Marsh*	21. The Lord is full of compassion	*Cath. Mag.*
11. I will sing unto the Lord *(Fragment.)*	*Fitzw.*	22. The Lord is my strength *(Thanksgiving for Victory of Ramillies, 1706.)*	*Page*
12. My song shall be of mercy	*Playford's Div. Com.*	23. This is the day which (MS.)	*Mann*

CLIFFORD, REV. JAMES. B. 1622; D. 1698.

Theological Writer. Author of "A Collection of Divine Services and Anthems," published 1663-64; Chorister of Magdalen College, Oxford, 1632; Minor Canon of St. Paul's, 1661; Senior Cardinal, 1682.

1. Instruct me, Lord *Clifford* |

COB, JOHN.

1. Let God arise *Clifford* |

---

* Different versions in MS. exist in some Cathedral libraries. The same words, set in an entirely different manner, are in a contemporary score book in possession of J. S. Bumpus. This copy has the following *colophon* :—"Thanksgiving Anthem, Sep. 23, 1705, at S. Paul's. The Queen present for the Victory and Success in Flanders in passing the French lines."

COOKE, Captain HENRY.   B. *c.* 1610; D. 1672.
First Master of the Children of the Chapel Royal after the Restoration (1660)

1. Blessed is he that considereth	*Clifford*	11. O clap your hands	*Clifford*
2. Christ rising again	,,	12. O Lord my God	,,
3. Darkness, a rest	,,	13. O sing unto the Lord	,,
4. Hear my cry, O God	,,	14. Praise the Lord, for it is	,,
5. Hear'st thou, my soul?	,,	15. Sing and rejoice	,,
6. I will alway give thanks	,,	16. The King shall rejoice	,,
7. Let my prayers	,,	17. The Lord in His wrath	*Husk*
8. Look up, languishing soul	,,	18. The Lord is my Shepherd	*Clifford*
9. My ravisht soul	,,	19. The twelve apostles in a ring	,,
10. My song shall be always	,,	20. Unto Thee, O Lord	,,

COOPER, JAMES.   D. 1721.
Org. Norwich Cathedral.

1. Glory to God in the highest	*Calvert*	3. Not unto us	*Norwich*
2. I waited patiently	*Tudway*	4. O give thanks	*Marshall*
		5. The Lord is King	*Mann*

CRANFORD, WILLIAM.   B. *c.* 1635.
Chorister in St. Paul's Cath., 1650; assisted in compiling Ravenscroft's Psalter.

1. How long, O Lord?	*Husk*	4.*The King shall rejoice	*Peterh.*
2.*I will love Thee	*Peterh.*	(*Identical with No. 3.*)	
3.*O Lord, make Thy servant Charles	*Husk*		

CREYGHTON (CREIGHTON), Rev. ROBERT, D.D.   B. 1640; D. 1733.
Son of the Bishop of Bath and Wells of the same name.   Professor of Greek in Cambridge University, 1662; Canon and Precentor of Wells, 1674.

1. Behold now, praise	*Cope*	6. O praise the Lord of heaven	*Wells*
2. God is our hope	*Husk*	7. Praise the Lord, O my soul	*Novello*
3. I will arise	*Boyce*	8. Thou, O God, art praised	*Husk*
4. Lord, let me know	*Husk*	9. Thy mercy, O Lord	*King's*, 1706
5. O praise God	*Wells*	10. Who shall ascend?	*Husk*

CROFT, WILLIAM, Mus. Doc., Oxon.   B. 1678; D. 1727.
Chapel Royal boy; Org. St. Anne's, Soho, 1700-11; Gent. Chapel Royal, 1700; Org. (with Jer. Clarke), 1704; and sole Org. 1707; succeeded Blow at St. Peter's, Westminster, 1708.

1. All the world	*Calvert*	10.†Cry aloud and shout	*Novello*
2. Behold, how good	*Div. Har.*	(*Part of No.* 58.)	
(*With J. Clarke and Blow*).		11. Deliver us, O Lord	*Page*
3. Behold, now praise *Chap.Roy.*,1724		12. Eternal Father	*Warren*
4. Be merciful unto me	*Arnold*	13. Give ear, O Lord	*Durham*
5.†Blessed are all they	*Novello*	14. Give thanks unto the Lord	*Marshall*
6. Blessed be He that cometh	*Durham*		
7. Blessed be the Lord	*Dublin*	15. Give the King thy judgments	*Boyce*
8. Blessed is the man	*Chap. Roy.*		
9. Blessed is the people	*Page*	16. God is gone up	,,

---

* Also attributed to *Thomas* Cranford.
† "Thirty Select Anthems," 2 vols., 1724.   New edition by Vincent Novello, 1847.

CROFT, WILLIAM (*continued*).

17. Hear me, O Lord   *York*, 1782
18. Hear my crying   *Birchall*
19. Hear my prayer, O God,
    and hide not   *Div. Har.*
20.*Hear my prayer O Lord,
    and consider
21.*Hear my prayer, O Lord, and let.
22. He loveth righteousness
    Chichester, 1868
    (*Part of No.* 74.)
23. Help us, O God   *Calvert*
24. Holy, Holy, Holy   ,,
25.*How dear are Thy counsels *Novello*
    (*2nd part of No.* 61.)
26.†I am the Resurrection   ,,
27.*I cried unto the Lord   ,,
28.†I heard a voice   ,,
29.†In the midst of life   ,,
30. I waited patiently   *King's*
31.*I will alway give thanks   *Novello*
    (*A thanksgiving for the Victory
    at Oudenard*, 1708. *Words
    appointed by Queen Anne.*)
32. I will give thanks   *Novello*
    (A.T.B.)
    (*A thanksgiving for the Victory
    at Blenheim.*)
33. I will give thanks   *Arnold*
    (5 *voices.*)
34. I will lift up mine eyes   *King's*
35. I will magnify Thee,
    O God   *Marshall*
36. I will magnify Thee,
    O Lord   *Div. Har.*
37.*I will sing unto the Lord   *Novello*
38. Let my complaint   *Calvert*
39. Lift up your hands   *Durham*
40. Like as the hart   *Warren*
41.*Lord, what love have I   *Novello*
42.†Man that is born   ,,
43. My song shall be alway   *Warren*
44. My soul, be thou joyful *Cath. Mag.*
45.*O be joyful in God   *Novello*
46. O clap your hands   *Cath. Mag.*
47. O come hither   *Calvert*
48. O come, let us sing   *Div. Har.*
49. Offer the sacrifice   *Tudway*
50. O give thanks unto the
    Lord, and call   *Joule*
51. O give thanks unto the
    Lord, for He *Chap. Roy.*, 1749
52.*O give thanks unto the
    Lord, for He   *Novello*
    (S.A.T.B.)

53. O God of Hosts   *Durham*
54. O how amiable   *Ely*
55.*O Lord God of my
    salvation   *Novello*
    (A.T.B.)
56.*O Lord God of my
    salvation   ,,
    (4 *and* 6 *voices.*)
57.*O Lord, grant the King   ,,
58.*O Lord, I will praise Thee   ,,
59. O Lord our Governour   *Joule*
60.*O Lord, rebuke me not *Novello*
61.*O Lord, Thou hast
    searched   ,,
62. O Lord, Thy Word
    endureth   *Div. Har.*
63. O praise the Lord, all
    ye heathen   *Boyce*
64.*O praise the Lord, ye
    that fear
65. O praise the Lord
    (*Psalm* 147.)   *Chap. Roy.*
66. O sing praises unto
    our God   *King's*
    (2 *movements ; the 2nd from No.* 16).
67. O sing unto the Lord *Marshall*
68.*Out of the deep   *Novello*
69. Praise God in His Holiness *Husk*
70. Praise God in His
    sanctuary   *King's*
71.*Praise the Lord, O
    my soul   *Chap. Roy.*
72. Put me not to rebuke *Novello*
    (4 *voices.*)
73. Put me not to rebuke   *Boyce*
    (3 *voices.*)
74.*Rejoice in the Lord, O ye *Warren*
75.*Sing praises to :he Lord *Boyce*
76. Sing unto God   *Wells*
77.*Sing unto God, O ye kingdoms
    York
78.*Sing unto the Lord and
    praise   *Novello*
79. Sing unto the Lord, for He ﹀ *York*
80. Teach me, O Lord *Chap. Roy.*, 1724
81.*The earth is the Lord's *Novello*
82.*The heavens declare   ,,
83. The Lord hath
    appeared   *Birchall, c.* 1780
84. The Lord is a Sun   *St. Paul's*
85.*The Lord is King   *Novello*
86. The Lord is my Light   *Page*
87. The Lord is my Light *Jesus Coll.*
    (*Psalm* 27).

* " Thirty Select Anthems," 2 vols., 1724. New edition by Vincent Novello, 1847.
† Burial Service.

CROFT, WILLIAM (*continued*).

88.*The Lord is my strength   *Novello*
      (*A thanksgiving for the Victory
      at Brabant.*)
89. The Lord is my strength   *Dublin*
      (*Different from No. 88.*)
90. The Lord of Hosts   *Cath. Mag.*
91. The Lord shall make
      good   *Marshall*
92. The souls of the righteous   *King's*
      (*Performed at Queen Anne's funeral.*)

93.*This is the day   *Novello*
94.*Thou, O God, art praised   ,,
95. Try me, O God   *King's*
96. Unto Thee, O Lord   *Fitzw.*
      (*Organ part only.*)
97.*We wait for Thy loving   *Novello*
98.*We will rejoice   ,,
      (*A thanksgiving for Quadruple
      Alliance or for Victory off
      Cape Passaro, 1718.*)

DAVIES, HUGH, Mus. Bac., Oxon.   B. *c.* 1600; D. *c.* 1664.
   Org. Hereford Cathedral, 1630-44.

   1. Thou, O God   *Ely* |

DAVIS (DAVIES), WILLIAM.
   Org. Worcester Cath., *c.* 1712-26.

   1. Help, Lord, for the
      godly   *Div. Har.*
   2. I will give thanks   ,,
   3.†Let God arise   *Bumpus*

   4. They that go down   *Joule*
   5. They that put their
      trust   *Div. Har.*
   6. Unto Thee will I cry   ,,

ELLIS, WILLIAM, Mus. Bac., Oxon, 1639.   D. 1674.
   Org. Eton College ; Org. St. John's College, Oxon., 1646, and later.

   1. Almighty God   *Bumpus*
      (*St. John Baptist's Day.*)
   2. O Lord our Governour   *Bumpus*

   3. This is the record of John   *Bumpus*
      (*For St. John Baptist's Day.*)

FERRABOSCO (FERABOSCO), JOHN, Mus. Doc., Cantab.   D. 1682.
   Org. Ely Cath., 1662-82.

   1. Behold, now, praise   *Ely*
   2. Be Thou exalted   ,,
   3. Blessed is the man   ,,
   4. Bow down Thine ear   ,,
   5. By the waters   ,,
   6. I will sing a new song   ,,

   7. Let God arise   *Ely*
      (*Verses by Lawes. Chorus by Ferabosco.*)
   8. Like as the hart   *Ely*
   9. O Lord our Governour   ,,
   10. The King shall rejoice   ,,
   11. The Lord hear thee   ,,
   12. The Lord is my strength   ,,

FINCH, Hon. and Rev. EDWARD.   B. 1664; D. 1737.
   Prebendary of York Minster and brother of Dean Finch.

   1.‡By the waters of Babylon   *Joule* | 2. Grant, we beseech Thee   *Tudway*

FISHER, LAWRENCE.

   1. I beheld and lo!   *Clifford* |

---

* " Thirty Select Anthems," 2 vols. 1724. New edition by Vincent Novello, 1847.
† Autograph score, " Humbly presented to the Ld. Bishop of Oxford."
‡ Partly adapted to the music of Steffani.

FOSTER, JOHN. D. **1677.**
Org. Durham Cath., 1661-77.

1. Almighty and everlasting *Durham*
2. Almighty God, Who art
   always   ,,
3. Almighty God, Who seest ,,
4. Glory be to God   ,,
5. I am the Resurrection ,,
6. If the Lord Himself   ,,
7. I heard a voice from heaven
                     Durham
8. Lord, what is man   ,,
9. My song shall be of mercy ,,
10. Set up Thyself   ,,
11. What reward shall I give ,,
12. When the Lord turned ,,

GALE, ——
1. O how amiable   *Durham* |

GATES, BERNARD. B. **1685**; D. **1773.**
Master of the Choristers of Chapel Royal and Westminster, 1740-58.

1. How long wilt thou? *Bumpus*
2. I will give thanks   ,,
3. I will lift up   ,,
      (*Psalm* 121.)
4. O be joyful in the Lord *Bumpus*
5. Rejoice in the Lord, O ye ,,
6. The Lord is my Light   ,,

GIBBONS, CHRISTOPHER, MUS. DOC., OXON. B. **1615**; D. **1676.**
Son of Orlando Gibbons. Org. Winchester Cath., 1640-44; joined Royalist Army 1644; Org. Westminster Abbey, 1660-65; Chapels Royal, 1660-76

1. Above the stars my Saviour.
2. How long wilt Thou
   forget?   *Tudway*
3. Let Thy merciful ears.
4. Sing unto the Lord.
5. Teach me, O Lord *Div. Har.*
6. The Lord said.

GIBBS, RICHARD. D. *c.* **1630.**
Org. Norwich Cath., (?) 1622-30.

1. Have mercy   *Ely*
2. If the Lord Himself *Clifford*
3. Look, shepherds, look!   ,,
4. Lord, in Thy wrath *Clifford*
5. O give thanks   *Tudway*
6. See, sinful soul   *Clifford*

GOLDWIN (GOLDING), JOHN. B. **1670**; D. **1719.**
Pupil of Dr. Child, whom he succeeded at St. George's Chapel, Windsor, 1697.

1. Ascribe unto the Lord *Tudway*
2. Behold, my servant *Boyce*
3. Blessed be the Lord God *Gloucester*
4. Come, ye children *Calvert*
5. Do well, O Lord   ,,
6. Hear me, O God *Div. Har.*
7. Holy, Holy, Holy *Warren*
8. I am well pleased.
9. I have set God alway *Boyce*
10. I will dwell in Thy
    tabernacle *Div. Har.*
11. I will magnify   *Ely*
12. I will sing unto the Lord *Page*
13. O be joyful   *Tudway*
14. O clap your hands   *Ely*
15. O Lord God of Hosts *Tudway*
16. O Lord, how glorious *Marshall*
17. O Lord my God   *Boyce*
18. O love the Lord   *Cope*
19. O praise God in His holiness *Page*
20. O praise the Lord, all ye
    heathen   *Cope*
21. Ponder my words *Gloucester*
22. Praise the Lord, ye
    servants *Div. Har.*
23. The Lord is King *Warren*
24. Thy way, O God *Tudway*

GOODSON, RICHARD, Senr., Mus.B., Oxon.   B. 1655 ; D. 1718.
Org. New Coll., Oxford, and Professor of Music in the University, 1682 ;
   Org. Christ Church Cath. 1691-1718.

1. I am the Resurrection
                    Dr. Cooke's MSS.

GREENE, MAURICE, Mus. Doc., Cantab.   B. 1695 ; D. 1755.
Chorister of St. Paul's under Jer. Clarke, Charles King, and Brind, whom he
   succeeded as Org. St. Paul's, 1718-55, after having been Org. St. Dunstan's,
   Fleet Street, and St. Andrew's, Holborn ; Org. and Comp. Chapel Royal,
   1727 ; Professor of Music, Cambridge University (after Tudway). He
   helped (with Festing) to found the Royal Society of Musicians.

1.*Acquaint thyself with God
2. All the kings of the earth *Durham*
3.*Arise, shine, O Zion
4.*Behold, happy is the man
   (*Only the last movement of No. 37.*)
5.*Behold, I bring you
6. Behold, the Lord is my Salvation
7.*Blessed are they   [*Boosey*
8.*Blessed are those
9. Blessed is he that
   considereth *Foundling Hymn Bk.*
10. Blessed is the man   *Dublin*
11. Blest is the man (Ps. 1)
            Foundling Hymn Bk.
12. Bow down Thine ear   *Page*
    (*Composed ætat 23.*)
13. But be not Thou far   *Rochester*
14. Glory be to God   *Chap. Roy.*
15.*God is our hope and strength
16.*Have mercy upon me
    (*Alto solo.*)
17. Have mercy upon me   *Lonsdale*
18. Hearken unto me   *Ely*
19. Hear my crying   *Lonsdale*
20. Hear my crying   *Page*
    (*Verse, 2 voices.*)
21. Hear my prayer, O God   *Arnold,*
    (*Verse, 4 voices*).   [1790.
22.*Hear my prayer, O Lord
23. Hear my prayer, O Lord *Birchall*
    (*Verse, 3 voices.*)
24. Hear, O Lord, and consider *King's*
25.*Hear, O Lord, and have mercy
26.*How long wilt Thou forget?
27. I call with my whole heart *Birchall*
28. I cried unto the Lord   ,,
29. I have longed for Thy saving
    health   *Calvert*
30. I will alway give thanks
            Lonsdale & Page
31. I will be glad and rejoice *Dublin*

32.*I will give thanks.
33. I will love Thee   *Chap. Roy.*
34. I will magnify Thee
            Lonsdale & Arnold
35. I will pay my vows   *Durham*
36. I will praise the name   ,,
37.*I will seek unto God
38.*I will sing of Thy power
39.*Let God arise
40.*Let my complaint
    (*Alto solo.*)
41.*Let my complaint
    (*Verse,* S.S.A.T.B.)
42. Like as the hart *Lonsdale & Arnold*
43.*Lord, how are they increased
44.*Lord, how long wilt Thou ?
    (*Full, with verse,* S.S.A.T.B.)
45. Lord, how long wilt
    Thou ?   *Chap. Roy.*
    (*Different from* 44.)
46.*Lord, let me know
47. Lord, teach us to number *Calvert*
48.*My God, my God
49. My heart is fixed   *Novello*
50. My song shall be alway *Marshall*
51.*My soul truly waiteth
52. O be joyful 1726, *Coll. of Anthems*
53.*O clap your hands
54. O give thanks   *Lonsdale*
    (*Verse, 2 voices.*)
55.*O give thanks unto the Lord
    (*Verse,* A.B.)
56.*O God of my righteousness
57.*O God, Thou art my God
58. O God, Thou hast cast us out
                            Arnold
59.*O how amiable
60.*O Lord, give ear
61. O Lord God of Hosts   *Arnold*
62.*O Lord, grant the King
63. O Lord, I will praise Thee *Arnold*

* These were published by Greene himself in his "Forty Select Anthems." 2 vols.
1743. Later editions were issued by Lonsdale and Novello.

MAURICE GREENE.

GREENE, MAURICE (*continued*).

64. O Lord, look down   *Page*
65. O Lord, our Governor
        Lonsdale's reprint
66.*O praise our God
67. O praise the Lord all ye *St. Paul's*
68. O praise the Lord of
    Heaven   *Arnold*
69.*O sing unto God
70.*O sing unto the Lord (*Psalm* 96)
    (*Solo tenor.*)
71.*O sing unto (*Psalm* 149)
    (*Full, with verse,* S.S.A.T.B.)
72.*O sing unto the Lord
    (*Verse,* T.)
73. O that men   *Lichfield*
74. Ponder my words   *Page*
75. Praise the Lord, O
    Jerusalem   *Durham*
76.*Praise the Lord (*Psalm* 113)
    (*Solo treble.*)
77. Praise the Lord (*Psalm* 146) *Arnold*
78.*Praise the Lord, ye servants
    (*Verse,* S.S.)

79. Praise the Lord   *Clark*
    (*Full.*)
80.*Put me not to rebuke
81. Rejoice in the Lord *King's MSS.*
82. Save, Lord, and hear us *Durham*
83. Save me, O God   *Page*
84. Sing unto God, O ye   *Novello*
85. Sing unto the Lord and
    praise   *Chap. Roy.*
86.*Sing unto the Lord a new song
87. The eyes of all wait   *Durham*
88.*The King shall rejoice
89.*The Lord, even the most mighty
90. The Lord is gracious
    Chap. Roy., 1749
91.*The Lord is my Shepherd
92. The Lord is my strength
    Lonsdale & Page
93.*Thou, O God, art praised
94 *Thou visitest the earth
    (*Part of* 93.)
95. Try me, O God
96. We praise Thee, O God *Chap. Roy.*

GREGGS, WILLIAM. B. 16 —; D. 1710.
Succeeded John Foster as Org. Durham Cath., 1677-1710.

1. My heart is inditing   *Durham* |

HALL, HENRY, Senr. B. *c.* 1655; D. 1707 (1706, *Ely*).
Pupil of Capt. Cooke and Blow; took Deacon's Orders, 1696; Org. Exeter Cath., 1674; Org. and Vicar-Choral of Hereford Cath., 1688.

1. Arise, O Lord   *Marshall*
2. Behold, now praise   *Joule*
3. Blessed be the Lord my
    strength   *Ely*
4. By the waters of Babylon   ,,
5. Comfort ye, My people *Tudway*
6. In Thee, O Lord   *Calvert*
7. It is a good thing   ,,
8. I will cry   *Ely*
9. Let God arise   ,,
10. Lift up your heads   *Dublin*
11. My soul is weary   *Fitzw.*

12. O clap your hands   *Ely*
13. O God, Thou art my God *Calvert*
14. O Lord, rebuke me not   *Ely*
15. O praise the Lord, all ye
    heathen   *Marshall*
16. Righteous art Thou, O Lord *Joule*
17. Sing we merrily   *King's,* 1706
18. The souls of the righteous *Tudway*
19. Thou, O God, art praised *Calvert*
20. When the Lord   *King's,* 1706
21. Why do the heathen?   *Ely*

HALL, HENRY, Junr. B. 16 —; D. 1713.
Org. Hereford Cath., 1707-13.

1. Blessed be the Lord God   *Wells*
2. Deliver us, O Lord God *Marshall*
(*Attributed by Calvert to H. Hall, Senr.*)

3. Praise the Lord, ye servants
    Bumpus
4. We will rejoice   *Wells*

---

* These were published by Greene himself in his "Forty Select Anthems." 2 vols. 1743. Later editions were issued by Lonsdale and Novello.

HANDEL, GEORGE FREDERICK. B. 1685 (1684) ; D. 1759.

(12 CHANDOS ANTHEMS, 1718-20).

1. As pants the hart   *No. VI.*
2. Have mercy upon me   *No. III.*
3. In the Lord put I my trust   *No. II.*
4. I will magnify Thee   *No. V.*
5. Let God arise   *No. XI.*
6. My song shall be   *No. VII.*
7. O be joyful in the Lord   *No. I.*
8. O come, let us sing   *No. VIII.*
9. O praise the Lord with
   one consent   *No. IX.*
10. O praise the Lord, ye
    angels   *No. XII.*
11. O sing unto the Lord   *No. IV.*
12. The Lord is my Light   *No. X.*
*(Also arranged by him for the Chapel
            Royal in 1727.)*

(4 CORONATION ANTHEMS, 1727).

13. Let Thy hand be strengthened.
14. My heart is inditing.
15. The King shall rejoice.
16. Zadock the Priest.

(FUNERAL ANTHEM, 1727.)
17. The ways of Zion do mourn.

(FOUNDLING HOSPITAL ANTHEM, 1749.)
18. Blessed are they that consider*eth*
                                   (sic).

(WEDDING ANTHEMS, 1734 AND 1736.)
19. This is the day.
20. Sing unto God, ye kingdoms.

(DETTINGEN ANTHEM, 1743.)
21. The King shall rejoice.

HART, PHILIP. B. *c.* 1650 ; D. 1749.

Org. St. Mary Axe, London.

1. I will give thanks   *Ely* | 2. Praise the Lord, ye servants   *Ely*

HAWKINS, JAMES, Senr., Mus. B., Cantab., 1719. B. *c.* 1660 ; D. 1729.

Org. Ely Cath., 1682-1729.

1. Arise, O Lord   *Ely*
2. Ascribe unto the Lord   ,,
3. Behold, how good   ,,
4. Behold, how good *(No. 2)*   ,,
5. Behold, now praise   ,,
6. Behold, O God our Defender   ,,
7. Blessed be the Lord   ,,
8. Blessed be Thou   ,,
9. Blessed is He   ,,
10. Blow up the trumpet   ,,
11. Bow down Thine ear   ,,
12. Christ being raised   ,,
13. Deliver us, O Lord   ,,
14. Great is the Lord   ,,
15. Haste Thee, O God   ,,
16. Hear my prayer   ,,
17. Hear, O Thou Shepherd   ,,
18. Hold not Thy tongue   ,,
19. In Jewry is God known   ,,
20. In Thee, O Lord   ,,
21. In the Lord put I my trust   ,,
22. I waited patiently   ,,
            (Doubtful.)
23. I will call upon the Lord   ,,
24. I will exalt Thee   ,,
25. I will give thanks   ,,
            (Solo.)
26. I will give thanks   ,,
            (Trio, G minor.)

27. I will give thanks   *Ely*
            (Trio, G major.)
28. I will magnify Thee   ,,
29. Lord, let me know   ,,
30. Lord, remember David   ,,
31. Lord, Thou art become   ,,
32. Lord, Thou hast been   ,,
33. Lord, who can tell ?   ,,
            (Doubtful).
34 Lord, who shall dwell   ,,
35. Merciful God   ,,
36. Merciful Lord   *King's,* 1706
            (Collect, St. John's Day.)
37. My God, my God   *Ely*
38. O be joyful in God   ,,
39. O clap your hands   ,,
40. O come, let us sing   ,,
41. O give thanks unto the Lord
    and call   ,,
42. O give thanks unto the Lord,
    for He   ,,
            (T.T.B.)
43. O give thanks unto the Lord,
    for He   ,,
            (3 voices.)
44. O how amiable   ,,
45. O Lord God of my salvation   ,,
46. O Lord grant the King   ,,
47. O Lord my God, I have   ,,

Hawkins, James, Senr. (*continued*).

48. O praise God in His holiness	*Ely*	61. Sing joyfully	*Ely*
49. O praise the Lord, all ye	,,	62. Sing, O daughter of Zion	,,
(*Full.*)		63. Sing we merrily	,,
50. O praise the Lord, all ye	,,	(" *Else Daniel Purcell's.*")	
(T.T.)		64. The earth is the Lord's	,,
51. O praise the Lord, laud ye	,,	65. The King shall rejoice	,,
52. O sing unto the Lord	,,	66. The Lord is King	,,
(*Solo Bass.*)		67. The Lord is my strength	,,
53. O sing unto the Lord	,,	(*Full.*)	
(*3 voices, in key of G.*)		68. The Lord is my strength	,,
54. O sing unto the Lord	,,	(*Trio.*)	
(*3 voices, in key of D.*)		69. The Lord is risen	,,
55. O that the Salvation	,,	70. The souls of the righteous	,,
56. Praise the Lord, ye servants	,,	71. Thy righteousness	,,
(*Full.*)		72. Turn Thou Thy face	,,
57. Praise the Lord, ye servants	,,	73. Unto Thee, O Lord.	
(*Soprano and Bass.*)		74. Whoso dwelleth	,,
58. Praise the Lord, ye servants	,,	75. " An humble imitation of the	
(*Doubtful.*)		ancient way of composition	
59. Rejoice in the Lord alway	,,	upon the famous Miserere "	,,
60. Rejoice in the Lord, O ye	,,		

Hawkins, James, Junr.
Org. Peterborough Cath., 1714-59.

1. O praise the Lord.   *Tudway* |

Hecht (Hight), Andrew. d. 1693.
Org. Lincoln Cath. after Mudde, 1662-93. Brought over from Holland by Dean Honeywood at the Restoration.

1. God is our hope   *Lincoln* | 3. Out of the deep   *Lincoln*
2. O God, Whose never failing
providence   *Lincoln* |

Henman, Richard. d. 1741.
Org. Exeter Cath., 1694-1741.

1. Have mercy   *Ely* |

Henstridge, Daniel. b. latter part of 17th century ; d. 1736.
Org. Rochester Cath. and Canterbury Cath., 1699-1736.

1. Behold how good and   *Div. Har.* | 4. Hide not Thou Thy face   *Marshall*
2. Blessed be the Lord God   ,, | 5. O be joyful in God   *Div. Har.*
3. Blessed is the man   ,, | 6. The Lord is King   ,,

Hinde, Henry. d. 1641.
Org. Lichfield Cath. until his death.

1. Sing praises   *Barnard* |

Hinde, Richard.

1. O sing unto the Lord   *Clifford* |
(*Composed in 1652.*)

HINE, WILLIAM. B. 1687 ; D. 1730.
Lay-Clerk, Magdalen College, 1705 ; articled to Jer. Clarke; Org. Gloucester Cath., 1710 ; taught William Hayes.

1. I will magnify Thee	3. Save me, O God
2. Rejoice in the Lord	

These Anthems were published in " Harmonia Sacra Glocestriensis," 1730.

HINGSTON (HINKSON), JOHN. B. early in 17th century ; D. 1683.
Org. to Oliver Cromwell at Hampton Court Palace.

1. Blessed be the Lord my strength *Clifford*	2. Withdraw not Thy mercy *Clifford*

HIRDSON (HEARDSON), THOMAS.
1. Keep, we beseech Thee   *Durham* |

HOLDER, Rev. WILLIAM, D.D.   B: c. 1614 ; D. 1697.
Canon of St. Paul's ; Sub-Dean of Chapel Royal ; Prebendary of Ely, &c. Married a sister of Sir Christopher Wren. Sub-Almoner to King Charles II., and Rector of Bletchington, Oxford.

1. Arise, O Lord (*Psalm* 44.)	*Ely*	6. O praise our God, ye people	*Ely*
2. Great is the Lord	,,	7. Out of the deep	,,
3. I look for the Lord	,,	8. The Lord is King	,,
4. I waited for the Lord	,,	9. The Lord is my Shepherd	,,
5. My heart is fixed	,,	10. Thou, O God, art praised	,,

HOLMES, GEORGE. B. c. 1660 ; D. 1721.
Org. to the Bishop of Durham and Org. Lincoln Cath., 1704-21.

1. Arise, shine, O daughter	*Tudway*	4. Hear my prayer	
(*For the Union with Scotland*, 1706.)		5. I will love Thee	*Tudway*
2. As for me	*Div. Har.*	6. This is the day	*Lichfield*
3. Hear my crying	,,		

HUMFREY { So spelt by himself ; also found } , **PELHAM. B. 1647 ; D. 1674.**
  as HUMPHREYS, HUMPHRY, &c.
Chorister (1660) and Gentleman (1667) of Chapel Royal. Studied under Lulli in Paris. Master of the Chapel Children, 1672.

1. Behold, how good and joyful		12. Like as the hart	*Boyce*
	Warren	13. Lord, I have sinned	*Fitzw.*
2. Bow down Thine ear	,,	14. Lord, teach us to number	
3. By the waters of Babylon	*Tudway*		*Cath. Mag.*
4. Haste Thee, O God	*King's*	15. O be joyful	*Fitzw.*
5. Have mercy upon me	*Boyce*	16. O give thanks	,,
6. Hear my crying	*Fitzw.*	17. O Lord my God	*Boyce*
7. Hear, O heavens	*Boyce*	18. O praise God	*Warren*
8. It is a good thing to give		19. O praise the Lord, laud ye	*Fitzw.*
thanks	*Warren*	20. Put me not to rebuke	*Husk*
9. I will alway give thanks		21. Rejoice in the Lord	*Boyce*
	Club Anthem.	22. The heavens declare	*Warren*
(*1st part only by Humfrey*.)		23. The King shall rejoice	*Fitzw.*
10. I will magnify Thee	*St. Paul's*	24. The Lord declared	*Warren*
11. Lift up your heads	*Fitzw.*	25. Thou art my King	,,

HUTCHINSON, JOHN. B. 1615.
Org. Southwell Minster, and York Minster, 1633.

1. Behold, how good and joyful	*Ely*	4. O Lord, let it be Thy pleasure	
2. Grant, we beseech Thee	,,		*Mason*
3. Of mortall man	,,	5. Out of the deep	*Durham*
(*The " Southwell Anthem."*)		6. Ye that fear the Lord	*Ely*

HUTCHINSON, ROBERT.

1. Who shall ascend? *Clifford* |

ISAAC, BAT. OR BENJ.

1. Come unto Me *King's* |

ISHAM (ISUM), JOHN, Mus. Bac., Oxon. B. 1685 ; D. 1726.
Org. St. Margaret's, Westminster; St. Anne's, Soho, 1711 (after Croft) ; and St. Andrew's, Holborn, 1718.

1. O sing unto the Lord *Div. Har.* | 2. Unto Thee, O Lord *Div. Har.*

IVE (IVES), SIMON. B. 1600 ; D. 1662.
Lay-Vicar of St. Paul's Cathedral.

1. Almighty and ever-living God	2. If God be for us	*Bumpus*
Clifford		

JACKSON, JOHN. B. *c.* 1630 ; D. *c.* 1690.
Choirmaster of Ely Cath. for three months, 1669 ; Org. Wells Cath., 1676.

1. Christ our Passover	*Husk*	5. O God, let it be Thy pleasure	
2. God standeth	,,	6. O how amiable	*Husk*
3. I said, " In the cutting off"	,,	7. The days of man	
4. Many a time	,,	8. The Lord said	

JEFFERYS (JEFFRIES), GEORGE. D. 1685.
One of King Charles I.'s Organists (son of Matthew Jefferys, Mus. Bac., Oxon., Vicar-Choral of Wells).

1. Awake, my soul	*Husk*	11. In the midst of life	*Husk*
2. Brightest sun	,,	12. Praise the Lord the God	,,
3. Glory be to God	*Clifford*	13. See, the Word is incarnate	,,
4. Glory be to the Lamb	*Husk*	14. Shew me Thy ways	,,
5. Great and marvellous	,,	15. Sing unto the Lord	,,
6. Hark, shepherd swains	,,	16. The Paschal Lamb	,,
7. Hear my prayer	,,	17. Turn Thee again	,,
8. He beheld the city	,,	18. Turn Thou us	,,
9. Holy, holy, holy	*Clifford*	19. Unto Thee, O Lord	,,
10. How wretched	*Husk*	20. What praise can reach	,,

JEFFERYS (JEFFRIES), STEPHEN. B. 1662 ; D. 1712.
Org. Gloucester Cath., 1682; dismissed 1710.

1. Sing we merrily *Durham* |
Doubtful whether by him or George Jefferys.

JEWITT, Rev. RANDOLPH (RANDALL), Mus. Bac., Dublin. D. 1675.

Minor Canon and Almoner, St. Paul's Cath., 1660-75; Org. Christ Church and St. Patrick's Cath., 1631; Chester Cath., 1643 ; Winchester, 1667.

1. Bow down Thine ear   *Clifford*
2. I heard a voice   *King's*, 1706
3. O God, the King of glory *Bumpus*

4. O God, Who through the preaching   *Bumpus*
   (*Conversion of St. Paul.*)
5. The King shall rejoice   ,,

KELWAY, THOMAS. B. *c.* 1695 ; D. 1749.

Org. Chichester Cath., 1733.

1. Blessed be the Lord God   *Novello*
2. I will give thanks   ,,
3. Let the words of my mouth   ,,
4. Not unto us, O Lord   *Cope*
5. O praise the Lord, all ye heathen   *King's*
6. Rejoice in the Lord   *Chester*

7. Sing unto God, O ye   *Calvert*
8. Sing we merrily   ,,
9. Teach me, O Lord.
10. The mighty God   *St. Paul's*
11. Thy way, O God   *Novello*
12. Unto Thee, O Lord   *Cope*

KEMPTON, THOMAS. B. 1690; D. 1762.

Pupil of James Hawkins, Senr. Org. Ely Cath. (after his master), 1729-62.

1. Behold, it is Christ   *Ely*
2. O give thanks   ,,

3. Shew me Thy ways   *Ely*

KING, CHARLES, Mus. Bac., Oxon. B. 1687 ; D. 1748.

Pupil of Blow and Jeremiah Clarke; Almoner (1707), Vicar-Choral (1730) of St. Paul's Cath.; Org. St. Benet Fink, London. He married a sister of J. Clarke.

1. As pants the hart   *Chorister's Handbook*
2. Hear my crying   *Tudway*
3. Hear, O Lord, and have mercy   *Arnold*
4. I will alway give thanks   *Page*
5. Lift up your heads   *Calvert*
6. Lord, remember David   ,,
7. Not unto us   *King's*
8. O be joyful in God   *Page*
9. O give thanks   *Novello*
10. O pray for the peace   *Arnold*
11. Out of the deep   *Joule*
12. Rejoice in the Lord, O ye righteous   *Arnold*

13. Sing unto God   *Tudway*
14. The Lord hath prepared   *Div. Har.*
15. The Lord is full of compassion   *Page*
16. The Lord is my Shepherd   *Chap. Roy.*, 1749
17. Turn Thou us   *H. King* (*Doubtful.*)
18. Turn Thy Face from my sins   *Chap. Roy.*, 1769
19. Unto Thee, O Lord   *Page*
20. Wherewithal shall a young man?   *Arnold*

KING, ROBERT, Mus.B., Cantab. B. *c.* 1660 ; D. *c.* 1720.

Musician in ordinary to William and Mary and Queen Anne.

1. I will alway give thanks   *Congreg. Church Music*

KING, Rev. WILLIAM, B.A., Mus. Bac., Oxon. B. 1624; D. 1680.
Son of George King (Org. Winchester Cath.); Chaplain of Magdalen
College, Oxon., 1652-54; and Org. New College Chapel, 1664.

1. Have mercy upon me	*Bumpus*	4. The Lord is King	*Cope*
2. O be joyful in God	,,	(*Attributed also to Charles King.*)	
3. O Lord, our Governor	,,	5. Thou art gone up	*Husk*
		6. Turn Thee again	*Bumpus*

KNAPP, WILLIAM. B. 1698; D. 1768.
Parish Clerk of Poole, Dorset.

1. Blessed are all they   *Joule* |

LAMB, BENJAMIN.
Org. Eton College, *c.* 1687, and Verger of St. George's, Windsor.

1. If the Lord Himself	*Tudway*	5. O worship the Lord	*Tudway*
2. I will give thanks	,,	6. Thy righteousness	*Div. Har.*
3. I will praise the name	,,	7. Unto Thee have I cried	*Tudway*
4. O how amiable	*Durham*		

LAMB, WILLIAM, Junr.
Org. Lichfield Cath. about 1690.

1. Lord, who shall dwell?   *Lichfield* |

LOCKE (LOCK), MATTHEW, B. 1630; D. 1677.
Composer in Ordinary to the King. Turned Roman Catholic, and became
Org. to Queen Catherine.

1. Arise, O Lord	*Warren*	17. Not unto us	*Fitzw.*
2. Awake, awake!	,,	18. O be joyful in the Lord	*Warren*
3. Behold, how good	,,	19. O clap your hands	*Ely*
4. Blessed is the man	,,	20. O give thanks	*Husk*
5. From the depths	,,	21. O Lord, hear my prayer	*Warren*
6. God be merciful	*Fitzw.*	22. O Lord, how marvellous	,,
7. I know that my Redeemer	,,	23. O Lord, rebuke me not	,,
8. In the beginning, O Lord	*Cope*	24. O sing unto the Lord a new	,,
9. I will hear what the Lord	*Ely*	25. Praise the Lord, all ye	
10. Let God arise	*Cope*	gentiles	,,
11. Lift up your hearts	*Boyce*	26. Sing unto the Lord	*Cope*
12. Lord, how long?	*Calvert*	27. The Lord hear thee	*Fitzw.*
13. Lord, let me know	*Boyce*	28. Turn Thy face	,,
14. Lord, now lettest thou	*Warren*	29. When I was in tribulation	*Warren*
15. Lord, teach us	,,	30. When the Son of Man	*Cope*
16. Lord, Thou art become	,,		

LOOSEMORE, GEORGE, Mus. Doc., Cantab. Flourished 17th century.
Org. Trinity College, Cambridge; son of Henry Loosemore and brother of
John, who built the Exeter Cath. organ.

1. Glory be to God   *Cope* | 2. Hear my crying   *Ely*

LOOSEMORE, HENRY, Mus. Bac., Cantab, 1640. B. *c.* 1600 ; D. 1670.

Org. King's College, Cambridge.

1. Behold, it is Christ	*Peterh.*	11. O sing unto the Lord	*Clifford*
2. Behold, now praise	,,	12. O that mine eyes	*Ely*
3. Do well, O Lord	*King's,* 1706	13. Praise the Lord, O my soul	,,
4. Fear not, Shepherd	*Durham*	14. Put me not to rebuke	*Tudway*
5. Fret not thyself	*Peterh.*	15. Tell the daughter of Zion	*Ely*
6. Give the King Thy judg-ments	*Clifford*	16. The Lord hath done great things	*Clifford*
7. I will give thanks	*Durham*	17. Thou art worthy, O Lord	*Peterh.*
8. Lord, I am not high-minded	*Clifford*	18. To Jesus Christ	*Clifford*
9. O God, my heart is ready	*Peterh.*	19. Truly God is loving	*Peterh.*
10. O praise God in His holiness	*Marshall*	20. Turn Thee again	,,
		21. Unto Thee lift I up	*Ely*

LOWE, EDWARD. B. *c.* 1610 ; D. 1682.

Succeeded Stonard as Prof. Music, Oxford, and Org. Christ Church Cath., 1630 ; Org. Chapel Royal, 1660. He wrote "Short Directions for the performance of Cathedrall Service," 1661 ; revised in 1664.

1. If the Lord Himself	*Clifford*	5. O give thanks unto the Lord, for the	*Clifford*
2. My song shall be always	,,	6. O how amiable	*Ely*
3. O clap your hands	,,	7. When the Lord turned	*Clifford*
4. O give thanks unto the Lord, and call	,,	8. Why do the heathen ?	,,

MACE, THOMAS. B. 1613 ; D. 1709.

Clerk of Trinity College, Cambridge, 1633 ; Author of "Musick's Monument," 1676. Resided in London, 1690.

1. I heard a voice   *Peterh.* |

MOLLE, HENRY.

Org. Peterhouse College early in 17th century. A contemporary of Bishop Cosin.

1. God the Protector	*Clifford*	3. Thou art my Portion	*Clifford*
2. Great and marvellous	*Peterh.*		

NALSON, Rev. VALENTINE. B. 16 — ; D. 1722.

Succentor and Priest Vicar-Choral of York Minster ; Prebendary of Ripon.

1. Give thanks, O Israel	*Ely*	3.*O most blessed Redeemer	*Ely*
2.*O clap your hands	,,	4. Thou, O God	,,

NEWTON, Rev. JOHN, D.D.

Rector of Ross, 1677.

1. Be merciful unto me	*Old Norwich*	2. Rejoice in the Lord	*Old Norwich*

NICHOLLS, JOHN.

1. I will give thanks	*Durham*	2. O pray for the peace	*Durham*

---

* Partly adaptations from the Fiocco family.

NORRIS, WILLIAM. B. *c.* 1676 ; D. 1710.
Chapel Royal Boy in 1685, and, later, Choirmaster at Lincoln.

1. Behold, now, praise	*Ely*	4. I will give thanks	*Tudway*
2. Blessed are they	*Tudway*	5. My heart rejoiceth	*Ely*
3. In Jewry (Jury) is God known	*Ely*	6. Rejoice in the Lord	*Mason*

OLDHAM, ROBERT.

1. By the waters   *Ely* |

PECKOVER (PICKHAVER), ROBERT. D. 1678.
Org. New College, Oxon., 1660|; Winchester College, 1665.

1. Consider and hear   *Bumpus* | 2. Sing unto God   *Bumpus*

PEPUSCH, JOHN CHRISTOPHER, Mus. Doc., Oxon. B. 1667 ; D. 1752.
Org. to the Duke of Chandos, 1712, and to the Charterhouse, 1737.

1. I will give thanks *Chap. Roy.*, 1826 | 3. O praise the Lord   *Husk*
2. O God, Thou art my God
          Chap. Roy., 1749 |

PERCIVALL, —.

1. Bow down Thine ear   *Mann* | 3. Save me, O God   *Mann*
2. O be joyful   ,, |

PHILLIPPS, ARTHUR, Mus. Bac., Oxon. B. 1605.
Org., Bristol Cath., 1638 ; Org., Magdalen College, Oxford, and University Choragus, 1639; also Org. to Queen Henrietta Maria of France.

1. Blessed art Thou   *Clifford* |
     (*Epithalamium.*)

PIGOTT, FRANCIS, Mus. Bac., Cantab. B. *c.* 1650 ; D. 1704.
Org. Magdalen College, Oxon., 1686 ; Temple Church, 1688 ; Chapel Royal, 1697.

1. I was glad. |
     (*Mentioned in Hawkins's History.*) |

PLEASANTS, THOMAS. B. 1648 ; D. 1689.
Org. Norwich Cath., 1676.
1. O praise the Lord   *Joule* |

PLEASANTS, WILLIAM.
1. O sing unto the Lord   *Mann* |

POPELY, WILLIAM. D. 1718.
Org. Southwell Minster at the time of his death.

1. Not unto us   *Bumpus* | 3. We will rejoice   *Bumpus*
2. O be joyful   ,, |

PORTER, WALTER. B. *c.* 1600 ; D. 1659.
Entered Chapel Royal, 1617 ; Master of Westminster Abbey Children, 1639.

1. Behold, bless ye.
2. But O, thrice blessed.
3. Cast off and scattered.
4. Great God of Hosts.
5. How long?
6. I will lift up mine eyes.
7. Lord, show're on us.
8. My ravisht soul.
9. My soul, praise.
10. O blest estate.
11. O happy he who God obeys.
12. The bounty of Jehovah.
13. Thou mover.
14. When Israel.
15. When I the bold.
16. Who knows the terror?
17· Who knows what his offences be?

The words of all these two-part motets, excepting Nos. 1 and 6, are by George Sandys.

PORTMAN, RICHARD. B. *c.* 1610 ; D. *c.* 1650.
Pupil of Orlando Gibbons ; Org. Westminster Abbey after Thos. Day, 1633-42 ; entered Chapel Royal, 1638. (Called *William* Portman by *Tudway.*)

1. Behold, how good and joyful   *Bumpus*
2. I will alway give thanks   *Clifford*
3. Lord, who shall dwell ?   *Husk*
4. O God, wherefore art Thou absent   *Bumpus*
5. Rejoice in the Lord   *Husk*

PRESTON, THOMAS, Senr. B. 1662 ; D. 1730.
Org. Ripon Cath., 1690-1730.

1. Sing aloud unto God   *Bumpus*

PRICE, RICHARD.

1. Almighty and everlasting God   *Clifford*
2. O God, who thro' the preaching   *Clifford*
   (*For St. Paul's Day.*)

PURCELL, DANIEL. B. 1660 ; D. 1717.
Youngest brother of Henry Purcell ; Org. Magdalen College, Oxford, 1688-95 ; St. Andrew's, Holborn, 1713.

1.*Bow down Thine ear.
2. Deliver us, O Lord.
3.*Hear my prayer.
4.*I will alway give thanks.
5. I will magnify.
6. Let mine eyes run down with tears.
7. Lord, I have loved.
8. O be joyful.
9.*O give thanks.
10. O miserable man.
11.*O praise the Lord.
12. Thou, O God.

PURCELL, HENRY. B. 1658 ; D. 1695.
Chorister, Chapel Royal, 1664 ; Org. Westminster Abbey, 1680 ; Chapel Royal, 1682.

1. Ah, few full of sorrows.
2. Arise, my darken'd melancholy soul.
3. Awake, and with attention hear.
4. Awake, ye dead.
5. Begin the song, and strike.
6. Behold, I bring you.
7. Behold, now, praise.
8. Be merciful unto me.
9. Blessed are all they   *King's*
10. Blessed are they that fear.
  (*With instruments. Composed*, 1687, *for Queen Mary.*)
11. Blessed be the Lord my strength.

---

* Henry Purcell also set these texts.

PURCELL, HENRY (*continued*).

12. Blessed is he that considereth.
13. Blessed is he whose unright-
    eousness.
14. Blessed is the man that feareth.
    (*Funeral Anthem for Q. Mary.*)
15. Bow down Thine ear.
16. By the waters of Babylon.
17. Christ is risen from the dead
    Dublin
18. Close Thine eyes.
19. Early, O Lord, my fainting soul.
20. Full of wrath.
21. Great God and just.
22. Hear me, O Lord, and that
    soon.
23. Hear me, O Lord, the great
    support.
24. Hear my prayer, O Lord.
25. How have I strayed.
26. How long, great God?
27. How pleasant is Thy dwelling-
    place   *Marshall*
28. I am the Resurrection.
    (*Part of No. 14.*)
29. I heard a voice.
30. In guilty night.
31. In the black and dismal.
32. In Thee, O Lord, do I put.
33. In the midst of life.
34. It is a good thing.
35. I was glad.
36. I will alway give thanks   *Mason*
    ("*Adapted to the words by
    Mr. Knight.*")
37. I will give thanks
38. I will sing unto the Lord.
39. *Jehovah, how many (*quam
    multi*).
40. Let God arise.
41. Let the night perish
42. Lord, how long wilt Thou?
43. Lord, I can suffer.
44. Lord, not to us.
45. Lord, what is man?
46. Lord, who can tell?
47. Man that is born
48. My beloved spake.
49. My heart is fixed.
50. My heart is inditing. (*Coronation.*)
51. My opening eyes.
52. My song shall be always.
53. Now that the sun has veiled.

54. O, all ye people.
55. O be joyful in the Lord *Marshall*
56. O consider my adversity.
57. O give thanks (*Psalm* 105)
    Marshall
58. O give thanks (*Psalm* 106).
59. O God, they that love   *Durham*
60. O God, Thou art my God.
61. O God, Thou hast cast us out.
62. O happy man.
63. O, I am sick of life.
64. O Lord God of Hosts.
65. O Lord, grant the King.
66. O Lord, how manifold.
    (*Part of No.* 79.)
67. O Lord our Governour (*Hymn*).
68. O Lord our Governour.
69. O Lord, rebuke me not.
70. O Lord, Thou art my God.
71. O miserable man.
72. O praise God in His Holiness.
73. O praise the Lord, all ye heathen.
74. O sing unto the Lord.
75. O solitude.
76. Out of the deep.
77. Plunged in the confines of despair.
78. Praise the Lord, O Jerusalem
    Novello
79. Praise the Lord, O my soul,
    and all.
80. Praise the Lord, O my soul ;
    O Lord, my God.
81. Praise the Lord, ye servants
    Marshall
82. Rejoice in the Lord alway.
    (*Known as the "Bell Anthem."*)
83. Remember not, Lord.
84. Save me, O God.
85. Since God so tender a regard.
86. Sing unto God, O ye kingdoms.
87. Sing we merrily   *Lichfield*
88. Tell me, some pitying angel.
89. The earth trembled.
90. The Lord is King.
91. The Lord is my Light.
92. The night is come.
93. The way of God is an undefiled way.
94. They that go down to the sea.
    (*Thanksgiving for escape of
    King Charles II. and the
    Duke of York from shipwreck
    in Fubbs' yacht.*)

All the above, except Nos. 9, 17, 36, 55, 57, 59, 77, 80, 86, and 97, are in V. Novello's Edition of Purcell. 4 Vols., 1829-32.

---

* Later edition, "O Lord Jehovah."

PURCELL, HENRY (*continued*).

95. Thou knowest, Lord.
    (*Part of No. 14.*)
96. Thou wakeful Shepherd.
97. Thy righteousness, O God *Durham*
98. Thy way, O God, is holy.
99. Thy word is a lantern.
100. Turn Thee again.

101. Turn Thou us, O good Lord.
102. Turn Thou us.
103. Unto Thee will I cry.
104. We sing to Him.
105. Who hath believed our report?
106. Why do the heathen?
107. With sick and famished eyes.

QUARLES, CHARLES Mus.B., Cantab.   D. 1727.

Org. Trinity College, Cambridge, 1688, and York Minster, 1722-27.

1. I will love Thee, O Lord
                King's, 1706
2. O Lord, Thou hast searched   ,,

3. We will go into His taber-
     nacles   *King s*, 1706

RAMSAY, ROBERT, Mus.B., Cantab.   B. *c.* 1600;   D. 1664.

Org. Trinity College, Cambridge, 1628-64 (called *William* in *Tudway*).

1. Almighty and everlasting
     God   *Peterh.*
   (*Collect for Trinity Sunday.*)
2. Almighty and everlasting
     God   ,,
   (*Collect for the Purification.*)
3. Almighty God, Who hast
     given   ,,
   (*Collect for Christmas Day.*)
4. Almighty God, Who through
     Thine   ,,
   (*Collect for Easter Day.*)
5. God, Which as upon this
     day   *Ely*
   (*Collect for Whitsunday.*)

6. Grant, we beseech Thee   *Peterh.*
   (*Collect for Ascension Day.*)
7. Haste Thee, O Lord   *Tudway*
8. I heard a voice   *Peterh.*
9. My song shall be alway   *Ely*
10. O Almighty God   *Peterh.*
    (*Collect for All Saints' Day.*)
11. O Lord, let me know   *Clifford*
12. O Sapientia   *Peterh.*
    (*For the Annunciation.*)
13. She weepeth sore   *Tudway*
14. We beseech Thee, O Lord *Peterh.*

READING, JOHN.

Org. Chichester Cath., 1674-1720.

1. Blessed is He   *Bumpus*
2. If ye then be risen   ,,
3. I heard a voice   ,,

4. O be joyful in God   *Bumpus*
5. O Lord, give Thy Holy
     Spirit   ,,

It is doubtful which of the three John Readings composed the above five Anthems.

READING, JOHN.   B. 1677;   D. 1764.

Pupil of Blow; Chapel Royal Boy; Org. Dulwich College, 1700-2; Master of the Boys at Lincoln Cath., 1703; Org. of several London churches.

1. Be merciful unto me   *Reading*
2. I will love Thee, O Lord   ,,
3. I will magnify Thee, O God ,,

4. Lord, teach us to number *Reading*
5. Unto Thee, O Lord   ,,
(*All 5 published by subscription*, 1741.)

READING, JOHN.   B. Early 17th century;   D. 1692.

Org. Winchester Cath. and College.   Composed tune to "Dulce Domum."

1. All people that on earth.

2. Thou knowest, Lord   *Winch.*

RICHARDSON, VAUGHAN. B. *c.* 1670 ; D. 1729 (1715 *in Ely list*).
Pupil of Blow (in Chapel Royal) ; Org. Winchester Cath., 1693.

1. Blessed are all they   **Bumpus*
2. Blessed be the Lord   ,,
3. God standeth in the congregation   ,,
4. Hear my prayer   ,,
5. Hear, O Thou Shepherd   ,,
6. I call with my whole heart   ,,
7. Lift up your heads   ,,
8. Lord, who shall dwell ?   ,,
9. O come hither   ,,
10. O God, Thou art my God   ,,
11. O how amiable   *Novello*
12. O Lord God of my salvation   *Tudway*
13. O sing unto the Lord   *Croft*
14. Praise the Lord, O my soul   *Bumpus*
15. Praise the Lord, ye servants   *Croft*
16. Sing unto the Lord and praise   *Joule*
17. The earth is the Lord's   *Croft*
18. The King shall rejoice   *Bumpus*
19. The Lord hear thee   ,,
20. This is the day   ,,
21. To God on high   *St. Paul's*

ROGERS, BENJAMIN, MUS. DOC., Oxon. B. 1614 ; D. 1698.
Lay-Clerk, St. George's, Windsor; succeeded Randolph Jewett as Org. Christ Church, Dublin, 1639-41 ; Org. Eton College, 1660, and Magdalen College, Oxford, 1664-85.

1. Behold how good and joyful   *Cope*
2. Behold, I bring you glad tidings   *Bumpus*
3. Behold now, praise the Lord   *Boyce*
4. Bow down Thine ear   *MSS. New Coll.*
5. Everlasting God   *Clifford*
6. Haste Thee, O God   *MSS. New Coll.*
7. Hear me when I call   *Clifford*
8. How long wilt Thou forget me?   *Cope*
9. I beheld, and lo !   *Bumpus*
10. If the Lord Himself   ,,
11. I will magnify Thee   *MSS. New Coll.*
12. Laudate Dominum   *Bumpus* (*Act Song.*)
13.†Let all, with sweet accord.
14.†Lift up your heads.
15. Lord, who shall dwell ?   *Boyce*
16. O clap your hands   *Bumpus*
17. O give thanks   *Cope*
18. O pray for the peace   ,,
19. O sing unto the Lord   *MSS. New Coll.*
20. O taste and see   *Norwich*
21. O that the salvation   *Cope*
22. Praise the Lord, O my soul   *Cope, Ely*
23. Rejoice in the Lord   *Bumpus*
24. Save me, O God (*Psalm 54*)   *Cope*
25. Save me, O God (*Psalm 69*)   *Lichfield*
26. Teach me, O Lord   *Boyce*
27. Te Deum Patrem colimus (1660)   *Hymnus Eucharisticus*
28.†Tell mankind Jehovah reigns.
29. Who shall ascend   *Bumpus*

ROSEINGRAVE (ROSINGRAVE), DANIEL. B. *c.* 1650 ; D. 1727.
Chapel Royal Boy ; Pupil of Henry Purcell and Dr. Blow ; Org. Gloucester Cath., 1677 ; Winchester, 1682 ; Salisbury, 1692 ; Christ Church and St. Patrick's Caths., 1628-1727.

1. Bow down Thine ear   *Bumpus*
2. Haste Thee, O God   *Mann*
3. Lord, Thou art become gracious   *Bumpus*
4. O clap your hands   ,,
5. O Lord our Governour   *Old Chap. Roy.*
6. The voice of my beloved   *Bumpus*
7. We have a strong city   ,,

* All Mr. Bumpus's are autograph scores.
† These three anthems were published in "Cantica Sacra," 2nd set, London, 1674.

ROSEINGRAVE (ROSINGRAVE), RALPH. B. *c.* 1680 ; D. 1747.
Succeeded his father, Daniel, at Christ Church and St. Patrick's Caths.,
Dublin, 1727-47.

1. Blessed is He that cometh
   (*Ps.* 118) *Ch. Ch., Dublin, MSS.*
2. Bow down Thine ear,
   Lord   ,,
3. I will cry unto God with
   my voice (*Psalm* 77)   ,,

4. I will magnify Thee *Ch. Ch., Dublin*
5. O come hither   ,,
6. Praise the Lord, ye servants ,,
7. Rejoice in the Lord   ,,
8. Sing unto God   ,,

ROSEINGRAVE (ROSINGRAVE), THOMAS. B. *c.* 1685 ; D. (insane) 1750.
Younger son of Daniel Roseingrave. Org. St. George's Church, Hanover
Square.

1. Arise, shine!   *Tudway*
   (*Composed in* 1712 *at Venice.*)

2. Great is the Lord   *Husk*
3. One generation   ,,

RUTTER, GEORGE.

1. Blessed is the man   *Durham* |

SHAW, ALEXANDER. D. *c.* 1681.
Org. Durham Cath., 1677-81.

1. I will sing unto the Lord, *Durham* | 2. The Lord is my Shepherd *Durham*

SILVER (SYLVER), JOHN.
Org. King's College, Cambridge, and, subsequently, Winchester Cath., 1661-67.

1. Lay not up   *Bumpus* |

2. Lord, Thou art become
   gracious   *Bumpus*

SMEWENS, THOMAS.

1. I heard a voice from heaven *Bumpus* |

SMITH, ROBERT.

1. God, be merciful   *Clifford*
2. O God, my heart is ready   ,,
3. O sing unto the Lord a new
   song   ,,

4. O sing unto the Lord   *Clifford*
5. Sing unto the Lord   ,,
6. When the Lord turned   ,,

STANDISH, FREDERICK.

1. Out of the deep   *Ely* |

STRINGER, PETER. D. 1673.
Org. Chester Cath., 1661-73 ; Manchester Collegiate Church, 1666.

1. I will magnify Thee.
2. Let God arise.
3. Look, shepherds, look !

4. O Lord, make Thy servant Charles.
5. With my whole heart.

STROGERS, NICHOLAS.
Organist in King James I.'s reign.

1. O God, be merciful   *Ely* |

2. Praised be the God of
   love   *Clifford*, 1664
   (*To George Herbert's words, simply
   initialled N. S.*)

Stroud, Edward.

1. I will magnify Thee. |

Tayler, Daniel.

1. Sing we merrily   *Durham* |

Taylor (Tayler), Captain Silas.   b. 1624 ; d. 1678.

1. I will give thanks   *Ouseley MSS.* | 3. The Lord is even at hand   *Ely*
2. Lord, let me know   *Ely* |

Tozer, Solomon.

1. O Lord, let me know   *Durham* |

Travers, Henry.

1. Shall we receive ?   *Ely* |

Tucker, Rev. William.   b. *c.* 1630 ; d. 1678.
    Gent. of the Chapel Royal, and Junior Priest at Coronation of King
    Charles II. ; Minor Canon and Precentor of Westminster Abbey.

1. Comfort ye, My people   *Ely* | 8. O clap your hands   *Bumpus*
2. God is gone up   *Chester* | 9. O give thanks unto the Lord *Page*
3. I was glad   *Ely* | 10. The voice of one crying
4. I will love Thee   *Fitzw.* | *Westm. Abbey*
    (*Organ only.*) | 11. This is the day   *King's,* 1706
5. I will magnify Thee   *King's* | 12. Turn Thy face   *Chap. Roy.*
6. Lord, how long ?   *Ely* | 13. Wherewithall shall ?   *Ely*
7. My heart is fixed   *Fitzw.* |
    (*Organ only.*) |

Tudway, Thomas, Mus. Doc., Cantab.   b. *c.* 1650 ; d. 1730.
    Org. King's College, Cambridge, 1670 ; Prof. Music to University, 1705-30.
    Lived in London and formed Lord Harley's Collection of MSS.

1. Arise, shine   *Tudway* | 14. Let us now praise worthy
2. Behold, God is my sal- | men   *Ely*
    vation   *King's,* 1706 | 15. Man that is born   *Tudway*
3. Behold, how good   *Tudway* | 16. My God, my God   ,,
4. Behold, Thou hast made | 17. My heart rejoiceth   ,,
    my days   *King's* | 18. Not unto us   *Ely*
5. Blessed is the people   ,, | 19. O how amiable   ,,
6. By the waters. | 20. O praise the Lord   *Tudway*
7. Give the Lord the honour *Tudway* | 21. O sing unto the Lord   *Ely*
8. Hearken unto Me, ye holy | 22. Plead Thou my cause   *Tudway*
    children   *King's* | 23. Quare fremuerunt gentes?   ,,
9. I am the Resurrection   *Tudway* | (*Mus. Bac. Exercise.*)
10. I heard a voice   ,, | 24. Sing, O heavens   ,,
11. Is it true that God will | 25. Sing we merrily   ,,
    dwell ?   ,, | 26. The Lord hath declared   ,,
    (*Opening of Queen Anne's Chapel,* | 27. The Lord hear thee   ,,
    Windsor, 1712.) | 28. Thou, O Lord, hast heard   ,,
12. I will lift up mine eyes   *Tudway* | (*Mus. Doc. Exercise.*)
13. I will sing unto the Lord   ,, |
    (*Victory at Blenheim.*) |

TURNER, WILLIAM, Mus. Doc., Cantab. B. 1652 ; D. 1740.
Gent. Chapel Royal to seven monarchs!

1. Behold, God is my salvation	*Bumpus*	15. Lo! the poor crieth.	
2. Behold, now, praise the Lord	*Tudway*	(*Bass solo. 2nd part of the Club Anthem.*)	
3. Blessed is the man	*Warren*	16. My soul truly waiteth	*St. Paul's*
4. By the waters	*King's*	17. O God, Thou art	*Boyce*
5. Deliver me from mine enemies	*King's*, 1706	18. O let the people	*Ely*
6. Haste Thee, O God	*Ely*	19. O Lord God of Hosts	,,
7. Hear my prayer	*St. Paul's*	20. O Lord, the very heavens	*Bumpus*
8. Hold not Thy tongue	*Ely*	21. O praise the Lord	*Tudway*
9. If the Lord Himself	*Bumpus*	22. Praise the Lord, O my soul	*Bumpus*
10. I will alway give thanks	*Club Anthem*	23. Righteous art Thou	*Ely*
(*2nd part only by Turner.*)		24. Sing praises	*Warren*
11. I will magnify Thee	*Fitzw.*	25. Sing unto God	,,
12. Lift up your heads	*Parish Choir*, 1848	26. Sing the King shall rejoice	*Tudway*
13. Lord, Thou hast been our refuge	*Boyce*	(*For St. Cecilia's Day*, 1697.)	
14. Lord, what is man?	*Fitzw.*	27. The Lord is King	*Joule*
		28. The Lord is righteous	*Tudway*
		29. The Queen shall rejoice	,,
		(*Coronation of Queen Anne.*)	
		30. This is the day	*Croft*
		31. Try me, O God	*Wells*

WAKELEY (WALKLEY), ANTHONY. B. 1672 ; D. 1717.
Org. Salisbury Cath. 1698, following D. Roseingrave.

1. Arise, shine!	*Croft*	8. O God, the heathen are come	*Croft*
2. If the Lord Himself	*Husk*	9. O God, Thou hast searched me out	*Ely*
3. In my trouble	,,	10. O praise God in His Holiness	*Croft*
4. I said, "In the cutting off"	*Croft*	11. O sing to the Lord	*Husk*
5. Lord, I will praise Thee	,,	12. Save me, O God, for Thy Name's sake	*Croft*
6. Lord, Thou art become gracious	,,		
7. O how amiable	,,		

WALTER (WALTERS), JOHN. Flourished at end of 17th century.
Org. Eton College. Taught Weldon.

1. O give thanks   *Croft* | 2. O God, Thou art my God   *Ely*

WANLESS, THOMAS, Mus. Bac., Cantab. B. 16— ; D. 1721.
Org. York Minster, 1691.

1. Awake up, my glory!   *Tudway* |

WARNER, PETER.

1. O Jerusalem   *Clifford* |

WARWICK, THOMAS.
Lutenist to King Charles I.; Gent. and Org. Chapel Royal, 1625 ; Org. Westminster Abbey, 1642.

1. O God of my salvation   *Peterh.* |

WELDON, JOHN. B. 1676; D. 1736.
Org. New College, Oxon.; Gent. Chapel Royal, 1701; Org. 1708, and Composer, 1715; Org. St. Bride's and St. Martin's-in-the-Fields, 1726; Pupil of Walter at Eton and of H. Purcell.

1. Awake up, my glory　　*Novello*
2. Blessed are those that are undefiled　　*Croft*
3. Blessed be the Lord my strength　　*Weldon*
4. Blessed is the man that feareth　　*Croft*
5. Have mercy upon me.　　*Weldon*
6. Hear my crying, O God　　*Boyce*
7. In Thee, O Lord　　,,
8. I waited patiently　　*Ely*
9. I will lift up mine eyes　　*Weldon*
10. I will love Thee, O Lord　　*Collection*, 1724
11. Let God arise　　*Husk*
12. My help cometh　　*Rochester*
13. O be joyful in God *Collection*, 1724
14. O be Thou our help　　*Lichfield*
15. O give thanks unto the Lord, and call　　*Croft*
16. O God, Thou hast cast us out *Boyce*
17. O how pleasant　　*Ely*
18. O Lord, let me hear Thy loving.
19. O Lord, rebuke me not　　*Weldon* (*Organ part only in Fitzw.*)
20. O praise God in His Holiness　　*Playford*
21. O praise the Lord, for it is　　*Playford*
22. O praise the Lord, laud ye *Bumpus*
23. O praise the Lord of Heaven　　*Weldon*
24. O praise the Lord with one consent　　*Rochester*
25. O praise the Lord, ye that fear Him　　*Croft*
26. O Saviour of the World *Bumpus*
27. O sing unto the Lord　　*Chester*
28. Praise the Lord, ye servants　　*Joule*
29. Ponder my words, O Lord　　*Ely*
30. Rejoice in the Lord　　*Chap. Roy.* (*Thanksgiving Anthem*, 1708.)
31. Righteous is the Lord　　,,
32. The King shall rejoice　　,,
33. The Lord shall preserve thee　　*Calvert* (*Part of No. 9.*)
34. The princes of the people　　*Collection*, 1724
35. Thou art my portion　　*Weldon*
36. Turn Thou us　　*Croft*
37. Who can tell how oft　　*Arnold*

His solo anthems were written for the counter-tenor singer, John Elford.

WILDBORE, ROBERT.
Org. Trinity Coll., Cambridge, 1682-8.

1. Almighty and everlasting God　　*Tudway*

WILLIAMS, THOMAS.
Org. S. John's Coll., Cambridge, in 1680.

1. Arise, arise　　*Ely*
2. O clap your hands　　*King's*, 1706
3. O sing unto the Lord *King's*, 1706

WILSON, THOMAS. Lived in the 17th century.
Called in Peterhouse books " Organista Petrensis"; Org. Peterhouse College, Cambridge.

1. Almighty God, Who madest *Peterh.* (*Collect for Circumcision.*)
2. Behold, how good and joyful ,,
3. Behold, now, praise the Lord ,,
4. Blessed is the man that feareth　　,,
5. Lord, That art become gracious　　,, (*Psalm for Christmas Day.*)
6. Merciful Lord　　*Peterh.* (*Collect for St. John Evang. Day*).
7. Prevent us, O Lord　　*Peterh.*
8. Thy mercy, O Lord　　,,
9. Turn Thy face　　,,

WISE, MICHAEL.　B. 1638;　D. (killed in a street disturbance), 1687.

Chapel Royal Boy; Org. Salisbury Cath., 1668, and Gentleman of the Chapel Royal, 1675; Almoner, St. Paul's, 1686.

1.	Awake, put on thy strength	*Boyce*	21. O be joyful in God	*Marshall*
2.	Awake up, my glory	,,	22. O God, when Thou wentest	*Husk*
3.	Behold, how good	*Ely*	23. Open me the gates	*Warren*
4.	Blessed is everyone	*Husk*	24. O praise God in His	
5.	Blessed is he that con-		Holiness	*Tudway*
	sidereth	*Boyce*	25. Praise the Lord, O	
6.	Blessed is the man	*Warren*	Jerusalem	*Exeter*, 1793
7.	By the waters	*Ely*	26. Prepare ye the way of the	
8.	Christ being raised	*Bumpus*	Lord	*Boyce*
9.	Christ rising again	*Lichfield*	27. Sing we merrily	*King's*
10.	Glory be to God on high	*Bumpus*	28. The King shall rejoice	*Southwell*
11.	Have mercy upon me	*Bumpus*	29. The Lord is my Shepherd	*Husk*
12.	Have pity	*Ely*	30. The Lord saith	*St. Paul's*
13.	Hearken, O daughter	*Husk*	31. The prodigall	*Ely*
14.	How are the mighty fallen	*Ely*	32. The ways of Zion do mourn	*Boyce*
15.	How long?	*Husk*	33. Thou, O God	*King's*
16.	I charge you, O daughters	*Warren*	34.*Thy beauty, O Israel	*Boyce*
17.	I was glad	*Marshall*	35. When Judith had laid	
18.	I will arise, and go	*Old Lichfield*	Holofernes	*Heathcote MSS.*
19.	I will sing a new song	*Langdon*	36. Wherewithal	*Lichfield*
20.	My song shall be alway	,,		

WOODHAM, TWIFORD.　D. 1728.

Lay-Clerk of Ely Cathedral.

1. I will praise Thy Name　　　*Ely* |

WOODSON, LEONARD.　D. *c.* 1641.

Org. Eton College, 1615.

1. Arise, O Lord God　　　*Husk* |　　2. Give the King Thy judgments
   ("Made *for Mr. Barnard*.")　　　　　　　　　　　　　　　*Peterh.*
　　　　　　　　　　　　　　　　　　　3. Hear, O Lord　　　*Husk*

WOOLCOT, CHARLES.

1. O Lord, Thou hast cast us out　*Tudway*

YARROW, —

1. Almighty and everlasting *Durham* |

---

* The second part of this Anthem (in Boyce's copy) is said to have been composed by Dean Aldrich on hearing of the untimely death of his friend, Michael Wise.—*Bumpus.*

FOREIGN ANTHEM COMPOSERS.

BUONONCINI, GIOVANNI BATTISTA. B. 1672; D. 1750.
Came to England, 1708; Musician to the Duke of Marlborough.

1. When Saul was King   *Ely*
(*For the funeral of Prince John, Duke
of Marlborough.*)

DRAGHI, GIOVANNI BATTISTA.
Succeeded Matthew Lock in 1677 as Org. to Queen Katherine of Braganza.
Referred to in Pepys' Diary, 1667.

1. This is the day   *Ely*

ANONYMOUS ANTHEMS.

From CLIFFORD'S COLLECTION, 1663, made by Rev. JAMES CLIFFORD,
when Minor Canon of S. Paul's Cath.

1. Christ being raised.
   (*2nd part of No. 3.*)
2. Christ is risen.
3. Christ our Passover.
4. O clap your hands.
5. O God, my heart is ready.
6. When as we sate in Babylon.

From CLIFFORD'S COLLECTION, 1664.

1. All people clap your hands.
2. Almighty God, which in Thy wrath.
   (*For plague or sickness.*)
3. Almighty God, Who by Thy Son Jesus.
   (*St. Peter.*)
4. Almighty God, Who hast knit together.
   (*All Saints.*)
5. Almighty God, Who thro' Thine only begotten.
   (*Easter Day.*)
6.*Christ is risen.
7.*Christ our Passover.
8. Deliver me from mine enemies.
9. Give laud unto the Lord.
10. Give the King Thy judgments.
11. God the King of Glory.
12. God, Which hast caused.
(*Conversion of St. Paul, old version*).
13. Grant, O Holy Trinity.
14. Grant, we beseech Thee.
   (*Ascension Day.*)
15. Hallelujah! salvation.
16. Hear me, O Lord, and that soon.
17. Hear my cry, O God.
18. Hear, O My people.
19. I am well pleased.
20. I will lift up mine eyes.
21. I will magnify Thee.
   (*Printed twice.*)
22. I will preach the law.
23. Jesus came, when the doors were shut.
24. Let Thy merciful ears.
25. My God, my Rock.
26.*O clap your hands.
27. O give thanks.
28.*O God, my heart is ready.
29. O God, my strength.
30. O God, Whose nature.
31. O Lord, consider my distress.
32. O Lord, give ear.
33. O Lord God, the heathen.
34. O Lord, Which for our sakes.
   (*1st Sunday in Lent.*)
35. O praise the Lord of Heaven.
36. O pray for the peace.
37. O Thou that art the fulfilling.
38. Praise the Lord.
39. Rejoice in the Lord alway.
40. Save me, O God.
41. Soul, awake!
42. Stir up, we beseech Thee.
43. The Blessed Lamb.
44. The earth is the Lord's.
45. The eyes of all wait.
46. The Lord is only my support.
47. The Lord said unto my Lord.
48. Unto Thee, O Lord.
49. We praise Thee, O Father.
50. We will sing a new song.
51. What shall I render?
52.*When, as we sate in Babylon.

Those marked * appear in 1663 Edition also.

From the ELY CATALOGUE, mostly collected by JAMES HAWKINS, Senr., Org. Ely Cath., 1682-1729. A later edition, greatly added to by Rev. W. E. DICKSON, Precentor of Ely, 1858.

1. God sheweth me.
    (*With symphonies.*)
2. Great is the Lord.
3. Hear my prayer.
4. I waited patiently.
5. O Lord, Thou art my God.
6. O praise the Lord.
7. Praise the Lord, O my soul.
8. Remember, O Lord.
9. Sing unto God.
10. To Thee, O Lord.
11. Turn Thy face.

From the PETERHOUSE CATALOGUE, made by Rev. JOHN JEBB, D.D.

1. Hear my prayer (Psalm 143).
    (? *Same as in Ely Catalogue.*)
2. Let Thy merciful ears.
    (? *Same as in Clifford*, 1664).
3. O Jerusalem, Jerusalem.
4. This is the day which the Lord

THIRD PERIOD.

EIGHTEENTH CENTURY.

WILLIAM BOYCE.

CHAPTER XIV.

THE THIRD PERIOD. GREENE AND HANDEL.

The anthems of the Second Period, "Solo and Verse," are now fully established; but, for the first half of the eighteenth century, there are few fresh composers of much note, and gradually we observe, in passing, that our composers are beginning to combine Full with Verse anthems, after which the style, with a few exceptions, degenerates, until, at the lowest stage, original work is almost entirely replaced by an influx of adaptations from the works of foreign masters—and precious bad adaptations too. During the latter years of this eighteenth century, the low-water mark in the history of the anthem is approached.

The composer who first demands our attention in this Third Period, which we may fairly term "Mixed," is Maurice Greene, son of Rev. Thomas Greene, D.D., and grandson of John Greene, a Recorder of London. He was born in 1696, elected chorister of St. Paul's in 1706, where he sang under Clarke and his brother-in-law, Charles King, and where he was articled to, and succeeded, Brind as organist in 1718. He had previously played at St. Dunstan's, Fleet Street, and St. Andrew's, Holborn.

In 1727 Greene, now a very distinguished musician and organist, succeeded Dr. Croft as organist of the Chapel Royal, and in 1730, when Dr. Thomas Tudway died, he was appointed to the chair of music at Cambridge, and, at the same time, had the degree of Mus. Doc. conferred upon him. His degree exercise was a setting of Pope's " Ode to St. Cecilia."

In 1743 he published " Forty select Anthems," the work upon which, as Mr. Husk says, his reputation mainly rests.

In an article in *The Harmonicon* for 1829 a writer expresses the opinion that "these Anthems place him at the head of the list of English ecclesiastical composers, for they combine the science and vigour of our earlier writers with the melody of the best German and Italian masters, who flourished in the first half of the eighteenth century."

From 1750 Greene was so fortunate as to have an estate, situated near Abridge, Essex, of the value of £700 a year, bequeathed to him by a wealthy uncle.

The leisure which this windfall ensured him, and the consequent freedom from the necessity of teaching, enabled him to commence an undertaking which he had long desired an opportunity to carry out—namely, the publication in score of the finest specimens of our English Cathedral music.   In five years he brought together a collection of anthems and services, of which, as before mentioned, only the separate parts were obtainable, and he brought them together in vocal score.

But, realising that his strength was failing, he felt that he was not destined to carry through his admirable project, and he willed the whole of his valuable materials to Dr. Boyce, desiring him to complete the work.   How well Boyce carried out his friend's dying wishes all the world knows.   As "Boyce's Cathedral Music" this great collection was published in three volumes between the years 1760 and 1778, the latter date being but a year before Boyce's death.

Greene died in 1755 and was buried beneath the church of St. Olave, Old Jewry.

When, for the sake of City "improvements," this quaint church was marked out for destruction, the late Sir John Stainer and W. A. Barrett were instrumental in removing Dr. Greene's remains to the Cathedral of which he had been organist for nearly forty years, and he was reverently re-interred in the grave of his faithful executor, Dr. Boyce, on May 18th, 1888.

Dr. Greene has given us several proofs of his ability to write fine full anthems and of how interesting his chorus parts can be made, and yet in some of his anthems the solo and verse have been over-elaborated to the exclusion of any chorus excepting a mere *Finale* of a few bars.

One of his finest solos is "Acquaint thyself with God," and one of the sweetest and most popular is "Thou visitest the earth." The more frequently heard of his verse anthems are the grand, vigorous "God is our hope and strength," "Let God arise," while amongst his fine full anthems, "O clap your hands" and "I will sing of Thy power" deserve mention.

In the year of Greene's death, 1755, it is interesting to note in passing that Haydn was just twenty-three years old, and was, perhaps, writing his first quartet; Mozart was not yet to grace the earth for a year; Gluck had not composed his "Orpheus," and John Sebastian Bach had only been dead five years.

There was another great musician, born about the same time as Bach, with whom Dr. Greene had much to do.   I allude to George Frederick Handel, who paid his first visit to this country in 1710. Greene, then only fourteen years old, was evidently attracted by the genius of the great German, and, probably on Handel's second visit to London two years later, did everything in his power to court his friendship.   There are some who assert that Handel's influence is visible in the style of Dr. Greene's anthems, but I am more inclined to agree with those who, on the contrary, state that Greene had a distinct style of his own, and that, however much our composers may have been affected by temporary influence, foreign or otherwise, few were actual imitators of Handel, and none of them successful.

On the other hand, it has been proved beyond question that Handel, not content to repeat himself and to transfer themes from his instrumental to his vocal works, drew largely and fearlessly from the creations of his predecessors and contemporaries. Whatever Handel appropriated he adorned, and by his genius exalted into a masterpiece.

When Handel paid England his third visit, in 1718, he accepted the appointment of Capellmeister to the Duke of Chandos, whose place, Cannons, was just beyond the town of Edgware. Here, with singers and orchestra at his disposal, he wrote the twelve Chandos anthems. I place Handel amongst *English* anthem composers because, in 1726, he became a naturalised British subject.

The Rev. William Mason, precentor of York Minster, speaking of the Sixth Chandos Anthem in 1782, criticises thus : " Mr. Handell has taken more liberty with the words than is usually done. So much indeed as might lead one to conclude that he formed the composition out of his musical commonplace, and adapted the words to airs previously invented ; which it is probable enough was the case, not only in this, but in many of his later productions."

It is matter for regret that these Chandos anthems are not more frequently heard ; the general idea of a Handel anthem being limited to excerpts from " Israel in Egypt," " Judas," and " The Messiah." His anthems, rightly so called, will be found in the list on page 72, and include four Coronation anthems for King George II. (1727), a Funeral Anthem for Queen Caroline (1736), and others.

In an interesting life of Handel, written anonymously within twelve months after his death, the writer (Mainwaring) criticises him in much the same way that Wagner was at first criticised by certain fault-finders ; it is difficult indeed in these modern days to understand the complaint that he sacrificed melodic charm for the sake of orchestral effect, and made his instruments too frequently take the place that should have been entirely allotted to the voice. The crudeness of his harmonic progression was also objected to ! It was only needed to add a hint that he did not possess the gift of melody to make this curious survey of Handel's work a complete parallel to the treatment of Wagner at the hands of certain pedants !

Handel's favourite afternoon employment, at one time, was a visit to Dr. Greene in the St. Paul's organ loft. He used to attend the afternoon service at 3 p.m. and then play to his heart's content on Father Schmidt's fine organ, which contained what was then quite a rarity, a set of pedals, and a compass extending to CC. Dr. Burney, in his account of the Handel Commemoration, alludes to these visits, and says: "Handel, after 3 o'clock prayers used frequently to get himself and young Greene locked up in the church together: and in summer often stript unto his shirt, and played away until 8 or 9 o'clock at night."

CHAPTER XV.

BOYCE AND THE HAYES FAMILY.

With Dr. Greene perhaps the best days of the *Verse* anthem came to an end; for the comparatively poor productions of Nares and Kent cannot be accounted of much value, and the two writers whose names head this chapter were, in my humble opinion, better in " Full " anthems with verse than in genuine " Verse " anthems.

William Boyce was the son of a cabinet maker and was born in 1710. After serving as articled pupil to Greene in St. Paul's, he became organist of the church in Vere Street, then known as Oxford Chapel.

When quite young his hearing became defective, a terrible trouble for any musician; but in spite of this trial, to which the ardour of most music-lovers would have succumbed, Boyce pursued his art with a keen zest and indomitable perseverance. Quite appropriately might the pathetic words written nearly a century later by that greater sufferer from the same affliction, Beethoven, be repeated in regard to Boyce. Beethoven wrote to Wegeler: " I will, as far as I can, defy my fate." " I will grapple with fate ; it shall never drag me down."

In 1736 Boyce gave up the Vere Street appointment to go to St. Michael's Church, Cornhill (and was at the same time sworn in a Gentleman of the Chapel Royal). It will appear to my readers by this time that everyone capable of writing a good anthem and service became, *ipso facto*, a Gentleman of the Chapel Royal. Well, this was, to a certain degree, the case. Musical services were few in those days, and the few good writers were much sought after. Boyce was organist and composer to the Chapel Royal.

He wrote some really fine anthems, full and verse, such as " O where shall wisdom be found " and " Great and marvellous." Those which he composed when acting as conductor of the Festival of the Sons of the Clergy had orchestral accompaniments.

In 1758, owing to his increasing deafness, he gave up teaching and church duties, and devoted himself to carrying out Dr. Greene's great wish, which, as I stated previously, was that he should edit the large collection of Cathedral music which the latter had formed, but which his failing health prevented him from completing. This valuable collection brought Dr. Boyce his meed of fame, but barely paid the expenses of publication !

It is interesting to note that William Boyce for several years was conductor of the Three Choirs Festival (Hereford, Worcester, and Gloucester)—festivals over 150 years old, but flourishing to-day, and perhaps at no time so strong as now, under the generalship of Dr. George Sinclair and his clever *confrères*.

Whilst Boyce was at work in St. Paul's, William Hayes, born in 1707, was equally industrious in the West country as articled pupil to Hine at Gloucester. Showing conspicuous ability as an organist, he proceeded to that post in St. Mary's Church, Shrewsbury, and, in 1731, he was organist of Worcester Cathedral; this position he resigned in 1734 to become organist and Master of the Choristers at Magdalen College, Oxford. Here he took his Bachelor's degree, and succeeded Goodson as Professor of Music. He was created Mus. Doc. on the occasion of the opening of the Radcliffe Library. He conducted the Gloucester Festival in 1763, and wrote several Prize Canons, Glees, Cantatas, &c., in addition to his Cathedral music. He died at Oxford in 1777, and was buried there. Two of his sons distinguished themselves in music—Dr. Philip Hayes and Rev. William Hayes. The former, born in 1738, followed his father at Oxford, succeeding to both his organ and professorship. In 1790 he was organist of St. John's College, and, prior to being at Magdalen, he had been organist of New College. He wrote fifty-four anthems.

The Rev. William Hayes was born in 1741, and, eight years later, became a choirmaster of Magdalen, under his father. He took his M.A. degree there. He was made Minor Canon of Worcester in 1765, and next year a Minor Canon of St. Paul's, and in 1783 " Junior Cardinal." He was at one time vicar of Tillingham, in Essex. He wrote an article in the *Gentleman's Magazine* for May, 1765, on " Rules necessary to be observed by all Cathedral singers in the kingdom."

CHAPTER XVI.

LESSER LIGHTS OF THE EIGHTEENTH CENTURY.

In the midst of mediocrity and the decline of original composition, the lesser lights of the Cathedral school shone in those dark times with a comparative splendour, to which they were scarcely entitled, and which a more considered judgment, matured by the almost infallible test of age, denies them now-a-days.

James Kent, born in 1700, a Winchester chorister under Vaughan Richardson, and Chapel Royal boy under Dr. Croft, is still known by his rather feeble " Hear my prayer" and his Service in C. He wrote some twenty-seven anthems. He was organist of Finedon, Northampton, where, as the late C. E. Stephens tells us, there may yet be seen an organ stool carved with his initials, " J. K.," followed by the date, " 1717." He was organist of Trinity, Cambridge, till 1737, and of Winchester Cathedral, 1737 to 1774.

He died at Winchester two years later, in 1776.

Hogarth's criticism of his anthems is that "he followed the style of Dr. Croft, though his compositions are less elaborate and of a more modern cast than his master's." One would naturally add that they were much weaker.

John Travers, about six years younger than Kent, was largely indebted to Maurice Greene and to Pepusch for education and assistance in his musical career. The latter eminent theorist bequeathed to him one half of his valuable library.

Travers was organist of St. Paul's, Covent Garden, in 1725, of Fulham Parish Church about 1730, and of the Chapel Royal from May 10, 1737. He died in 1758. His Canzonets made his temporary popularity, but one or two of his anthems, of which there were over twenty, still survive, notably "Ascribe unto the Lord." He published, in 1746, " The Whole Book of Psalms for one, two, three, four, and five voices."

Even more prolific, having written fifty-three anthems, and perhaps rather stronger in style and more able contrapuntally, was James Nares, born at Hanwell, Middlesex, in 1715.

He studied, when a Chapel Royal boy, under Bernard Gates, and later on was a pupil of Dr. Pepusch. After serving as deputy-organist at St. George's, Windsor, he became organist of York Minster in 1734, of the Chapel Royal, 1756, and Master of the Children, 1757-1780. His death took place in 1783 in London.

Another anthem writer to be named in this chapter is Dr. Benjamin Cooke. He is most likely to be remembered as a writer of simple and very melodious glees, but he wrote at least thirty anthems. Where are those anthems now ? as Hans Breitmann would ask.

He was the finest organ-player of his day, and reached the height of his fame as full organist of Westminster in 1762, succeeding John Robinson. He also followed Kelway at St. Martin's-in-the-Fields in 1782. Eleven years later he died, and was buried in the Cloisters of the Abbey with which so much of his career had been connected. His anthems are almost entirely forgotten, but his fine Service in G will live.

William Jackson, of Exeter, as distinguished from his namesake of Masham, was a man of very many gifts ; an essayist, a composer, organist, and *painter*. Redgrave tells us that " he was a friend of Gainsborough, had a good taste for art, and was known in his day by his clever landscapes." He exhibited in the Royal Academy in 1771, copied Gainsborough, and wrote a sketch of his life. Paddon published three volumes of anthems and services by him. His ever-green Te Deum in F contains, in some unaccountable way, the property of an apparently endless existence ! His anthems, nineteen of which are recorded here, were " meritorious," and at one time extremely popular, although now scarcely ever used. His essays proved him to be possessed of considerable knowledge and a somewhat didactic style of writing.

Thomas Sanders Dupuis, also reported to have been an able executant on the organ, left some forty-four anthems, many of which were written for the Chapel Royal during his tenure of the organist's post there. In 1790 he accumulated the degrees of Bachelor and Doctor of Music at Oxford. He died at his house in Park Lane in 1796. His anthems are of all kinds—Full, Solo, Verse, and Full with Verse. His son-in-law, John Spencer, edited and published fourteen of them in 1798.

Thomas Ebdon, who was born at Durham in 1738, spent his life there in the service of the Cathedral. From twenty-five years of age until his death, in 1811 (*i.e.*, during forty-eight years), he was organist, and was apparently composing Anthems to the end of his life, the date on one of those in MS. being June, 1811, three months before he died. He published Cathedral music in 1790 and 1810, but several of his thirty-eight anthems are still in MS. His Service in C has outlived them all.

The great period of glee writing, another essentially British form of composition, had now set in, and was scarcely an improving factor to the Church musician. From 1740 to 1816 the best glees appeared, and divided the interests of such Anthem writers as Theodore Aylward, Dupuis, J. W. Callcott, and Thomas Linley. Their Anthems will be found in the list appended to the history of this century (p. 105 onwards), but by their glees they will stand in the history of English music.

Amongst those who are best known as Glee composers, but have been attracted towards the Anthem, we must specially allude to Samuel Webbe, born in Minorca in 1740. His father having left the family destitute, young Samuel, at the age of eleven, was apprenticed to a cabinet maker, but, at the end of his apprenticeship, he turned to his favourite, Music, first composing, about 1763, unaccompanied Catches, Canons, and Glees, for many of which he obtained prizes from the Catch Club. Of this Club he was secretary from 1784 to 1816, and librarian of the Glee Club from its foundation.

CHAPTER XVII.

ADAPTATIONS AND ARRANGEMENTS.

From about the year 1770 until 1817, or, in other words, during the best part of the long reign of King George III., there followed a period of forty years' dearth in Anthem writing: a famine longer than that of the Egyptians, and in which no Joseph arose to help; no one, with the exception of Jonathan Battishill and Dr. Crotch, appeared on the "trackless desert" to render any support or supply any strength to what must be considered as the very weakest part of the History of the Anthem, until at length Attwood returned to England from the Continent and began to write and redeem the situation.

This was the opportunity for adaptations and arrangements!

It seems strange to us that a composer so recently dead as Handel then was, whose Anthems were scarcely known to the general public, should become the victim of the adapter. But it was so, and Bond was the perpetrator. His methods are perhaps less obnoxious than others to be referred to, in that he limited the various ingredients of the "Compound" Anthem to the works of the one master.

But incongruity was assured by taking one number from one work, a second from another work, which illustrated a totally different subject, and so on. And all this time the great Chandos Anthems had been composed, and were, I expect, available; for Handel had made an arrangement of them himself, to suit the requirements of the Chapel Royal service.

The next medley to notice is that in which different composers are jumbled together. The masters to suffer from this treatment have been mostly of the Italian and German school, and the greatest offender in this line of blending composers was John Pratt. Not only were the styles of the various writers placed in opposition, but in place of the Latin, Italian, or German words, the notes had tacked on to them, patched over them, without fit, without fitness, passages from the Holy Scriptures, principally from the Book of Psalms.

The Rev. W. Mason, already quoted, differs from my view. He says: " It is somewhat singular that Italian music, adapted to English words, as it has been by Aldrich from Palestrina, and Carissimi (and by Nalson from Fiocco) *should produce so good an effect;* it is still more singular that the very ingenious Mr. Garth, of Durham, should have been able to adapt the music of fifty Psalms in succession, which Benedetto Marcello originally composed for a poetical version in Italian."——"*It is not easy to account for the phenomenon;* for, though we are able frequently to perceive that these transmutations have been for the worse (which, besides other reasons, the different degrees of softness in the two languages must necessarily occasion), yet still these attempts must be allowed to have been attended with greater success than might in any reason have been expected, in so much that we may venture to assert *that the English Cathedrals have gained some of their best Anthems* from this kind of naturalisation, as it may be called, of Italian masters." The italics are my own.

And this leads us to another form of the trouble.

As though our grand Church service were destitute in the matter of anthems, as though the grand school of the Madrigalian era, and the geniuses of the Restoration had never enriched this essentially Protestant form of composition, this offspring of the Reformed Church of England, the Masses of the Roman Church and other parts of its Liturgy have been seized by the ruthless adapters, bereft of their Latin, and not, mind you, *translated* into English, but deprived even of their appropriateness in the connection between words and music, by having some mild, harmless texts, in no way illustrated by the musical passages, put in their place. If the music of an anthem be not suggested by the very essence of the words, it were better never to have been written. One cannot insist too forcibly that music must be inspired by some definite sentiment; but in the words, apparently selected haphazard, to which many of the masterpieces of the age were attached, that sentiment was largely ignored; the music was hacked about in some instances and cut and crippled in order to pick out some pretty phrase or showy passage.

All such adaptations or arrangements are really bad in principle, and should appear hateful to all right instincts and healthy tastes.

They catered for the irreverent ear-tickling of the wealthy noblemen of the time, but were quite inappropriate to the solemn service of the Church of God.

What a pity that the authorities of the time did not unearth and publish some of the hundreds of anthems, scattered about the country in parts, many of which are by now irretrievably lost.

We ask, " Where are they, all these treasures of the past ? " and echo not only answers—"where?" but gently suggests that they may have been used to wrap butter in, for all the interest that was taken in good work at this degenerate period !

Grateful, indeed, should we be to Day, Barnard, Boyce, Arnold, Page, Vincent Novello, and Sir Gore Ouseley, to whom we are indebted for the possession and knowledge of many an anthem, which might have suffered a like fate, even after surviving the pillage of the seventeenth century.

CHAPTER XVIII.

JONATHAN BATTISHILL AND DR. CROTCH.

In addition to the compounding and adapting prevalent at this time, there were some few writers of florid melodies with paltry accompaniments, but poor imitations of all that had been much better and more scholarly in the preceding years.

Their work conveys an air of indifference and carelessness, which one is glad to know is, at the present day, giving way very largely to reverent fitness and thought, both as regards subject and treatment. There is no doubt that now, at the end of the nineteenth century, Church composers (rightly so named) are approaching their responsibilities in a spirit of deadly earnestness, and one is convinced that this must bear good fruit in time.

An exception to the weak writers referred to above is to be found in the person of Jonathan Battishill, son of a solicitor, who was born in London in 1738.

Although, in his younger days, he was connected more closely with the theatre than with Church music, in after life he abandoned the former connection and devoted his abilities to the composition of anthems, amongst which his setting of the words " Call to remembrance " stands pre-eminent, with its happy combination of melody and clever part-writing.

In the year 1775 the loss of his wife so preyed upon his mind that he gave up composition altogether, and spent most of his time studying in the solitude of his library, in which he had collected some 7,000 books, mostly classics.

Battishill died in 1801, and was buried, according to his dying wish, near his friend and master, Dr. Boyce, in the crypt of St. Paul's Cathedral.

In the second volume of Dr. Busby's History, the writer speaks of Battishill's anthems as being "characterised by the learning and sober majesty of Boyce's best Cathedral compositions : and his choruses may be compared with those of his early friend and favourite master."

The other good musician who stands as an oasis in this desert of mediocrity is Dr. William Crotch.

He was born in Norwich in 1775. His father, a master carpenter, combining a taste for music with his mechanics, built himself a chamber organ, upon which the small Willy, at the age of two, appears to have produced *sounds*, which the fond parent distinctly recognised as " God save the King " !

Obviously the elder Crotch had a more sensitive ear than the gentleman who was only able to distinguish our national anthem from " Cherry Ripe " by the fact that people stood up for the one and sat down for the other !

If we find the " God save the King " tale hard to credit, we know one thing as true—viz., that William Crotch had a marvellously acute ear, and the gift—a precious gift to the musician—of exact pitch, a fixed tonality which is not granted to every follower of the Divine Art.

When he was five years old his father brought him to London, where he gave a performance on the organ, showing the evidence of distinct genius; and, besides this, he displayed great skill in drawing. He must, indeed, have been as surprising a little prodigy as Mozart had been some twenty years earlier.

At the youthful age of eleven he went to Cambridge as assistant to the music professor, Dr. Randall, and, when fourteen years old, he composed an oratorio, entitled " The Captivity of Judah."

In 1788 he removed to the sister University of Oxford, where he studied with a view to entering the Church.

On the death of his patron, Rev. A. C. Schomberg, of Magdalen College, Oxford, he turned again to music, becoming, in 1790, organist of St. John's College and, seven years later, Professor of Music to the University, in the place of Dr. Philip Hayes, already alluded to as the son of Dr. William Hayes, each of whom held the professorship in turn.

On the establishment of the Royal Academy of Music in 1822, the admirable school where so many of us have received our musical training, and from which the majority of modern anthem writers were equipped for service, Crotch became its first principal.

After over sixty years of hard work, he died in December, 1847, while seated at dinner in his son's house at Taunton.

He wrote several anthems, one at least, " The Lord is King," having orchestral accompaniment.

JONATHAN BATTISHILL.

LIST OF ANTHEMS AND COMPOSERS OF THE EIGHTEENTH CENTURY.

ABINGDON, WILLOUGHBY, EARL OF. B. 1740; D. 1799.
Amateur Composer and Flautist.

1. Grant, we beseech Thee
   Longhurst's " Short Anthems."

ADAMS, THOMAS. B. 1785; D. 1858.
Org. St. Dunstan-in-the-West and St. George's, Camberwell.

1. O how amiable   *Husk* | 2. Like as the hart   *Novello*
(*Composed for the Consecration of St. George's, Camberwell, 1824.*)

ADCOCK, JAMES. B. 1778; D. 1860.
Lay-Clerk of St. George's Chapel, Windsor, 1797, and Eton, 1799, and singer at Trinity, St. John's, and King's Colleges, Cambridge.

1. I will praise   *King's* | 3. O God, the King of glory *Marshall*
2. My soul truly waiteth *Cramer* | 4. Thou knowest, Lord   *Joule*

ALCOCK, JOHN, Senr., Mus. Doc., Oxon. B. 1715; D. 1806.
Chorister of St. Paul's, under C. King; Org. and Vicar-Choral of Lichfield Cath., 1749-60; Org. of Sutton Coldfield, 1761-86, &c.; Private Org. to Earl of Donegal.

1. Arise, O Lord, into Thy resting
   place   *Alcock*
2. Arise, shine, O Zion.
3. Behold, how good and joyful *Joule*
4. Behold, I bring you glad tidings
                           Alcock
5. Be Thou my Judge   ,,
6. Blessed is he whose un-
   righteousness   ,,
7. Bow down Thine ear   *Joule*
8. Hear, O Thou Shepherd *Alcock*
9. Hold not Thy tongue   ,,
10. I have set God alway   ,,
11. It is a good thing to give
    thanks   ,,
12. I will alway give thanks
13. I will magnify Thee   *Alcock*
14. I will sing a new song   ,,
15. Let every soul be subject
                      St. Paul's MSS.
16. Lord, teach us   *St. Paul's*
17. Lord, what love have I *Alcock*
18. Miserere mei, Deus   ,,
19. O give thanks unto the
    Lord   ,,

20. O Lord, grant the King *Alcock*
21. O Lord, Thou hast searched ,,
22. Omnis spiritus laudet
    Dominum   ,,
(*8 voices and instruments in 21 parts,
    1771.*)
23. O praise our God, ye people *Alcock*
24. Out of the deep   *Durham*
25. Praise the Lord, O my soul *Calvert*
26. Praise the Lord, ye servants *Joule*
27. Rejoice in the Lord, O ye
    righteous   *Calvert*
28. Righteous art Thou   ,,
29. The heavens declare   *Alcock*
30. The Lord hath prepared *Joule*
31. The Lord liveth, and blessed ,,
32. The souls of the righteous *Calvert*
33. The ways of Zion do mourn ,,
34. Unto Thee have I cried *Gloucester*
35. When the Lord turned *Alcock*
36. Wherewithal shall a young
    man?   *Alcock*
37. Why do the heathen? *St. Paul's*
38. Why standest Thou so far
    off?   *Mann*

Anthems marked *Alcock* were published by him in 1771.

ALCOCK, JOHN, Junr., Mus. Bac., Oxon. B. 1740 ; D. 1791.

Son of Dr. Alcock and Org. St. Mary Magdalene, Newark-on-Trent, 1758, and Walsall Parish Church, 1773.

1. Arise, O Lord, and lift up.
2. *Awake up, my glory.
3. *Behold, God is my salvation.
4. Blessed are they that fear.
5. *Hark, the herald angels.
6. *Let all that are to mirth inclined.
7. Lord, Thou hast been our refuge.
8. *O clap your hands.
9. *O praise God in His holiness.
10. *O Lord, our Governour.
11. Praised be the Lord.
12. *Rejoice in the Lord.
13. The Lord is King   *Joule*
14. *This is the day.
15. Thy throne, O God.

Those marked with an * published in a volume by C. & S. Thompson, St. Paul's Churchyard. N.D. (but *c.* 1770).

ARNOLD SAMUEL, Mus. Doc., Oxon. B. 1740 ; D. 1802.

Chorister and Org. Chapel Royal (after Nares) ; Org. Westminster Abbey (after Dr. Cooke), and founder of the Glee Club, with Callcott.

1. All Thy works praise Thee *Calvert*
2. Except the Lord   ,,
3. Give the Lord the honour due   ,,
4. God is our hope   ,,
5. Hallelujah ! salvation and glory   ,,
6. Have mercy upon me   ,,
7. Hear, O Thou Shepherd   ,,
8. Honour, glory, salvation.
9. I will praise the Name of God ,,
10. My song shall be of mercy   ,,
11. O be joyful in God, all ye lands ,,
    (*Composed for the Peace,* 1783.)
12. O give thanks   ,,
13. O how amiable   *Calvert*
14. O praise the Lord, all ye heathen   ,,
15. O sing unto the Lord   ,,
16. O teach us to number   ,,
17. Praise the Lord, ye house of ,,
18. The heavens declare   ,,
19. The Lord is King   *Westr. Abbey MSS.*
20. Thou, O Lord, art just   ,,
    (*Composed for the Fast, April* 19, 1793.)
21. Wherewithal shall a young man ?
22. Who are these ?   *Calvert*
23. Who is this that cometh   *Page*

ASPINWALL (ASPINALL), JOSEPH.

1. Give ear, O Lord   *Addison*
2. I will judge you   ,,
3. The Lord is nigh *Singer's Library*

ATTWOOD, THOMAS. B. 1765 ; D. 1838.

Pupil of Nares and Ayrton ; later on, of Latilla and Mozart. Sent to Italy by King George IV. (then Prince of Wales). Composer and Org. Chapel Royal and to King George IV. ; Org. St. Paul's Cath., following John Jones, 1796.

1. Be Thou my Judge, O Lord   *Calvert*
2. Blessed is he that considereth   ,,
3. Bow down Thine ear   *Novello*
4. Come, Holy Ghost   ,,
5. Enter not into judgment
    Sacred Minstrelsy, 1835.
6. Grant, we beseech Thee *Attwood*
7. I was glad (*Full orchestra*) *Novello*
    (*Coronation of King George IV.*)
8. Let the words of my mouth   *Attwood*
9. Let thy hand be strengthened
    Unpublished
    (*2nd Anthem, Coronation of King George IV.*)
10. My soul truly waiteth
    Welsh and Hawes
11. O God, who by the leading   *Attwood*
12. O Lord, grant the king
    (*Full orchestra*)   *Novello*
    (*Coronation of King William IV.*)
13. O Lord, we beseech Thee *Attwood*
14. Teach me, O Lord   ,,

ATTWOOD, THOMAS (*continued*).

15. Teach me Thy way   *Attwood*
16. They that go down to the sea ,,
17. Turn Thee again   *Novello*
(*Princess Charlotte's Memorial Service
    at St. Paul's*, 1817.)

18. Turn Thy Face from my
     sins   *Sacred Minstrelsy*, 1835
19. Withdraw not Thou   *Attwood*

AVISON, CHARLES. B. 1710; D. 1770.

Essayist, Composer, and Org. St. Nicholas Church, Newcastle-on-Tyne.

1. Glory be to God   *Marshall* |

Avison is the subject of a poem by Robert Browning.

AYLWARD, THEODORE, Mus. Doc., Oxon. B. 1730; D. 1801.

Gresham Professor, and Org. of several London Churches and of St. George's
    Chapel, Windsor, 1788.

1. I will cry unto God with
     my voice   *Calvert*
2. O God, the King of Glory *King's*

3. O how amiable   *Calvert*
4. Ponder my words   ,,

AYRTON, EDMUND, Mus. Doc., Cantab. (et Oxon.). B. 1734;
    D. 1808.

Pupil of Nares; Org. Southwell Minster, 1755; Vicar-Choral St. Paul's
    and Gent. Chapel Royal, 1767; Lay-Vicar Westminster Abbey, 1780;
    Master of Chapel Royal Boys, 1783-1805.

1.*Begin unto my God with
     timbrels.
     (*With orchestra.*)
2. Bow down Thine ear   *Calvert*
3. By the waters of Babylon   *Joule*
4. Give the King Thy judg-
     ments   ,,

5. I will arise   *Calvert*
6. I will sing unto the Lord *King's*
7. O come, let us sing   *Calvert*
8.†O come, let us worship.
9. Thy righteousness, O God.
10. Unto Thee, O Lord.

BACON, Rev. ROBERT, B.A., Oxon. B. —; D. 1759.

Priest-Vicar of Salisbury Cath., 1753.

1. My soul truly waiteth   *Calvert* |
2. The eyes of the Lord   *Novello* |

3. The Lord is King   *Bumpus*

BAILDON, JOSEPH. B. 1727; D. 1774.

Pupil of C. King; Gent. of the Chapel Royal and Lay-Vicar of Westminster
    Abbey; Org. All Saints', Fulham, and St. Luke's, Old Street.

1. Behold, how good and
     joyful   *Page* |

BAKER, GEORGE, Mus. Doc., Oxon. B. 1773; D. 1847.

Org. at Stafford, Derby, Rugeley, &c.

---

* Sung in St. Paul's, July 29, 1784, as a Thanksgiving for the Peace of Paris, and
originally composed for his Doctor's degree exercise.   Published by him, 1788.
† No. 8 was printed in the Winchester Choral Festival Book, 1878.

BANKS, RALPH. B. 1767 ; D. 1841.

Pupil of Ebdon; Chorister in Durham Cath.; Org. Rochester Cath. for 52 years, 1788-1840.

Creator, Spirit, by Whose aid
                Chappell
2. Give ear, O heavens   ,,
3. Lord, Thou art become gracious
                Marshall
4. Lord, Thou hast been our refuge
                Marshall
5. O Lord, grant the King
        Page and Chappell

6. O sing unto the Lord   *Chappell*
(*Re-opening of Rochester Cath. Organ, 1840, and an adaptation from Handel.*)
7. Praise the Lord, O my soul
                Marshall
8. Sing praises to the Lord. *Chappell*
9. The souls of the righteous *Chappell*
(*For Funeral of Ven. Archdeacon Law, D.D., Rochester, 1825.*)

All these Anthems, except Nos. 3, 4, and 7, were published in Banks' Cathedral Music.

BATTISHILL, JONATHAN. B. 1738 ; D. 1801.

Pupil of Wm. Savage; Chorister in St. Paul's Cathedral; Org. St. Clement, Eastcheap, and (1767) Christ Church, Newgate Street.

1. Again my mournful sighs *Novello*
2. Behold, how good and joyful *Page*
3. Call to remembrance   ,,
4. Deliver us, O Lord our God ,,
5. Hear my prayer   *Gloucester*
6. How long wilt Thou forget me
                  Page
7. I waited patiently   *Calvert*
8. I will magnify Thee   *Page*

9. I will sing of the Lord *Novello*
10. Lord, remember David *Calvert*
11. O Lord, look down from heaven
                  Page
12. Save me, O God (*Psalm 54*) ,,
13. Save me, O God (*Psalm 69*)
               Salisbury
14. The heavens declare   *Page*
15. Unto Thee lift I up   ,,

Nos. 3 and 8 were published during the composer's lifetime by C. and S. Thompson.

BEALE, WILLIAM, B. 1784 ; D. 1854.

Pupil of Drs. Arnold and Cooke; Chorister in Westminster Abbey; Gent. of the Chapel Royal, 1816-20; Org. Trinity and St. John's Colleges, Cambridge, 1820; subsequently, St. John's Church, Clapham Rise.

1. Bow down Thine ear   *Novello*
(*Edited by Dr. Mann.*)

BECKWITH, JOHN (Senr.). B. 1728 ; D. 1800.

Uncle of J. Christmas Beckwith and of Rev. Edward James Beckwith; Lay-Clerk of Norwich Cath.

1. Blessed is he that provid-
  eth   *Norwich*, 1789
2. Bow down Thine ear   ,,
3. Cry aloud and shout   ,,
4.*God is our hope and
  strength   ,,
5. Great and marvellous   ,,
6.*Hear my crying, O God *Mann*
7. Hear my prayer   *Norwich*
8. Hear, O Thou Shepherd   ,,
9.*I will alway give thanks *Mann*

10.*I will give thanks to Thee *Norwich*
11. Let Thy merciful ears   ,,
12. Lift up Thy voice   ,,
13.*Lift up your heads   ,,
14. O all ye works of the Lord ,,
15. O give thanks unto the
    Lord, and call *Norwich*, 1789
16.*O give thanks unto the
    Lord, for He   ,,
17. O how amiable   ,,
18. O Lord, my God   ,,

---

* In King's College Library attributed to Dr. Beckwith—*i.e.*, J. Beckwith, Junr.

BECKWITH, JOHN (Senr.) (*continued*).

19. On Thee, great Ruler
              Norwich, 1789
20. O praise our God, ye
    people   ,,
21. O praise the Lord, laud
    ye   *Mann*
22. O sing unto God, sing
    praises   *Norwich*
23. O sing unto the Lord
    a new song   ,,

24. Praise the Lord, O my
    soul   *Norwich*
25. Sing unto the Lord,
    for He   ,,
26. This is the day which
    the Lord   *Mann*
27. Unto Thee, O God, do
    we give   ,,
28. Worthy art Thou, O
    Lord, of all   *Norwich*

BECKWITH, JOHN CHRISTMAS, Mus. Doc., Oxon. (BECKWITH Junr.).
    B. December 25, 1759; D. 1809.

Son of Edw. Beckwith. Org. St. Peter Mancroft, Norwich, and succeeded
John Garland as Org. Norwich Cath., 1808.

1. As pants the hart.
2. Blessed is the man that
    hath not walked   *Publ.* 1790
3. I bow my knee.   ,,
4. I cried unto the Lord.
5. I heard a voice.
6. I will sing unto the
    Lord   *Publ.* 1790
7. Let God arise
8. Let God, the God of Battles, rise.
9. Lift your voice and thankful sing.

10. My soul is weary   *Novello*
11. O Lord, Thy word.
12. Ponder my words   *Publ.* 1790
13. Sing unto the Lord a
    new song   ,,
14. Sing ye to the Lord, for He hath.
15. The Lord is my Light.
16. The Lord is very great
    and terrible   *Publ.* 1790
17. Trust ye in the Lord for ever.

BELLAMY, RICHARD, Mus. Bac., Cantab. B. *c.* 1745-50.; D. 1813.

   * Fine Bass singer; Almoner St. Paul's Cath., 1793-99; Lay-Vicar Westminster Abbey; Gent. Chapel Royal.

1. Blessed is the man
        C. and S. Thompson
2. Come, Holy Ghost   ,,
3. I waited patiently   ,,
4. O God, whose nature   ,,

5. Sing ye merrily
        C. and S. Thompson
6. The ways of Zion   ,,
7. When Saul was King over us ,,

    Adaptations of Mozart were known as "Anthems" by him.

BENNETT, THOMAS. B. 1779; D. 1848.
   Org. Chichester Cath., 1817-48.

1. I will magnify Thee, O God *Joule* | 2. O Lord, the very heavens *Joule*

BISHOP, Sir HENRY ROWLEY, Kt., Mus. Doc., Oxon. B. 1782; D. 1855.
   Founded (with others) Philharmonic Society; Operatic Conductor and Composer; Professor of Music in Edinburgh University, 1841-3, and of Oxford
(after Crotch), 1848.

1. I have kept the ways   *Bumpus.* |
    (*Contralto solo. Composed for Queen Charlotte's Funeral.*)

---

   * Some of Boyce's Anthems were specially composed to exhibit Bellamy's fine
baritone-bass voice.

BLAKE, Rev. EDWARD, D.D. B. 1708 ; D. 1765.

Perpetual Curate of St. Thomas's, Salisbury, 1740; Vicar of St. Mary the Virgin, Oxford, 1754 ; Prebendary of Salisbury Cath. and Rector of Tortworth, 1757.

1. I have set God alway   *Page* | 2. Thou, O God, art praised *Bumpus*

BLOOMFIELD, ISAAC WILLIAM.

Of Hornington, near Bury St. Edmunds.

1. Behold, the Lord is my salvation. | 4. Let them give thanks.
2. Give thanks unto the Lord. | 5. Seek ye after God.
3. I am well pleased. | 6. The King shall rejoice.

All in Dr. Mann's library ; composed for "when there is no organ."

BLYTH, BENJAMIN, MUS. DOC., Oxon., 1833. B. c. 1800 ; D. —
Organist of Richmond Parish Church.

1. I will arise   *Bumpus* |

BOND, CAPEL L. D. 1790.

Org. and Conductor of the first Birmingham Festival, 1768 ; Organist of Holy Trinity, Coventry.

1. Blessed be the Lord God *Marshall* | 4. O Lord our Governour *Winchester*
2. Have mercy upon me   *Salisbury* | 5. Praise the Lord, ye servants *Joule*
3. I will alway give thanks   *Joule* | 6. The glory of the Lord   *Marshall*

All published by the Composer, 1 vol., folio, 1769.

BOND, HUGH. B. c. 1710. ; D. 1792.

Org. St. Mary Arches, Exeter, and Lay-Vicar, Exeter Cath., 1762.

1. Have mercy upon me   *Lincoln* | 7. O Lord, our Governour *Marshall*
2. How blest is he who ne'er | 8. O 'twas a joyful sound   *Exeter*
    Exeter, 1793 | 9. Praise the Lord, ye servants
3. How numerous, Lord   ,, | *Marshall*
4. I will alway give thanks *Gloucester* | 10. The Lord is my Light   *Lincoln*
5. My lot is fallen   *Salisbury*, 1852 | 11. To my complaint   *Exeter*
6. O Lord, hear my prayer
    Norwich, 1789 |

Adaptations by him of Handel's music were used as Anthems.

BOYCE, WILLIAM, MUS. DOC., Cantab. B. 1710 ; D. 1779.

Pupil of C. King, Greene, and Pepusch ; Org. St. Peter's, Vere Street, 1734 ; St. Michael's, Cornhill, 1736-68 ; Allhallows, Thames Street, 1749-69; Composer (1736) and Org. of the Chapel Royal, 1758, and Master of the King's Band, 1755.

1. Begin unto my God with timbrels   *Chap. Roy. MSS.* | 5. Blessed is he that considereth the poor.
2. Be glad, O ye righteous   *Durham* | 6.*Blessed is he that considereth the poor.
3. Behold, O God, our Defender   *Chap. Roy. MSS.* | *(Differing from 5.)*
4.*Be Thou my Judge. | 7.*Blessed is the man.

* All those marked * were published in the four volumes known as "Boyce's own."

Boyce, William (*continued*).

8. Blessing and glory   *King's*
     (*With verse.*)
9.*Blessing and glory.
     (*Full, 8 voices.*)
10.*By the waters.
11. Come, Holy Ghost.
12.*Give the King Thy judgments.
13.*Give unto the Lord, O ye
     mighty.
14.*Hear my crying.
15. Hear my prayer *Chap. Roy. MSS.*
(*Full Score, with double discant in two
     keys.*)
16.*Here shall soft charity.
17.*How long wilt Thou forget
     me?
18. I am the Resurrection   *Page*
(*Burial Service, composed for the
     Funeral of Capt. Coram, at the
     Foundling Hospital.*)
19.*I cried unto the Lord.
20.*If we believe that Jesus died.
21.*I have set God alway.
22.*I have surely built.
23. I was glad   *Chap. Roy. MSS.*
24.*I will alway give thanks.
25.*I will magnify Thee.
26.*Let my complaint.
27.*Like as the hart.
28.*Lord, teach us to number.
29.*Lord, Thou has been our
     refuge.
30. Lord, what is man, that
     Thou art?
31.*Lord, what is man, that
     Thou shouldest?
32.*Lord, who shall dwell?
33.*My heart is fixed *Chap. Roy.*, 1749
34. My heart rejoiceth
     Chap. Roy. MSS.
35.*O be joyful in God.
36.*O be joyful in God.
     (*Verse, 4 voices.*)
37. O come hither   *Wells*
38.*O give thanks unto the
     Lord, and call *Chap. Roy.*, 1749
39.*O give thanks unto the
     Lord, for He is.

40. O Lord God of Hosts
     (*Psalm* 89)   *Dublin*
41. O praise the Lord with me *Marshall*
42.*O praise the Lord, ye that
     fear.
43.*O sing unto the Lord.
     (*Psalm* 149.)
44. O sing unto the Lord
     (*Psalm* 96)   *Chap. Roy. MSS.*
45.*O where shall wisdom?
46.*Ponder my words.
47.*Praise the Lord, ye servants.
48. Remember, O Lord.
     (*Treble Chorus.*)
49.*Save me, O God.
50.*Sing, O heavens.
51.*Sing praises to the Lord.
52.*Sing unto the Lord, and
     praise.
53.*Teach me, O Lord.
     (*Differing from* 54.)
54. Teach me, O Lord
     Chap. Roy. MSS.
55.*The Heavens declare.
56. The King shall rejoice
     Chap. Roy. MSS.
     (*For King George III.'s wedding.*)
57.*The Lord is full of com-
     passion.
58.*The Lord is King, and
     hath put on.
59.*The Lord is King, be the people.
60.*The Lord is my Light.
61.*The Lord liveth.
62.*The Lord my pasture.
63. The souls of the righteous
     Chap. Roy. MSS.
64.*Turn Thee unto me.
     (*Verse,* s.s.)
65. Turn Thee unto me.
     (*Verse,* a.)
66. Unto Thee, O Lord
     Chap. Roy. MSS.
67.*Wherewithal shall a young man.
     Eight Coronation Anthems
     (*Unpublished.*)

Bridgewater, Thomas. d. 1831.
Org. St. Saviour's Church, York.

1. I will give thanks unto
     Thee   *Novello*

---

* All those marked * were published in the four volumes known as "Boyce's own."

BRODERIP, JOHN.   B. *c.* 1710 ; D. 1774.
Org. Wells Cath., 1741-74 ; also at Shepton Mallet.

1. As pants the hart.
2. How good and pleasant.
3. How long wilt Thou forget?
4. In vain the dusky night.
5. Lo, my Shepherd's Hand
   Divine.
6. To God in ceaseless strains.
7. To God with mournful
   voice.
8. To Thee, O Lord, my cries.
9. The Lord Himself.
10. Where Babylon's proud
    water flows.

BRODERIP, ROBERT.   B. *c.* 1750 ; D. 1808.
Org. St. James's Church, Bristol.

1. Awake up, my glory !   *Calvert*
2. Is there not an appointed
   time ?   *Calvert*

BUCK, ZECHARIAH, Mus. Doc., Cantuar.   B. 1798 ; D. 1879.
Pupil of Garland and J. Beckwith.   Organist of Norwich Cath., 1828-77.

1. Blessed is the people   *Norwich*
2. Come hither, angel tongues
   invite   *Bunnett's Sac. Har.*

(*For the Enthronement of Bishop
Hinds, by whom the words were
written,* 1849.)

3. Have mercy upon me   *Norwich*
4. I heard a voice
        Bunnett's Sac. Har.
(*For the Funeral of Bishop Stanley,*
        1849.)
5. Lord, who shall dwell ?   *Norwich*
6. O Lord, give Thy Holy
   Spirit   *Bunnett's Sac. Har.*
7. They that put their trust   *Norwich*

BURGHERSH, LORD.   (*See* WESTMORELAND, EARL OF.)

BUSBY, THOMAS, LL.D., Mus. Doc., Cantab.   B. 1755 ; D. 1838.
Scholar, Historian, and Musician.   Pupil of Battishill.

1. O God, Thou art my God   *Page* |

BUSWELL, JOHN, Mus. Doc., Oxon., 1759.   B. and D. in the 18th
century.
Gent. of the Chapel Royal.

1. Lord, how are they increased   *Marshall*

CALAH, JOHN.   B. 1758 ; D. 1798.
Org. Peterborough Cath., 1785-98.

1. Behold, how good and joyful   *Marshall*

CALLCOTT, JOHN WALL, Mus. Doc., Oxon.   B. 1766 ; D. 1821.
Org. to the Female Orphan Asylum and of St. Paul's, Covent Garden ;
Founder (with Arnold) of the Glee Club ; Pupil of Haydn.

1. Awake, put on strength   *Boosey*
2. Blessed is he that considereth   *Marshall*
3. Christ being raised   *Gloucester*
4. Forgive, blest shade   *Joule*
5. Grant, we beseech Thee
        Turle and Taylor
6. I heard a voice
        Hullah's Singer's Library
7. I was glad (*Psalm* 122)   *Boosey*
8. Let the words of my
   mouth   *Marshall*
9. Praise the Lord, O my
   soul   *Novello*
10. Propter Sion non tacebo
        (*Degree Exercise*)
11. The Lord Himself, the mighty
    Lord   *Turle and Taylor*
12. Thou, Lord, hast been a
    defence   *Hullah's Voc. Scores*
13. Thou shalt shew me   *Novello*

CAMIDGE, JOHN, Senr. B. c. 1734; D. 1803.

Pupil of Greene and Handel; Org. York Minster, 1756, in succession to Nares.

1. Blessed are all they that fear *Mason*
2.*Blessed is He that con-sidereth *Marshall*
3. Blessing and glory ,,
4. Hear my prayer, O God ,,
5. I will alway give thanks *Mason*
6.*Lift up your heads *Marshall*
7. Lord, how are they in-creased ,,
8. O be joyful in God *Marshall*
9.*O save Thy people ,,
10. O turn away mine eyes *Beverley*
11. Sing unto the Lord *Trinity Library*
12. The King shall rejoice *Marshall*
13. The Lord hear thee ,,
14. The Lord is King ,,
15. The Lord shall preserve *Beverley*

CAMIDGE, JOHN, Junr., Mus. Doc., Cantab. (and Cantuar., 1855). B. 1790; D. 1859.

Son of Matthew Camidge; Org. York Minster, 1844-59.

1. Fret not thyself.
2. Holy, Holy, Holy.
3. I will cry unto God.
4. Sing unto the Lord.

All published in the composer's Cathedral Music.

CAMIDGE, MATTHEW. B. 1764; D. 1844.

Son of John Camidge, Senr.; Org. York Minster, 1803-44 (following his father).

1. Blessed is he that considereth.
2. Consider and hear me.
3. Lift up your heads.
4. O save Thy people.
5. Teach me, O Lord.
6. Thy way, O God, is holy.

All published in the composer's Collection of Cathedral Music, c. 1800.

CARNABY, WILLIAM, Mus. Doc., Cantab. B. 1772; D. 1839.

Chapel Royal Boy under Nares and Ayrton; Org. at Eye, Suffolk, Huntingdon, and Hanover Chapel, Regent Street.

1. O God, Whose nature and property *Haycraft* 1837 |

CARTER, THOMAS. B. 1735 $\left\{ {1758 \atop 1768} \right\}$; D. 1804.

Org. of St. Werburgh's Church, Dublin.

1. Hear my prayer, O God *Husk*
2. Like as the hart *Dublin*
3. Sing unto the Lord (Psalm 68) *Dublin*

CECIL, Rev. RICHARD. B. 1748; D. 1810.

Amateur Musician; Vicar of Cobham, Surrey.

1. I will arise *Nov. Cat.* |

---

* Probably attributed to J. Camidge, in mistake, by Marshall. *See* MATTHEW CAMIDGE.

CHAPPLE, SAMUEL. B. 1775; D. *c.* 1845.
Blind from childhood. Org. at Ashburton, Devon.

1. Christ is our passover.
2. Hearken unto me.
3. I am the Resurrection.
4. I'll wash my hands
5. It is a good thing.
6. I waited patiently.
7. I will sing unto the Lord.
8. My soul truly waiteth.
9. O come, let us sing.
10. Ponder my words.
11. Praise the Lord.
12. Praise the Lord, O my soul.
13. Rejoice in the Lord.
14. Show us Thy mercy.
15. Sing unto the Lord.
16. The earth may be glad.
17. The Lord is King.
18. Who can express.

CHARD, GEORGE WILLIAM, Mus. Doc., Cantab., 1812. B. 1765;
D. 1849.
Pupil of Hudson as Chorister of St. Paul's; Org. Winchester Cath. and
Coll., 1802.

1. Almighty and everlasting
                         Gloucester
   (14th *after Trinity.*)
2. Behold, I bring you   *Calvert*
3. Blessed are the people   ,,
4. Forsake me not   *Winchester*
5. Glory be to God on high   *King's*
6. Grant, we beseech Thee *Winchester*
   (21st *after Trinity.*)
7. Happy the man   *Bumpus*
   (*Written* 1836.)
8. Have mercy upon me   *Calvert*
9. Hearken unto my voice *Winchester*
10. He brought them out of
    darkness   *Bumpus*
11. Holy, Holy, Holy   *King's*
12. In humble faith *Pub. by Composer*
13. Is there not an appointed time
                          Bumpus
14. It is good for me to hold *Winchester*
15. Let Thy merciful ears   ,,
16. Lord, we beseech Thee   *Bumpus*
17. Not unto us   *Marshall*
18. O God, the King of Glory
                Pub. by Composer
19. O how amiable   *Marshall*
20. O Israel, trust in the Lord
                      Winchester
21. O Lord, from whom   *Gloucester*
22. O Lord my God   *Marshall*
23. Rejoice in the Lord   *Marshall*
24. The earth, O Lord, is full
                        Binfield
25. Thy righteousness, O God
26. To celebrate Thy praise *Longhurst*
27. Turn Thee again   *Bumpus*
28. Turn Thee unto me   *Winchester*

He also adapted from Handel and Paisiello.

CHEESE, GRIFFITH JAMES. B. 1751; D. 1804.
Blind. Org. Leominster Par. Church, 1771, and of Manchester Collegiate
Church, 1783.
1. Teach me, O Lord   *Joule* |

CLARKE, CHARLES ERLIN JACKSON. B. 1795; D. 1844.
Org. Durham Cath., 1812, and Worcester Cath., 1814.
1. Gather yourselves together *Calvert* | 2. May the grace of Christ (*Nat. Psal.*)

CLARK, THOMAS. B. 1775; D. 1859.
Psalm-tune composer (of Canterbury).

1. Awake up, my glory   *Joule*
2.*God came from Teman   *Clarke*
3. In that day shall this song   *Joule*
4. I will arise   ,,
5. O be joyful in the Lord   ,,
6.*Praise the Lord, O my soul *Clarke*
7. Rejoice in the Lord, O ye   *Joule*
8. Since I have placed my trust
                        Marshall
9. Why do the heathen   *Joule*

* From Clark's "Seraphim," 1834.

CLARKE-WHITFELD (until 1814, *Clarke* only), JOHN, Mus. Doc.,
Dublin (Cantab. et Oxon. *ad eundem*). B. 1770; D. 1836.

Org. Ludlow, 1789-94; Armagh, 1794-97; Master of Choristers, Ch. Ch. and
St. Patrick's Cath., Dublin; Org. of Trinity and St. John's, Cambridge, 1799
(succeeding Randall); and of Hereford Cath. (following Hayter); Professor
of Music of Cambridge University, 1821.

1.*Behold, God is my salvation.
2.*†Behold how good and joyful.
3.*Behold now, praise the Lord.
4.*Blessed are all they (*Psalm* 128)
        Bumpus Aut. MSS.
5.*†Blessed is the man (*Psalm* 112).
6.*Bow down Thine ear (*Psalm* 86).
7.*By the waters   *Pub. by Lonsdale*
8.*Enter not into judgment.
9.*Hear, O Thou Shepherd.
10.*I am the Resurrection.
11.*In Jewry is God known.
12.*†I will alway give thanks.
13.*I will arise.
14.*I will lift up mine eyes.
15. Make a joyful noise   *Boosey*
16.*†My heart sheweth me.
17.*O give thanks.
18. O God,wherefore art Thou? *Bumpus*
19.†*O Lord God of my salvation.
   (*Psalm* 88.)
20.*O praise God in His Holiness.
21.*O sing unto the Lord a new song.
22.*Out of the deep.
23.*Praise the Lord, ye servants.
   (*Psalm* 113.)
24.*Sing unto the Lord, and praise.
25.*The Heavens declare.
26.*The Lord's Prayer.
27.*Wherewithal shall a young man?
28.*Who will rise up?
   (*Part of No.* 1.)

And an adaptation from Handel.

CLIFTON, JOHN CHARLES. B. 1781; D. 1841.

Chorister in St. Paul's Cathedral. Pupil of Bellamy and C. Wesley. For a
time a merchant, then taught in Bath, Dublin, and London. An advocate
of Logier's system.

1. As pants the hart (*Canon*)
2. The Lord is my light   *Cramer*
3. Wash me throughly
   Chichester, 1823

COLE, WILLIAM. B. *c.* 1764; D. 1848.

Org. in Colchester and London.

1. Behold, how good and
   joyful   *E. Gaffe's Library*
2. Blessed are the undefiled ,,
3. Come, behold the works ,,
4. Hear My law, O My people ,,
5. Hear my prayer, O Lord ,,
6. I will praise Thee, O Lord ,,
7. Let my complaint ,,
8. O sing unto the Lord ,,
9. O worship the Lord
   E. Gaffe's Library
10. Ponder my words ,,
11. Praise waiteth for thee ,,
12. The Lord hear thee ,,
13. The Lord is nigh unto all ,,
14. They that put their trust ,,
15. Thy mercy, O Lord ,,
16. Turn us, O God ,,

COMER, —

1. Let God arise   *Exeter*, 1793 |

---

* Anthems marked * were published in the Composer's "Cathedral Music."
4 vols., 1806-1825.
† Autograph copies of these Anthems in Trinity College, all dated 1818.

COOKE, BENJAMIN, Mus. Doc., Cantab. (et Oxon.). B. 1734 ; D. 1793.
Org. St. Martin's-in-the-Fields, 1782; Master of the Boys, Westminster
Abbey, 1757 ; Pupil of Pepusch ; Lay-Vicar of the Abbey, 1758, and Org.,
after John Robinson, 1762.

1. *All the earth calleth upon truth.
   (*With orchestra,* 1786.)
2. All the earth rejoiceth   *Husk*
3. As the hart panteth   ,,
4. Behold, how good and joyful   ,,
   (*For the installation of the Bishop of
   Osnaburgh as Knight of the Bath,*
   1772.)
5. Call to remembrance   ,,
   (*With orchestra,* 1764.)
6. *Forgive, O Lord.
   (*Hymn before Sacrament, written for
   the Foundling Hospital,* 1791.)
7. How good and pleasant   *Husk*
   (*For Founder's Day at Charterhouse,*
   1748.)
8. How long wilt thou forget? *Calvert*
9. I heard a great voice   *Husk*
   (*With orchestra,* 1764.)
10. I will magnify Thee, O God   ,,
    (*With orchestra,* 1749.)
11. Let all the just   ,,
    (*For Founder's Day at Charterhouse,*
    1748.)
12. Let your light so shine   *Husk*
13. Like as the hart   *Bumpus*
    (*Composed in* 1749.)
14. May God His favouring ear *Husk*
    (*For 2 choirs,* 1789.)

15. Not unto us   *Husk*
16. O Lord, I will praise Thee   ,,
    (*With orchestra,* 1752.)
17. O praise God in His holiness ,,
    (*Composed,* 1762.)
18. O praise the Lord   ,,
19. Out of the deep   ,,
    (*Written in* 1750.)
20. Praised be the Lord daily   ,,
21. Resound His praise
                 Hullah's Singer's Library
22. *Spirit of God.
    (*For Whitsunday. Composed for the
    Foundling Hospital,* 1791.)
23. *The Lord in His wrath.
    (*With orchestra.*)
24. The Lord is great in Zion *Husk*
25. *The Lord said unto the woman.
    (*For the Lying-In Charity,* 1770.)
26. To Father, Son, and Holy
    Ghost   *Husk*
27. To Thee, great God   ,,
    (*For two choirs,* 1792.)
28. Vouchsafe, O Lord   ,,
29. When all Thy mercies   ,,
30. Wherewithal shall a young
    man ?   ,,
    (*Published in* 1793.)

COOKE, HENRY. B. 1769 ; D. 1840.
Third son of Benjamin Cooke. Held an appointment in the General Post
Office.

1. Blessed be the Lord God. | 3. God's providence for needy souls.
2. Give the King. |

All from Dr. B. Cooke's MSS.

COOKE, ROBERT. B. 1768 ; drowned in the Thames, 1814.
Son of Benjamin Cooke, whom he succeeded at St. Martin's, 1793, and Westminster, 1802.

1. How long wilt Thou forget? *Joule* | 3. Thou, O Lord, art my Defender
2. I looked, and lo ! a Lamb | *Marshall*
                 Cooke's MSS. |

COOMBS, JAMES MORRIS, Senr. B. 1769 ; D. 1820.
Chorister of Salisbury Cath. ; Org. Chippenham Parish Church, Wilts.

1. Blessed is the man that | 2. Out of the deep   *Bumpus MSS.*
           feareth   *Gloucester* |

---

* All from Dr. B. Cooke's MSS. (19 Vols.) now in possession of the Royal College of Music.

COOMBS, JAMES MORRIS, Junr. B. 1799. D. 1873.
Org. Chippenham Parish Church and the private Chapel at Bowood, 1831.
1. Give ear, O Lord   *Novello* |

CORFE, ARTHUR THOMAS. B. 1778 ; D. 1863 (while kneeling in prayer).
Son of Joseph Corfe ; Org. Salisbury Cath., 1804-63.
1. Lord, Thou art become | 2. Teach me, O Lord   *Salisbury*
   gracious   *Salisbury* |
He also adapted from Carissimi, Mozart, Sacchini, and others.

CORFE, JOSEPH. B. 1740 ; D. 1820.
Org. Salisbury Cath., 1792-1804.

1. Almighty and everlasting God	*Corfe*	11. O praise God in His Holiness	*Joule*
2. Be Thou my Judge	,,	12. Ponder my words	*Corfe*
3. Call to remembrance	*Marshall*	13. The heavens have declared	*Salisbury*
4. Hear me, O Lord	*Calvert*	(*Part of No.* 16.)	
5. Hosanna to the Son of David	*Corfe*	14. The King shall rejoice	*Corfe*
6. I will magnify Thee (*Psalm* 30)	,,	15. The Lord is King	,,
7. Lord, remember David	*Calvert*	16. The rich and poor meet together	*Salisbury*
8. O God, the Protector of all	*Corfe*	17. This is the day	*Corfe*
9. O God, Who hast prepared	,,	18. Thou, O God, art praised	,,
10. O Lord, rebuke me not.			

Also adaptations from Steffani, Jomelli, &c.

COTES, Rev. DIGBY H., M.A.
Author of sermon, "Music, a rational assistant in the duty of praise, when united with charity." Published in 1756.
1. In the beginning   *Novello* |

CROTCH, WILLIAM, Mus. Doc., Oxon. B. 1775 ; D. 1847.
Pupil of Randall ; Org. Christ Church Cath., 1790-1807 ; St. John's College, 1797-1806 ; Professor of Music at Oxford University, 1797 ; First Principal of the R.A.M., 1822.

1.*Behold, thy King cometh. (*Part of No.* 15.)		12. O Lord, from Whom all good things	*Pettet,* 1825
2.*Be merciful unto me.		13. O Lord, give ear	*King's*
3.*Blessed is he whose un-righteousness		14.*O Lord God of Hosts.	
4. Comfort the soul	*Novello*	15.*Rejoice in the Lord.	
5.*God is our hope.		16. Remember, O Lord	*King's*
6. Holy, Holy, Holy (*For Trinity,* 1827. *Hymn by Heber.*)	*Novello*	17.*Sing we merrily.	
7.*How dear are Thy counsels.		18. The joy of our heart is ceased (*Death of the Duke of York,* 1827.)	*Bumpus*
8. In God's Word	*Novello*	19.*The Lord, even the most mighty.	
9. Methinks I hear	,,	20. The Lord is King	*Novello,* 1843
10.*My God, my God, look.		21. Weep not for me (*Words by Milman.*)	*Pettet*
11. O come hither, and hearken	*Cramer*	22.*Who is like unto Thee ?	

Selections from his Oratorio "Palestine" are used as Anthems.

* These anthems were published in "Ten Anthems," *c.* 1793. New Edition, by W. H. Monk (Novello).

CUTLER, WILLIAM HENRY, Mus. Bac., Oxon.   B. 1792 ; D. —.
Chorister in St. Paul's ; org. St. Helen's, Bishopsgate, 1818, and Quebec
Chapel, 1823 ; sang at Drury Lane in oratorio ; taught on Logier's system.
1. O praise the Lord   *Bumpus*
    (*With orchestra.*)

CUZENS, BENJAMIN.   Flourished late in the 18th century.
Published and wrote " The Portsmouth Harmony " and "Divine Harmony."

1. Almighty and everlast-ing *Thompson* (*Collect for 2nd Sunday after Epiphany.*)	5. Christ, seeing the multi-tude *Thompson*
2. Almighty God, give us grace ,, (*1st Sunday after Advent.*)	6. God, Who as at this time ,,
	7. If ye then be risen ,,
	8. In the beginning ,,
	9. I will magnify *Div. Har.*
3. Almighty God, Who hast given us ,, (*Christmas Day.*)	10. Now the God of peace *Thompson*
	11. O be joyful *Div. Har.*
	12. O give thanks ,,
	13. O the depth of the riches ,,
4. Almighty God, Who through ,, (*Easter Day.*)	14. Ponder my words ,,
	15. Sing we merrily ,,
	16. Whom have I in heaven ? ,,

DARE, CHARLES JAMES.   D. 1820.
Org. Hereford Cath., 1805-18.   Conducted Hereford Festivals, 1807-16.
1. I will call upon the Lord *Gloucester* |

DAVY, JOHN.   B. 1763 ; D. 1824.
Pupil of W. Jackson ; Teacher in Exeter and London ;   Violin in Covent
Garden Theatre Orchestra.

1. I will give thanks *Exeter*	3. Ponder my words
2. Lord, who shall dwell (Op. 9) *Bumpus*	*Appendix to Gloucester.*

DIXON, WILLIAM.   B. *c.* 1760 ; D. 1825.
Music Engraver, Teacher, and Writer in Liverpool and London.

1. Almighty God, give us grace *Joule*	6. I am the Resurrection *Joule* (*Burial Anthem.*)
2. Behold, how good ,, (*After a Club Sermon.*)	7. Most gracious God ,, (*In time of war.*)
3. Blessed are all they ,, (*For Weddings.*)	8. O Lord, Who hast taught us ,,
4. Bow down Thine ear ,, (*After a Charity Sermon.*)	9. Turn Thou us, good Lord ,, (*For First Day of Lent.*)
5. Come unto Me ,, (*For Communion Sunday.*)	

DOBNEY, MICHAEL.
Flourished at Maidstone, *c.* 1810.

1. Be merciful to me, O God *Joule*	2. Unto Thee, O Lord, will I lift up *Joule*

DRUMMOND, GEORGE, Mus. Bac., Oxon.   B. 1798 ; D. 1839.
Blind from infancy ; Pupil of Crotch.
1. Lord of all power and might *Husk* | 2. O give thanks (*Psalm* 105)   *Husk*

DUPUIS, THOMAS SANDERS, MUS. DOC., OXON. B. 1730; D. 1796.
Pupil at Chapel Royal of Gates and Travers; Org. and Composer of the
Chapel Royal, 1779, after Boyce.

1. Arise, O Lord God *Old Chap. Roy.*
2.*Arise, shine „
3. Be Thou my Judge *Chap. Roy.*
4.*Be Thou my Judge *Metrical Anthem*
5. Blessed are all they *Chap. Roy.*
6. Blessed is he that considereth „
7.*Bow down Thine ear.
8. By the waters *Joule*
9. Hearken unto Me *Chap. Roy.*
10. Hearken unto My voice „
11. Hear my prayer „
12.*How long wilt Thou forget.
13. I cried unto the Lord *Chap. Roy.*
14. If the Lord Himself „
(*For the 5th of November.*)
15. It is a good thing „
16. I was glad „
17. I will magnify Thee, O God „
18. I will sing of the Lord „
19.*Lift up your heads.
20. Lord, teach us to number
Chap. Roy.
21. Lord, we pray Thee „
22. Lord, what is man? „
23.*Lord, what love have I.

24. My God, my God *Chap. Roy.*
25. My heart is fixed „
26.*Not unto us, O Lord.
27. O God, my God *Chap. Roy.*
28.*O God, whose nature.
29. O how amiable *Chap. Roy.*
30. O Lord God of Hosts „
31. O Lord, how manifold „
32. O Lord, how many „
33. O praise our God, ye people „
34. Ponder my words „
35. Put me not to rebuke „
36.*Rejoice in the Lord.
37.*Save me, O God, for Thy
Name's sake.
38.*Sing unto God, O ye
kingdoms.
39. Sing unto the Lord, and
praise *Chap. Roy.*
40.*Teach me, O Lord.
41. The Lord, even the most
mighty *Chap. Roy.*
42. The Lord is my Light „
43.*The Lord is my Shepherd.
44.*The souls of the righteous.
45. Thou art my King *Chap. Roy.*

EBDON, THOMAS. B. 1738; D. 1811.
Chorister and Org. (1763) of Durham Cathedral.

1.†Behold, God is my salvation.
2.†Behold how good and joyful.
3.†Blessed is he that considereth.
4. Blessed is he that hath the God
Durham
5.†Blessed is the man.
6.†Cry unto the Lord.
7.†Deliver me from mine enemies.
8. Have mercy upon me, O Lord *Calvert*
9.†Hear me when I call.
10. Help us, O God *Joule*
11. Holy, Holy, Holy *Calvert*
12. How still and peaceful *Durham*
13.†I did call upon the Lord.
14. I will alway give thanks *Marshall*
15. I will give thanks *Durham*
16.†I will magnify Thee.
17.†I will remember.
18. I will sing of the Lord *Durham*
19. Lord, Thou knowest all my
desires „
20. Lord, who shall dwell? *Joule*
21. Many a one there be *Durham*

22.†O give thanks unto the Lord.
(*Psalm 106.*)
23. O give thanks unto the Lord
(*Psalm 136.*) *Mann*
24.†O Lord my God, I cried
25.†O Lord my God, I will exalt
Thee.
26.†O Lord, rebuke me not.
27.†O sing unto the Lord.
28.†Praised be the Lord daily.
29. Praise the Lord, O my soul *Dublin*
30. Praise the Lord, ye servants
Marshall
31. Sing unto the Lord, and praise
Durham
32.†Teach me, O Lord.
33. The eyes of the Lord *Durham*
34.†The Lord is my Shepherd.
35.†The souls of the righteous.
36.†To God, O my soul.
37. To God the mighty Lord *Durham*
38.†Wherewithal shall a young
man?

---

* These were published in Dupuis's "Cathedral Music." 3 vols. Edited by John
Spencer, 1797.
† These were published in Ebdon's "Cathedral Music." 2 vols., 1790-1810.

EVANS, CHARLES SMART. B. 1770; D. 1849.

Gent. of the Chapel Royal; Org. St. Paul's, Covent Garden. Gained prizes for Glees at the Catch Club, &c.

1.*Almighty Father, Who hast	*Husk*	5. Teach me, O Lord	*Joule*
2. I will alway give thanks	,,	6. The Lord is my Shepherd	,,
3. I will love Thee	*Pettet*	7. The scene of death is closed	*Husk*
4.*O God, the Strength of all	*Husk*		

EVANS, WILLIAM. D. 1740.

Org. Wells Cath., 1734-40.

1. In Thee, O Lord   *Wells* |

FISH, WILLIAM. B. 1775; D. 1863 (1864).

Violinist at Norwich Theatre; Composer and Teacher in Norwich. Taught E. Taylor and G. Perry.

1. The Lord that made the
      heavens   *Durham*, 1848 |

FULLER, ROBERT, Mus. Bac., Cantab. B.— ; D. 1743.

Org. King's College, Cambridge, 1727-42; to the University, 1731.

1. Behold, I bring you	*Ely*	5. I will alway give thanks.	*Ely*
2. Behold, Thou hast made	,,	6. Lift up your heads	,,
3. Glorious and powerful	,,	7. Sing unto the Lord	,,
4. Hosanna !	,,		

GARDINER, WILLIAM. B. 1770; D. 1853.

A clever amateur, resident in Leicester. Author of " The Music of Nature " and " Music and Friends."

1. Great God Divine	*Husk*	3. One thing have I desired	*Husk*
2. Holy, Holy, Holy	,,		

He compiled an Oratorio " Judah," from works of Haydn, Mozart, and Beethoven !

GARLAND, THOMAS. B. 1731; D. 1808.

Org. Norwich Cath., 1749-1808

1. Behold, now praise the Lord	*Mann*	5. Save me, O God	*Marshall*
2. Come, Holy Ghost	*Bunnett*	6. Sing unto the Lord	,,
3. Like as the hart	*Mann*	7. Sing we merrily	,,
4. Not unto us	,,		

---

* Published *c.* 1830, and dedicated to Bishop Barrington (of Durham).

GARTH, JOHN. B. 1722; D. 1810.

Was responsible for adaptations of music by Marcello to words of the Psalms. He composed music to the following thirty Collects :—

1. 1st Sunday after Epiphany	*Birchall*	16. 12th Sunday after Trinity	*Birchall*
2. 2nd Sunday after Epiphany	,,	17. 13th Sunday after Trinity	,,
3. 5th Sunday after Easter	,,	18. 14th Sunday after Trinity	,,
4. Sunday after Ascension	,,	19. 15th Sunday after Trinity	,,
5. 1st Sunday after Trinity	,,	20. 16th Sunday after Trinity	,,
6. 2nd Sunday after Trinity	,,	21. 17th Sunday after Trinity	,,
7. 3rd Sunday after Trinity	,,	22. 18th Sunday after Trinity	,,
8. 4th Sunday after Trinity	,,	23. 19th Sunday after Trinity	,,
9. 5th Sunday after Trinity	,,	24. 20th Sunday after Trinity	,,
10. 6th Sunday after Trinity	,,	25. 21st Sunday after Trinity	,,
11. 7th Sunday after Trinity	,,	26. 22nd Sunday after Trinity	,,
12. 8th Sunday after Trinity	,,	27. 23rd Sunday after Trinity	,,
13. 9th Sunday after Trinity	,,	28. 24th Sunday after Trinity	,,
14. 10th Sunday after Trinity	,,	29. 25th Sunday after Trinity	,,
15. 11th Sunday after Trinity	,,	30. Prevent us, O Lord	,,

All published in a small oblong quarto vol., dated 1794.

GREEN, JAMES.

Org. at Hull in the first half of the century. Published in 1724, " A book of Psalmody."

1. Arise, O Lord, we pray Thee.	10. O give thanks unto the Lord.
2. Behold, I bring you.	11. O how amiable.
3. Behold, the Lord is my salvation.	12. O praise the Lord, for it is.
4. Blessed are all they.	13. O sing unto God, sing praises.
5. Hear my prayer, O Lord.	14. Praise the Lord, O my soul.
6. How long wilt Thou forget?	15. Sing unto the Lord.
7. Lift up your heads.	16. Sing we merrily.
8. O be joyful in God.	17. They that put their trust.
9. O clap your hands.	18. Thou, O God, art praised.

All published in his "Book of Psalmody," of which the 11th edition appeared in 1751.

GREGOR, Rev. CHRISTIAN.

" Bishop" of the Unitas Fratrum, 1802.

1. Glory to God in the highest *Joule* | 2. Hosanna, blessed is He   *Joule*

GREVILLE, Rev. ROBERT.

Composer of " Now the bright morning star" (Prize Glee, 1787).

1. Turn Thee, O Lord   *Marshall* |-

GRIESBACH, JOHN HENRY. B. 1798 ; D. 1875.

Composer, and 'Cello Player in the Queen's Band.

1. I shall see Him, but not now *Fowle* |

GUISE, RICHARD, Mus. Bac. B. 1735 ; D. 1808.
Lay-Clerk of St. George's, Windsor, and Eton College, 1760-73 ; Gent. of the Chapel Royal, 1779, and Master of the Boys, Westminster Abbey, 1793.

1. Hear me, O Lord   *Calvert*
2. Praised be the Lord   ,,
3. The King shall rejoice   ,,
4. Unto Thee lift I up   *Calvert*
5. Wherewithal   ,,

HARGREAVES, GEORGE. B. 1799 ; D. 1869.
Miniature Painter and Composer. Son of Thomas Hargreaves, a famous Miniature Painter

1. Let God arise   *Joule* | 2. The earth is the Lord's   *Joule*

HARRINGTON, HENRY, M.D., M.A., Oxon. B. 1727 ; D. 1816.
Physician and Mayor of Bath. Founded the Bath Musical Society.

1. O render thanks   *Norwich* | 2. There was darkness *Exeter*, 1793

HARRIS, JOSEPH JOHN, Mus. Bac., Oxon. B. 1799 ; D. 1869
Chapel Royal Boy ; Org. St. Olave's, Southwark, Blackburn, and Manchester Cath.

1. Blessed be the Lord God.
2.*Except the Lord   } *Hime and*
3. If the Lord Himself   } *Addison*
4. If we say that we have no sin.
5. I will arise.
6. My soul truly waiteth   *Joule*
7. O Lord, correct me } *Hime and*
8. Rend your heart   } *Addison*
9. The Lord hear thee   *Joule*
10.†The Lord is my strength.
11. To the Lord our God
Hime and Addison

HART, CHARLES. B. 1797 ; D. 1859.
Pupil of Dr. Crotch ; Org. St. Dunstan's, Stepney, 1829-33 ; Tredegar Square Church and St. George's, Beckenham.

1. Almighty and everlasting
        Lyra Eccles., 1844
2.‡Sing unto God.   *Novello*
3.‡Teach me, O Lord.   *Novello*
4.‡The Lord is my Shepherd.   ,,
5. Thou, O God, art praised *Marshall*

HARWOOD, EDWARD (TEDDY). B. 1707 ; D. 1787.
Of Hoddleson, near Blackburn.

1. Have mercy upon me   *Joule* | 2. Vital spark of heavenly flame   *Joule*

HAVERGAL, Rev. WILLIAM HENRY, M.A. B. 1793 ; D. 1870.
Educated at Merchant Taylor's School and Oxford ; Rector of Astley, Worcestershire, 1829-42 ; Rector of St. Nicholas, Worcester, and Hon. Canon of Worcester Cath., 1845 ; Rector of Shareshill, 1860.

1. Arise, O Lord God
        Lyra Eccles., 1844
2. Give thanks to the Lord *Shepherd*
        (*Gresham Prize*, 1841.)
3. God so loved the world
        Lyra Eccles., 1844
4. O Saviour of the world
        Hackett, 1842
5. Praise ye the Lord *Lyra Eccles.*

---

* Dr. Mann attributes this to another Harris ; no initials.
† On laying the Foundation Stone of new tower to Manchester Cath., 1864.
‡ Dedicated to Dr. Crotch.

HAYES, PHILIP, Mus. Doc., Oxon.   B. 1738 ; D. ·1797.

Son of William Hayes, and his pupil; Gent. Chapel Royal, 1767; Org. New College, Oxford, 1776 ; Magdalen, 1777 ; St. John's, 1790; Professor of Music in University, 1777.

Sixteen Psalms, selected from Merrick's Version.   Printed for Richard Frith, Oxford :—

1. Behold, my God.
2. Be Thou my Judge.
3. Come celebrate your God and King.
4. How blest the man, whose conscious grief.
5. How shall my tongue Thy justice sing.
6. Jehovah reigns—ye nations own.
7. Let Zion's heaven-devoted mount.
8. Lord, let Thy clemency divine.
9. O turn, great Ruler of the skies.
10. The Lord, th' eternal sceptre rears.
11. Thy eyes in me, nor lofty mind.
12. To Thee above the starry spheres.
13. When various griefs.
14. Who o'er the waves.
15. Who trust in God's protecting hand.
16. Ye tribes of earth.

The following Anthems in Score, in the autograph of Dr. Philip Hayes, are in the possession of Mr. John S. Bumpus :—

VOLUME I.

1.*Blessed is he that considereth   *July* 31, 1767
2. Hear my prayer   *June*, 1759
3. In Jewry is God known   *May* 10, 1778
4. I will receive the cup of salvation   1769
5. Lo, this is our God   *December* 8, 1771
6.*O how amiable   *June* 30, 1768
7.*Righteous art Thou   *May* 9, 1778
8.*The Lord descended from above   *November* 10, 1769
9.*The Lord is full of compassion
(*Composed, with bassoon accompaniment, for a country church, September* 18, 1770.)

VOLUME II.

10. Arise, O Lord God *January*, 1790
11. Begin unto my God with timbrels
(*Composed for the University Sermon at New College, Oxford, Trinity Sunday*, 1779.)
12.*Behold, O God, our Defender
13. Blessed be the Lord God   *November* 4, 1779
14. Christ being raised   (*Solo.*) *Easter Eve*, 1796
15. Christ being raised   (*Full.*) *February* 19, 1787
16. Come, Holy Ghost   *October* 2, 1783
17. Fixed in the heavens   *November* 14, 1779
18. Hearken unto my voice   *October* 9, 1779
19. Hear the voice of my humble petitions
20. Hear, ye children
(*For the Infirmary Meeting at the Octagon (Episcopal) Chapel, Bath, December* 16, 1787.)
21. I am the Resurrection
(*Complete Burial Service in E flat, March* 24, 1772.)
22. I have longed for Thy saving health
23. O consider my adversity   *October* 9, 1779
24. O Lord, my God   *Unfinished*
25. O praise the Lord, all ye heathen   *August* 30, 1793
26. O praise the Lord of heaven
27. O pray for the peace of Jerusalem
28. Remember not, Lord, our offences
(*For the General Fast, April* 19, 1793.)
29. Sing ye merrily
(*Composed at Finedon, Notts., the seat of the Dolben Family, September* 12, 1787.)
30. The ways of Zion do mourn
(*For the General Fast, February* 21, 1781.)
31. Thy mercy, O Lord *April* 12, 1781

The following are in a third volume, unaccountably missing, but probably uniform with the two in the possession of Mr. Bumpus. The composer has inserted a list of its contents in Volume I. :—

32. Behold, God is great.	41.*O Lord our Governour.
33. Behold, God is highly.	42. O Lord, Thou hast dealt.
34. Behold, I bring you.	43. Our soul hath patiently tarried.
35. Have mercy upon me.	44.*Rejoice in the Lord.
36. Hear the right, O Lord.	45. Return unto the Lord.
37. I have longed for Thy saving health.	46. Show me Thy ways.
	47. The Lord hear thee
38. I will magnify Thee.	48.*The Lord is my Shepherd
39. Lord, let me know mine end.	49. The sacrifices of God.
40. O Israel trust.	

The following are in the possession of Mr. A. M. Broadley, great grandson of the composer :—

50. Blessed is he that considereth.	51. O praise the Lord(*With instruments*)
(*With instruments*.) *Same as No. 1*	52. Sing unto God ,,

In the possession of Mr. T. C. Taphouse, of Oxford :—

53.*The heathen make much ado.	54. Try me, O God
	Words in Marshall's Collection

HAYES, WILLIAM, MUS. DOC., OXON. B. 1707; D. 1777.

Pupil of Hine; Org. St. Mary's, Shrewsbury, 1729-31; Worcester Cath., 1731-34, and Magdalen, 1734; Professor of Music in the University of Oxford, 1741, and Conductor, Gloucester Festival, 1763.

1.†All people that on earth.	23.†Not unto us, O Lord.
2.‡A race by God unblest.	24.†O be joyful in God.
3.‡Arise, ye people.	25.†O give thanks unto the Lord.
4.†Blessed are all they.	26.†O God, Thou art my God.
5.†Blessed art Thou, O Lord.	27. O how amiable.
6.†Bow down Thine ear.	28. O Lord God of Hosts *Durham*
(*Verse*, s.s.)	29. O Lord, look down *Husk*
7.†Bring unto the Lord.	30.†O worship the Lord.
8.‡Great is our God.	31.†Praise the Lord, O Jerusalem.
9.†Great is the Lord.	32.†Praise the Lord, O my soul.
10.‡Haste to my aid.	33.†Save, Lord, and hear.
11. Hear me, O God *Dublin*, 1881	34.‡The Festal morn, my God, is come.
12.‡How blest the sight.	35.†The Lord, even the most mighty.
13.*I have set God alway.	36.†The Lord is good.
14.‡Is this a dream?	37. The Lord is my Light *Marshall*
15.†I will give thanks.	38.†The Lord preserveth.
16.‡Let thy various realms, O earth.	39.‡To God above, from all below.
17.‡Lift your voice, and thankful sing.	40.‡To God I cried with anguish stung.
18.‡Lo! from the hills my help descends.	41.‡To Thee, from out the depths I pray.
19.‡Lo ! my Shepherd's hand divine.	42.†Unto Thee, O God, do we give.
20.‡Lord, how long wilt Thou ?	43.†Who is the King of Glory ?
21.†Lord, Thou hast been.	44.†Whoso dwelleth.
22.‡My soul, with sacred zeal inspired.	45.‡Ye servants of th' Eternal King.

* These have been printed.
† All edited and published by Dr. P. Hayes in 1795.
‡ Sixteen Psalms, selected from Merrick's New Version. Printed by Randall. New Editions by W. Cross and E. Clare.

THOMAS ATTWOOD.

HEATHCOTE, EDWARD. B.— ; D. 1835.
Org. Bakewell Church and afterwards Southwell Minster, 1818-35.
1. Keep, we beseech Thee   *Southwell* | 2. O Lord, we beseech Thee *Southwell*

HEATHCOTE, Rev. GILBERT. B. 1765 ; D. 1829.
Fellow of Winchester Coll. and of New Coll., Oxford; Archdeacon of Winchester; Vicar of Hursley.

1. Awake, my soul, lift up thine eyes *Bumpus, Aut. MSS.* (*May*, 7, 1792.)
2. Behold, how good and joyful ,,
3. Behold now, praise the Lord ,, (*Winchester*, 1822.)
4. Blessed are the people ,,
5. Blessed is he that considereth ,, (*February*, 7, 1783.)
6. Come, Holy Ghost, Eternal God ,, (*May*, 1811.)
7. God so loved the world ,,
8. Hosanna to the Son of David ,, (*New Coll., Oxford, March 26, 1787.*)
9. I am the Resurrection ,, (*Complete Burial Service in A minor, New Coll., Oxford, September,* 1799.)
10. O come, loud anthems let us sing *Bumpus, Aut. MSS.*
11. O praise the Lord, laud ye ,, (*August* 9, 1791.) (*For a country church, with accompaniment for two flutes, bassoon, or 'cello*).
12. Save me, O God ,, (*New Coll., Oxford, December* 17, 1794.)
13. When we our wearied limbs ,, (1805.)
14. While I live I will praise the Lord ,, (*May*, 1811.)

HEMPEL, CHARLES WILLIAM. B. 1777 ; D. 1855.
Org. of St. Mary's Church, Truro.

1. Like as the hart   *Joule* | 4. Praise the Lord, O my soul   *Joule*
2. Man that is born   *Marshall* | 5. Unto Thee, O God   *Marshall*
3. Ponder my words   *Joule* |

HENLEY, Rev. PHOCION, M.A. B. 1728 ; D. 1764.
Rector of St. Andrew by the Wardrobe with St. Anne's, Blackfriars, 1759.

1. Hear my prayer, O God   *Page* | 3. The Lord is my Shepherd
2. O let my mouth be filled   *King's* | *Durham*, 1848

HERSCHELL, Sir FREDERICK WILLIAM, K.C.B., F.R.S., D.C.L. B. 1738 ; D. 1822.
Bandsman in the Hanoverian Guards; Org. Halifax Parish Church; Private Astronomer to King George III.; Scientist and Musician.

1. O come, loud anthems   *Norwich*, 1789 |

HESLETINE (HESELTINE), JAMES. D. 1763.
Org. St. Katherine's Hospital, London; Durham Cath., 1710-63; Pupil of Blow.

1. I cried by reason of my affliction (*Collection of Anthems*, 1724.)
2. I will give thanks unto Thee   *Div. Har.*
3. I will love Thee, O Lord   *King's*
4. O let my mouth   *Dublin*, 1881
5. Praise the Lord, ye servants   *Durham*, 1848
6. This is the day   *Durham*
7. Unto Thee will I cry   *Collection*, 1714
8. We have a strong city   *Div. Har.*

He destroyed several of his Anthems to spite the Dean and Chapter, in return for some supposed slight.

HODGES, EDWARD, Mus. Doc., Cantab. B. 1796; D. 1867.
Org. of several Bristol churches; went to U.S.A., 1838; Org. St. John's
Episcopal Church, New York, and Trinity Church, New York, 1846;
returned to England, 1863.

1. I heard a voice from heaven	*Mann*	4. O Lord God, to whom vengeance.	*Psalm* 94
2. In the beginning	*Marshall*		(*Oratorio Anthem.*)
3. I was glad	,,	5. O pray for the peace of Jerusalem	*Novello*
		(*Part of No.* 3.)	

HOLDER, JOSEPH WILLIAM, Mus. Bac., Oxon. B. 1764; D. 1832.
Pupil of Nares; Org. St. George the Martyr, Queen Square; St. Mary's Church,
Bungay, and Chelmsford.

1. Arise, O Lord, why sleepest Thou?	*Ely*	6. O praise our God	*Ely*
2. Great is the Lord	,,	7. Out of the deep	,,
3. I look for the Lord	,,	8. The Lord is King	,,
4. I waited for the Lord	,,	9. The Lord is my Shepherd	,,
5. My heart is fixed	,,	10. Thou, O God	,,

HOLLAND, Rev. W. W.
1. Grant, we beseech Thee. *Marshall* |

HOLMES, WILLIAM. B. 1764; D. 1829.
Leader of the choir in the Parish Church, Teigngrace, Devonshire.

1. O Lord, Thou hast searched *Joule* |

HOOK, Rev. WALTER.
Son of Dean Hook; sometime Succentor of Chichester; Rector of Lavington.

1. Blessed is the man that trusteth	*Chichester*, 1868	4. Out of the mouth of very babes	*Chichester*, 1868
2. Forth from the dark and stormy sky	*Novello*	5. The pains of hell came	,,
3. Mine eyes are ever looking	*Chichester*, 1868	6. These have left a name	*Novello*
		7. We work for the Saviour	*Chichester*, 1868

HORSLEY, WILLIAM, Mus. Bac., Oxon. B. 1774; D. 1858.
Org. Ely Chapel, Holborn; Belgrave Chapel, Charterhouse (following
Stevens); and to The Asylum for Female Orphans. Married daughter of
J. W. Callcott.

1. Awake, thou that sleepest	*Novello*	5. I heard a voice from heaven.	
2. Come, Holy Spirit	*Nat. Psal.*	(*Canon* 4 *in* 2.)	
3. Hear me, when I call	*Novello*	6. Let Thy merciful ears	*Novello*
4. Hear, O Lord, and have mercy.		7. Thee we adore	*Nat. Psal.*
		8. When Israel came out.	
		(*Degree exercise.*)	

HOWARD, SAMUEL, Mus. Doc., Cantab. B. 1710; D. 1782.
Pupil of Croft and Pepusch; Org. St. Bride's and Clement Dane, London;
assisted Boyce in forming his Collection.

1. Blessed is the man	*King's*	3. Wherewithal shall a young man?	*Dublin*, 1881
2. This is the day	*Husk*		
(*With orchestra.*)			

HOWGILL, WILLIAM.

Org. at Whitehaven (1794); later on in London.

1. The righteous souls.
(*Printed at the "Whitehaven Gazette"
Office in 1805.*)

2. My song shall be alway.

ISAAC, ELIAS. B. 1734; D. 1793.

Pupil of Dr. Greene; Org. Worcester Cath., 1748-93; Conductor of the Festivals.

1. O Lord, grant the King   *Durham*

JACKSON, WILLIAM (of Exeter). B. 1730; D. 1803.

Pupil of Silvester and J. Travers; Org. Exeter Cath., 1777-1803; Essayist and Landscape Painter.

1.*Awake, put on thy strength.
2.*Blow ye the trumpet.
3.*Come unto Me.
4.*God came from Teman.
5. Hear me, O God   *Husk*
6. How numerous, Lord *Jesus College*
7. I beheld, and lo!   *Exeter*, 1793
8. I looked and behold   ,,
9. Lift up your heads   ,,
10. Lord, hear the voice *Jesus College*

11. O be joyful   *Exeter*
12. O come, let us worship   ,,
13.*O Lord, how manifold   ,,
14. Praise the Lord.
15. Sing to the Lord   *Marshall*
16. There shall be signs   *Exeter*
17. Through all the chang-
      ing   *Jesus College*
18. To the Lord our God   *Exeter*
19. When the day

JONES, JOHN. B. *c.* 1730; D. 1796.

One of the two Organists of the Middle Temple, 1749; Charterhouse (following Pepusch), 1753; St. Paul's, 1755. Held all three posts together!

1. Arise, O Lord   *Durham*, 1848
2. Blessed is he that considereth
                        Marshall

3. I will give thanks   *Husk*
4. O magnify   *Marshall*

JONES, Rev. WILLIAM (of Nayland), M.A., F.R.S. B. 1726; D. 1800.

Successively Rector of Paston, Northamptonshire; Curate of Finedon; Vicar of Stoke-by-Nayland; Rector of Pluckley, Kent. Author of several learned treatises.

1. From Thy seat.
   Longman and Broderip, 1798

2. Thou, Lord, in the beginning
   Longman and Broderip, 1798

KEMP, JOSEPH, Mus. Doc., Cantab. B. 1778; D. 1824.

Pupil of W. Jackson, of Exeter; Org. of Bristol Cath. Teacher in London.

1. A sound of battle.
   (*To the Duke of Cumberland.*)

2. I am Alpha and Omega.

---

* Published in Jackson's Cathedral Music, edited by James Paddon.

KENT, JAMES. B. 1700 ; D. 1776.

Pupil of Richardson and Croft; Org. Finedon, 1717, Trinity College, Cambridge, 1727, and Winchester Cath., 1737-74 (following J. Bishop).

1.*All Thy works praise Thee.
2.*Blessed be Thou, Lord God of Israel.
3.*Give the Lord the honour.
4. Hearken unto My voice   *Arnold*
5.*Hearken unto this, O man.
6.*Hear my prayer, O God.
7.*In the beginning was.
8.*It is a good thing.
9.*Lord, how are they increased.
10.*Lord, what love have I.
11.*Lord, who shall dwell?
12.*My song shall be of mercy.
13.*My soul truly waiteth.
14. O Lord our Governour (with Amen).
15.*O Lord our Governour (with Hallelujah).
16.*Rejoice in the Lord, O ye.
17.*Sing, O Heavens.
18. Teach me, O Lord.
19.*The Lord hath prepared.
20.*The Lord is my Shepherd.
21.*When the Son of Man.
22.*Who is this that cometh?
23.*Why do the heathen?

KNYVETT, WILLIAM. B. 1779 ; D. 1856.

Alto Singer and Composer ; Gent. and Composer, Chapel Royal, and Lay-Vicar, Westminster Abbey ; Principal Alto Singer and Conductor at "Antient Music" Concerts.

1. I will sing a new song   *Joule*
2. The King shall rejoice   *Calvert*
(*Coronation of King George IV.*, 1821.)
3. This is the Day.
(*Coronation of Queen Victoria*, 1838.)

LANGDON, RICHARD, Mus. Bac., Oxon. B. before 1730 ; D. 1803.

Org. Exeter (1753), Ely (1777), Bristol (1777), and Armagh (1782-94) Caths.

1. Be Thou my Judge   *Calvert*
2. Blessed is he that considereth   *Gloucester*
3. Lord, Thou hast been our refuge   *Exeter*, 1793
4. Not unto us, O Lord   ,,
5. O Lord, our Governour   ,,
6. O pray for the peace of Jerusalem   *Bumpus*
7. Turn Thee unto me.   *Weekes*
†8. Turn Thou us   *Husk*
9. Wherewithal shall a young man   *Dublin*, 1881

LATROBE, Rev. CHRISTIAN IGNATIUS. B. 1758 ; D. 1836.

Secretary to the United Moravian Brethren in England ; Writer and Composer.

1. Behold, the Lamb of God   *Mann*
2. Blessed be Thou that dwellest   ,,
3. Bless the Lord, O my soul   ,,
4. Cheer up, my soul   ,,
5. Eden, from its flowery bed   ,,
6. Gloomy Garden   ,,
7. Gracious Lord, how great Thy love   ,,
8. Hark, what sing the heavenly choirs   ,,
9. Holy Redeemer, be Thy rest   *Joule*
10. How amiable are Thy tabernacles   *Mann*
11. How excellent is Thy loving-kindness   ,,
12. How shall I meet my Saviour   ,,
13. Make a joyful noise   ,,
14. My God, let, I beseech Thee   ,,
15. O be joyful (*Psalm* 100)   ,,

---

* First published in Two Volumes. Vol. 1 by the Composer, 1773. Vol. 2, edited by Joseph Corfe, of Salisbury, 1796. Modern reprints by Novello and others.
† Attributed by Dr. Mann to W. Langdon.

LATROBE, Rev. CHRISTIAN IGNATIUS (*continued*).

16. O how blessed is the
     station *Mann*
17. O send out Thy light ,,
18. O Thou great Power ,,
19. Out of the deep ,,
20. Praise waiteth for Thee ,,
21. See this transient mortal
     life ,,
22. Stand up and bless ,,
23. Surely He hath borne ,,
24. There is a river ,,

25. Thou for our grief didst
     mourn *Mann*
26. Tho' waves and storms ,,
27. Thy throne, O God *Wells*
28. Unto the Lamb that
     was *Mann*
29. Was ever grief like Thine? ,,
30. What shall we render? ,,
31. Worthy, O Lord, art
     Thou ,,

LEE, WILLIAM. B. —; D. 1754.
  Org. Southwell Minster, 1718-54.

1. O do well unto Thy
     servants *Marshall*
2. They that put their trust
     Marshall

LINLEY, Rev. OZIAS THURSTON. B. 1765; D. 1831.
  Minor Canon of Norwich and afterwards Fellow and Org. Dulwich Coll.

1. Lord, let me know my end *Mann*
     (*Incomplete.*)

LINLEY, THOMAS, Senr. B. 1725; D. 1795.
  Pupil of Chilcot and Paradies; Conductor of Oratorios in Bath; shared
  management of Drury Lane Theatre with Sheridan; Writer of Ballad-
  Operas, &c.

1. Bow down Thine ear *Page*
2. O how amiable *Mann*

LINLEY, THOMAS, Junr. B. 1756; D. 1778 (drowned).
  Studied under his father, Thomas Linley, Boyce, and (in Florence) Nardini.
  Met Mozart abroad. Leader of Bath Concerts and at Drury Lane.

1. Let God arise *Mann*

LINLEY, WILLIAM. B. 1767; D. 1835.
  Harrovian; Brother of the above; Pupil of Abel and his father; appointed
  (by Fox) to post in the East India Company's service; in India for a time.

1. God be merciful *Mann*
2. I called upon the Lord *Mann*

MACMURDIE, JOSEPH, Mus. Bac., Oxon. B. 1792; D. 1878.
  English Composer and Writer; Director of the Philharmonic Society; some
  time Org. Brixton Parish Church.

1. O give thanks *Norwich*

MALAN (DE MÉRINDOL), Rev. CÉSAR HENRI ABRAHAM, D.D. B. 1787;
  D. 1864.
  French Divine, Poet, and Musician; Pastor of Geneva.

  Lord my God *Novello*
  2. Unto Him that loved us.

MARSH, JOHN. B. 1752 ; D. 1828.

Clever amateur; articled to a Solicitor at Romsey; resided in Salisbury (1776), Canterbury (1785), and Chichester (1787), in which places he directed Subscription Concerts, and occasionally officiated for the Cath. Organists.

1. By the waters.
   (*Published* 1789.)
2. I will arise   *St. Paul's*
   (*Published* 1789.)
3. O give thanks (*Psalm* 106)   1789
4. O give thanks (*Psalm* 107)   ,,
5. O Lord, Who hast taught us   ,,

6. O praise God in His
   Holiness.   *Publ. 1789.*
   (*Composed for the opening of Green's organ in Canterbury Cathedral,* 1784.)
7. O praise the Lord   *Marshall*
8. Remove far from me vanity   ,,

MARSHALL, WORTH.

Lay-Clerk of Ely, 1759.

1. O my son, despise not thou
   Bumpus

MASON, REV. WILLIAM, M.A. B. 1725 ; D. 1794.

Rector of Aston, Yorks; Prebendary and Precentor, 1763, of York Minster; Essayist, Poet, and Writer.

1. All flesh is grass   *Bumpus*
2. Almighty God   *Marshall*
3. Give ear, O Thou Shepherd *Calvert*
4. Gracious and righteous   *Novello*
5. Hear my crying, O God *Marshall*
6. Help me, O God   *Calvert*
7. If ye love Me   ,,
8. I will go forth   ,,

9. Lord of all power and
   might   *Novello*
10. O God of my fathers   *Lincoln*
11. O Lord God of Hosts   *Marshall*
12. O Lord, how manifold   *Bumpus*
13. O Lord, we beseech Thee *Marshall*
14. O love the Lord   *Novello*

MATTHEWS, SAMUEL, Mus. Bac., Cantab. B. 1769 ; D. 1831.

Org. Trinity and St. John's Colleges, Cambridge.

1. Behold, how good   *Marshall*
2. Behold, I bring you   *King's*
3. Behold now, praise   ,,
4. Bow down Thine ear   ,,
5. Is there not an appointed
   time ?   *Calvert*

6. I was glad   *Marshall*
7. Lift up your heads   *King's*
8. O God the Protector   *Marshall*
9. Teach me, O Lord   *King's*
10. The Lord liveth   *Marshall*
11. The ways of Zion   ,,

And adaptations from the sacred works of Haydn, Mozart, Pergolesi, &c.

MORNINGTON, GARRETT COLLEY WELLESLEY, First Earl of, Mus. Doc., Dublin. B. 1735 ; D. 1781.

Professor of Music in University of Dublin, 1764-74 ; Father of the famous Duke of Wellington. Gained several prizes from the Catch Club.

1. O Lord, hear the prayer of Thy
   servants *Clark's " Seraphim,"*1833.

2. Rejoice in the Lord alway   *Joule*

MOSELEY, MISS LUCY.

1. Blessed are all they   *Exeter,* 1793

MOUNT-EDGCUMBE, RICHARD EDGCUMBE, Second Earl of. B. 1764; D. 1839.

Composer and Writer upon Italian Opera in England.

1. I will take heed unto my ways
    Lincoln, 1851 |

MUTLOW, WILLIAM. B. 1761; D. 1832.

Org. of Gloucester Cath., 1782-1832. Conducted Festival of the Three Choirs, 1790.

1. Unto Thee, O Lord *Novello* |

NARES, JAMES, Mus. Doc., Cantab. B. 1715; D. 1783.

Pupil of Gates and Pepusch; Org. York Minster, 1734, and Chapel Royal, 1756; Master of the Children, 1757-80.

1.*Arise, Thou Judge.
2.*Awake up, my glory.
3. Be glad, O ye righteous *Joule*
4.*Behold, how good and joyful.
5. Behold now, praise the Lord
 (*Longhurst's Short Anthems*) *Novello*
6.*Behold, O God, our Defender.
7. Blessed be the Lord God *Novello*
8. Blessed is he that considereth   ,,
9.†Blest, who with gen'rous
  pity flows.
10.*By the waters of Babylon.
11.*Call to remembrance.
12. Come hither *S. Paul's*
13. Do well, O Lord *Chap. Roy.*
14.*God is our hope and strength.
15. Haste Thee, O God *Calvert*
16. Have mercy upon me
  Sacred Minstrelsy,‡1834
17.*Hide not Thou Thy face.
18. I am well pleased *Calvert*
19.†If the Lord Himself.
20. I have set God alway *Joule*
21. I know that the Lord *Chap. Roy.*
22. In my prosperity, I said ,,
23.*It is a good thing to give thanks.
24. I will magnify Thee *Chap. Roy.*
25. Like as the hart *Joule*
26.*Lord, how long wilt Thou?
    (T.B.)
27. Lord, let me know my end *Joule*

28. Lord, remember David *Calvert*
29.*Not unto us, O Lord.
30. O clap your hands *Chap. Roy.*
31. O come hither
  Sacred Minstrelsy, 1834
32.*O come, let us sing.
33.*O give thanks unto the God
  of Heaven.
34. O Lord, grant the king *Arnold*
35.*O Lord my God.
36. O praise the Lord, all ye
  heaven   *Joule*
37. O praise the Lord, laud ye *Calvert*
38.†O what great troubles.
39. Praise the Lord, ye
  servants (*Psalm* 113) *Dublin*
40.*Rejoice in the Lord.
41. Save me, O God *Chap. Roy.*
42.†The eyes of the Lord.
43. The Lord hear thee *Chap. Roy.*
44.*The Lord is my strength.
45.*The Lord is righteous.
46.*The souls of the righteous.
47.†Thy praise, O God, shall wake
  my lyre.
48.-Try me, O God *Arnold*
49.*Turn Thee again
50.†Turn us, O God.
51.*Unto Thee, O God.
52. When the Lord turned again *Joule*
53. Wherewithal shall a young man
  Sacred Minstrelsy, 1834

---

* Anthems marked * published by the Composer, 1778. Modern edition by V. Novello.
† Anthems marked † published under the editorship of Dr. Ayrton, 1788. New edition by Dr. J. L. Hopkins.

NIGHTINGALE, JOHN CHARLES. B. 1785 ; D. 1837.
Org. Foundling Hospital.

1. Arise, shine !	*Bumpus* |

NORRIS, THOMAS, MUS. BAC., OXON. B. 1741 ; D. 1790.
Org. Christ Church Cath., 1776-90, and St. John's College, Oxon., 1765.
Tenor singer of repute.

1. Hear my prayer, O God
   (*Psalm* 55)	*Novello*
2. Hear my prayer, O Lord
   (*Psalm* 102)	,,
3. I will alway give thanks
   Chap. Roy., 1769

4. Rejoice in the Lord *Chap. Roy.*,1769
5. Sing we merrily	*St. Paul's*
6. The earth is the Lord's *Chap. Roy.*
7. The Lord is King	*Gloucester*
8. Thou, O God, art praised
   Chap. Roy.

NOVELLO, VINCENT. B. 1781 ; D. 1861.
Pupil of S. Webbe; Org. Portuguese Chapel, 1797-1822, and Duke Street,
Moorfields, 1840-43 ; founded firm of Novello, 1811 ; Editor of most of the
great Collections of Anthems ; retired to Nice, 1848.

1. Blessed is the people	*Novello*
2. Call to remembrance	,,
3. Drive far from us	,,
4. Glory be to God	,,
5. God be merciful	,,
6. God save the Queen	,,
   (*Arrangement*)
7. Hallelujah, Hallelujah !	,,
   (*Part of No.* 13.)
8. Hear me, O Lord	,,
9. Hear what God the Lord	,,
10. In manus tuas (Like as the
    hart)	,,
11. I will sing of mercy	,,
    (*Part of No.* 8.)

12. O how amiable	*Novello*
13. O praise the Lord	,,
14. Out of the deep	*Dublin*
15. Praise the Lord, O my soul *Joule*
16. Praise the Lord, ye servants *Novello*
17. Pray for the peace	,,
18. Rejoice in the Lord	,,
19. Sing unto the Lord a new
    song	,,
20. The Lord is great in Zion	,,
21. The Lord is my strength	,,
22. The Lord loveth	,,
23. Therefore with angels	,,
24. There is a river	,,

OLIVE, JOSEPH. B. *c.* 1710 ; D. 1786.

1. Blessed is he that considereth
   Cath. Mag. |

PEARSALL, ROBERT LUCAS DE. B. 1795 ; D. 1856.
Called to the Bar, 1821 ; pupil of Panny (Mayence) ; lived at Wartensee
Castle, Lake Constance (from 1832).

1.*Blessed is everyone that feareth.
2.*I heard a voice.
3. In dulci jubilo	*Novello*
4.*I will cry unto God.
5.*I will rejoice.

6.*Let God arise.
7.*My heart is fixed.
8.*O clap your hands.
9.*O come, let us sing.
10.*O give thanks.

PERKINS, WILLIAM. D. 1860.
Org. Wells Cath., 1819-60. Son of Dodd Perkins (1750-1820).

1. I cried unto the Lord	*Wells* |	2. O Lord, our Governour	*Wells*

* Published under the editorship of W. F. Trimnell.

PERRY, GEORGE, B. 1793 ; D. 1862.
Pupil of Beckwith in Norwich ; Conductor Haymarket Theatre ; Org. Quebec
Chapel and Trinity Church, Gray's Inn Road; composed Operas and
Oratorios.

1. Blessed be the Lord thy God
   Musical Standard, No. 8.
   (*Accession of Queen Victoria.*)
2. I will arise   *Husk*
   (*London Choir Association.*)

3. The Queen shall rejoice   *Husk*
   (*Birth of the Princess Royal.*)

PICKERING, JOHN. B. 1792 ; D. 1843.
Composer and Teacher in Preston and Manchester.

1. Every day will I give thanks
   Durham, 1848

PITT, THOMAS. D. 1806 (?)
Org. Worcester Cath., 1793-1806, after Isaac.

1. Arise, O Lord God   *Marshall*
2. Blessed are they that
   dwell   *Chap. Roy.*, 1826
3. O come, let us sing   ,,

4. O Lord, I need not   *Calvert*
5. O Lord, we beseech
   Thee   *Marshall*

PORTER, SAMUEL, Senr. B. 1733 ; D. 1810.
Chorister of St. Paul's under C. King and Pupil of Dr. Greene; Org.
Canterbury Cath., after W. Raylton (1757-1803).

1. Behold ! how good   *King's*
2. I will magnify Thee   ,,
3.*Not unto us.
4.*O be joyful.
5. O God, my heart is fixed.
   Published 1825.

6. O Lord God of Hosts   *King's*
7.*O Lord our Governour.
8.*Save me, O God.
9.*Thee will I bless.
10. Thou shalt open my lips   *King's*

PORTER, SAMUEL, Junr. B. *c.* 1750 ; D. 1823.
Member of the King's Band and Organist at Faversham for 37 years.

1. Behold, God is my salvation.
2. Blessed be the Lord my strength.

3. O God, the King of glory.
4. O where shall wisdom ?

All published by Goulding, Phipps and D'Almaine.

PORTER, Rev. WILLIAM JAMES, M.A. B. 17— ; D. 1865.
Son of Samuel Porter, Senr.; Head-Master of Worcester College School, and
Chaplain to Viscount Fitzwilliam ; Vicar of Himbleton, 1815-65.

1. Like as the hart. | 2. Ponder my words.

Both published by Preston.

PRATT, JOHN. B. 1772 ; D. 1855.
Pupil of Dr. Randall; Org. King's and St. Peter's Colleges, Cambridge,
and to the University.

1. Almighty and everlasting *King's*
2. O Lord, grant the King   ,,

3. O Lord, we beseech Thee   *King's*
4. Why art thou so vexed ?   ,,

Also adaptations from works of German and Italian masters.

---

* These were printed in a volume of his Cathedral Music, edited by his son, Rev.
W. J. Porter; folio, no date.

PRING, JACOB CUBITT, Mus. Bac., Oxon. B. 1771 ; D. 1799.
Pupil of Hudson, and Chorister in St. Paul's ; Org. St. Botolph, Aldersgate.

1.*Blessed is the man.
2.*Bow down Thine ear.
3.*Hold not Thy tongue.
4.*Lord, Thou art become gracious.
5.*O give thanks.
6.*Out of the deep.

7.*Save me, O God.
8. Unto Thee, O Lord.
      Turle and Taylor
     (*Canon, 3 in 1.*)
9.*Why do the heathen.

PRING, JOSEPH, Mus.D., Oxon. B. 1776 ; D. 1842.
Brother of the above ; Chorister of St. Paul's ; Org. Bangor Cath., 1793, and pupil of Hudson.

1.†Behold, God is my salvation.
2.†Behold, how good and joyful.
3.†Cenwch i'r Arglwydd Ganiad newydd.
4.†Come, Holy Ghost.
5.†Daughters of Jerusalem.
6.†Deliver us from our enemies.
7.†If the Lord Himself.
    (*Thanksgiving, Oct. 29, 1798.*)
8.†I waited patiently.
9.†I will sing unto the Lord.

10.†O Lord, our Governour.
11.†O Lord, we beseech Thee,
12.†O praise God in His Holiness.
13.†Plead Thou my cause.
14.†Ponder my words.
15.†Sing unto God, O ye kingdoms.
16.†Sing we merrily.
17.†The Lord said unto my Lord.
18.†Thy way, O God.
19.†Why boasteth thou thyself.
20.†With angels and archangels.

PYMAR, THOMAS. B. 1775 ; D. 1854.
Org. Beccles Parish Church for over 49 years.

1. O God our refuge   *Bumpus* |

RADCLIFFE, JAMES. B. 1751 ; D. 1818.
Lay Clerk of Worcester and afterwards of Durham Cathedrals.

1. Blessed is he.
2. How long wilt Thou forget me.
3. O be joyful in God.
4. O give thanks.
5. O how amiable.

6. O Lord, the very heavens.
7. Sing unto the Lord.
8. They that put their trust.
9. Thy Word is a lantern.
10. We wait for Thy loving-kindness.

All published by Riley, No. 8, Strand, in 1801.

RANDALL, JOHN, Mus. Doc., Cantab. B. 1715 ; D. 1799.
Pupil of Gates ; Org. King's Coll., Cambridge ; King's, 1743 ; Trinity, 1777 ; St. Mary's (University) Church and Pembroke Hall ; and Professor of Music in the University (after Greene), 1755.

1. O be joyful in God (*Psalm* 66.)
    Parts in St. John's College |

2. O Lord, grant the King   *King's*
3. Who hath believed?   ,,

RAYLTON (RAILTON), WILLIAM. D. 1757.
Pupil of Dr. Croft ; Org. Canterbury Cath., 1736-57.

1. Behold, I bring you   *Husk* |
2. Behold, O God   *Cath. Mag.* |

3. I am the Resurrection   *Joule*
4. O give thanks   ,,

---

* Published by Longman and Broderip.
† Published by Preston in 1805.

REYNOLDS, JOHN. D. 1778 (? 1770).
Gentleman of Chapel Royal, 1765-70.

1. My God, my God, look
   upon me !   *Page*

ROGERS (RODGERS), JAMES. D. (?) 1784.
Org. Ely Cath., 1774-7, and Peterborough, 1777-84.

1. Behold, I bring you.   3. The Lord is only my support.
2. Be light and glad.

All published by Longman and Broderip. Edited by his pupil, Henry Burdett.

ROGERS, Sir JOHN LEMAN, Bart. B. 1780 ; D. 1847.
Amateur Composer ; eldest son of Sir Frederick Leman Rogers, Bart., M.P.,
   Recorder of Plymouth ; President of the Madrigal Society, 1820-41.

1. Be Thou my Judge   *Joule*   3. I will give thanks   *Joule*
2. Hear the right, O Lord   *Bumpus*
(*Composed in memory of Philip Salter.*)

RUSSELL, WILLIAM, MUS. BAC., OXON. B. 1777 ; D. 1813.
Pupil of Shrubsole, Arnold, &c. ; Org. St. Ann's, Limehouse, 1798 ; Foundling
   Hospital, 1801 ; Pianist at Covent Garden Theatre.

1. Behold, the eye of the   3. Grant to us, Lord   *Fowle*
   Lord   *Winchester*   4. Hear, O Thou Shepherd   *King's*
2. Blessed Lord, Who hast   5. O Lord God of Hosts   *Lichfield*
   caused   *Novello*   6. Ponder my words   *King's*

SAFFERY, OSMOND.

1. The Lord's Prayer.
A curious metrical version, ending "Honour, glory, praise and power, Are His
exclusively."

SALTER, PHILIP. B. latter part of 18th century ; D. 1884.
Vicar-Choral of Exeter Cath.

1. Almighty and everlasting   2. Lord,how long wilt Thou ? *Joule*
   God   *Winchester*

SCOTT, JOHN. B. 1776 ; D. 1815.
Chorister in St. George's Chapel and Eton College ; Pupil of Aylward and
   Webbe ; Deputy to Dr. Arnold at Westminster Abbey, and subsequently
   Org. of Spanish Town, Jamaica.

1. Praise the Lord, O Jerusalem
                Novello

SEXTON, WILLIAM. B. 1764 ; D. c. 1824.
Pupil of Edw. Webb ; Org., Sub-Precentor, &c., at St. George's, Windsor.
Printed a mutilated edition of Handel's Chandos Anthems.

SHEELES, JOHN. B. 17— ; D. 18—.

Harpsichord Teacher in London, c. 1810.

1. How dear are Thy counsels   2. O Lord, Thou hast searched
                  Calvert   *Old Chap. Roy.*

SHENTON, Rev. ROBERT, M.A. B. c. 1730 ; D. 1798.

Vicar-Choral, Hereford Cath., and Dean's Vicar at Christ Church and St. Patrick's Caths., Dublin.

1. Behold, how good and joyful
                  Dublin, 1881
2. Blessed be the name   *Dublin*
3. By the waters of Babylon   ,,
4. I will magnify Thee   ,,
5. Lord, how are they increased *Joule*
6. Lord, Thou hast been our
     refuge   ,,
7. O be joyful in God.
8. O give thanks.
     (*Psalm* 105.)
9. O give thanks.
     (*Psalm* 136.)

10. O God, my heart   *Dublin*, 1881
11. O Lord, Thou hast searched
                        Dublin
12. Praise the Lord, O my soul *Joule*
     (*Psalm* 103.)
13. Praise the Lord, O my soul *Dublin*
     (*Differing from No.* 12.)
14. Praise the Lord, ye servants   ,,
15. Sing we merrily   ,,
16. The beauty of Israel   ,,
17. Try me, O God   ,,

SHIELD, WILLIAM. B. 1748 ; D. 1829.

Apprenticed to a North Shields boat-builder ; Pupil of Avison ; Master of the Royal Music, following Sir W. Parsons, 1817 ; Writer of Ballad Operas ; Principal Tenor player, Covent Garden Opera.

1. Behold, how good and joyful *Pettet*
2. How beautiful upon the
     mountains   *Joule*

3. When I was a child   *Pettet*

SIMPSON, PURVER.

1. In the midst of life *Durham*, 1848 |

SKEATS, HIGHMORE, Senr. B. 1760 ; D. 1831.

Org. Ely Cath., 1778, after R. Langdon, and of Canterbury Cath., after S. Porter, 1803.

1. Come unto Me   *Ely MSS.*
2. Haste Thee, O God   ,,
3. I will alway   ,,
4. Lord, how long   ,,
5. O God, our refuge   *Bumpus*

6. O Lord, let it be Thy
     pleasure   *Ely MSS.*
7. Praise ye the Lord   ,,
8. Teach us, O Lord   *Ely MSS.*

The following six Psalms (with interludes), in imitation of those composed by William and Philip Hayes, are printed in the Rev. J. Powell Metcalfe's " Metrical Anthems " (Novello) :—

9. How just and merciful is God.
10. My soul inspired.
11. O praise ye the Lord.
12. O render thanks.
13. Praise the Lord enthron'd on high.

14. Ye saints and servants of the Lord.
_____
15.*Thou, Lord, by strictest search
     hast known
     Bunnett's Sacred Music, 1865

SKEATS, HIGHMORE, Junr. B. 1786; D. 1835.

Org. Ely Cath., 1804, St. George's Chapel, Windsor, 1830.

1. The righteous souls that take
   their flight (Chorale)   *Novello*

Also attributed to his father.

SLATTER, Rev. GEORGE MAXIMILIAN, D.D. B. 1790; D. 1868.

Rector of West Anstey, Devon, and Priest-Vicar of Exeter Cathedral.

1.†Almighty and everlasting God, Who art.
2.†Almighty and everlasting God, Who hatest.
3.†Almighty and everlasting God, Who of.
4.†Almighty Father.
5.†Almighty God, give us peace.
6.†Grant to us, Lord.
7.†Grant, we beseech Thee.
8.*I will magnify Thee.
9.†Let Thy merciful ears.
10.†O Almighty God, Who out of.
11.†O God the King of Glory.
12. O Lord, my God, in Thee
   Marshall
13.*Rejoice in the Lord.
14.*Remember, O Lord.

SLY, R.

Organist in Lynn.

1. I will give thanks.

SMART, Sir GEORGE THOMAS, Knight. B. 1776; D. 1867.

Received Knighthood from Lord Lieutenant of Ireland, 1811; Pupil of Dupuis and Arnold; Org. St. James's Chapel, Hampstead Road; Conductor Philharmonic Society; Org. Chapel Royal, 1822; conducted at many festivals and the Coronation of King George IV. and Queen Victoria.

1.‡Blessed is He that considereth.
2.‡Except the Lord build the house.
3.‡God be merciful.
4.‡I will lift up mine eyes.
5.‡O God, Who art the Author.
6. Plead Thou my cause *Chap. Roy.*

SMITH, JOHN, Mus. Doc., Dublin. B. 1795; D. 1861.

Vicar-Choral, St. Patrick's, 1816; Org. Chapel Royal, Dublin, 1833-35; Professor of Music, Dublin University, 1847.

1.§Blessed be Thou.
2.§Blessed is he that.
3. Come, Holy Ghost   *Novello*
   (*Veni, Creator Spiritus.*)
4.§Come near, ye nations.
5.§Give the king Thy judgments.
6.§Grant, we beseech Thee.
7.§O clap your hands.
8.§O Lord, grant the king.
9.§O sing unto the Lord a new song.
10.§The Lord shall comfort Zion.
11.§The souls of the righteous.

---

* Published in his own Collection of Church Music, *c.* 1851 (Addison).
† Printed in his "Ten Collects as Anthems, &c.," 1827 (Payne and Hopkins).
‡ Published by the composer in a Collection of his Cathedral Music, 1860 (Addison).
§ All in MS. at Dublin.

SMITH, JOHN STAFFORD. B. 1750; D. 1836.

Pupil of his father, Martin Smith, and of Boyce. Gent. Chapel Royal, 1784;
  Lay-Vicar, Westminster Abbey, 1786; Org. Chapel Royal, 1802; gained
  several prizes for Glees. Master of Chapel Royal Boys, 1805-16.

1. Almighty and everlasting God
      Novello's Short Anthems
2. Behold, now praise   *Gloucester*
3.*Come unto Me.
4.*Come ye, and let us go up.
5. Give the King Thy judgments
      Calvert
6.*Have mercy upon me.
7.*Hear my crying.
8.*Horrible is the end of the
      unrighteous.
9.*How amiable.
10.*I will go forth in the strength.
11.*Jesus, seeing the multitudes
      Calvert
12.*My soul shall make her boast.
13. O come, loud anthems *Chap. Roy.*

14.*O Lord, grant the King.
15.*O Lord, my God.
16. O praise the Lord, for it is   *Joule*
17.*O where shall wisdom.
18.*Praise the Lord.
19.*Rejoice not against me.
20. Remember not, Lord   *Husk*
21.*The Lord hath prepared His
      throne.
22.*The souls of the righteous.
23. The spacious firmament on
      high   *Bumpus*
24.*Thus saith the High and Lofty
      One.
25.*Trust ye in the Lord.
26.*Try me, O God.
27.*What shall I render?

SMITH, MARTIN. D. 1782.

Father of the above. Org. Gloucester Cath., 1740 to 1782.

1. I will magnify Thee   *Marshall* | 2. Praise the Lord, call   *Marshall*

SMITH, ROBERT ARCHIBALD. B. 1780; D. 1829.

Apprenticed as a Weaver; Precentor in the Abbey Church, Paisley, and
  Musical Director of St. George's, Edinburgh.

1. As the cloud is consumed
      Gall and Inglis
2. Blessed is he that
      considereth   ,,
3. Give ear unto My voice ,,
4. God be merciful   ,,
5. Great and marvellous   ,,

6. How beautiful upon the
      mountains   *Wells*
7. Make a joyful noise
      Gall and Inglis
8. Sing unto God   ,,
9. The earth is the Lord's ,,

STANLEY, JOHN, Mus. Bac., Oxon. B. 1713; D. 1786.

Blind from infancy; Pupil of J. Reading and Greene; Org. All Hallows',
  Bread Street, 1724, and St. Andrew's, Holborn, 1726; Master of the King's
  Band, 1779; one of two organists, Temple Church, 1734-1786.

1. Arise, pour out thine heart like
      water.
2. Hearken unto Me, My people.
3. Jehovah, Lord, how great!

4. My strength will I ascribe
      Dublin, 1881
5. O Lord, my God   *Bumpus*
6. Praise the Lord, O Jerusalem
      Dublin, 1881

---

* Published by the Composer in 1793.

STEPHENS, JOHN, Mus. Doc., Cantab. B. *c.* 1718 ; D. 1780.
Chorister in Gloucester Cath. ; Org. Salisbury Cath., 1746-80.

1. Almighty God, give us grace	*Marshall*	8.*O praise our God.	
		9. Praise ye the Lord	*Marshall*
2.*Blessed is he that considereth.		10.*Teach me, O Lord.	
3.*Blessed is the man.		11. The Lord, even	*Chap. Roy.*
4. Bow down Thine ear	*Marshall*	12.*The Lord is in His holy temple.	
5. Let everything	*Lichfield*	13.*The rich and poor meet together.	
6. Like as the hart	*Chap. Roy.*	14.*Thy mercy, O Lord.	
7.*My heart is fixed.		15. Unto Thee, O Lord	*Joule*

STEVENSON, Sir JOHN ANDREW, Knight, Mus. Doc., Dublin.
B. 1762 ; D. 1833.
Pupil of Dr. Woodward ; Vicar-Choral of Christ Church, Dublin, 1800 ;
and St. Patrick's Cath., 1783.

1. Arise, O Lord God	*Dublin*	13.†I will magnify Thee.	
2. Behold, how good and joyful	,,	14.†Lord, how are they increased.	
		15.†O God, my heart is ready.	
3. Behold, I bring you	,,	16.†O Lord our Governour.	
4.†Blessed be the Lord my strength.		17. O praise God in His Holiness	*Dublin*
5.†Blessed is he that considereth.		18.†Rejoice in the Lord, O ye.	
6.†Bow down Thine ear.		19. Teach me, O Lord	*Dublin*
7. By the waters of Babylon	*Dublin*	20.†The earth is the Lord's.	
8. Grant to us, Lord	,,	21. The Lord is King	*Dublin*
9. I am the Resurrection	,,	22. The Lord is my Shepherd	,,
10.†I am well pleased.		23.†There were shepherds.	
11.†I looked, and behold a door.		24. When the day of Pentecost	*Dublin*
12.†I looked, and lo a Lamb.			

STOKES, CHARLES. B. 1784 ; D. 1839.
Chorister of St. Paul's Cath. ; Org. at Croydon, &c.

1. I will lay me down *Novello* |

STROUD, CHARLES. B. 1706 ; D. 1726.
Pupil of Croft ; Chorister, and afterwards Deputy-Org. Chapel Royal, Whitehall.

1. Hear my Prayer *Page* |

SUDLOW, WILLIAM. B. 1772 ; D. 1848.
Org. Manchester Cath., 1804-48.

1. O, my God, my sins *Manchester* |

TARGETT, JAMES. B. 1778 ; D. 1803.
Chorister, and afterwards Org. Chichester Cath., 1801-3.

1. Christ being raised.	3. O Saviour of the world.
2. Come, Holy Ghost.	4. Out of the deep *Clementi*

Nos. 1 to 3 edited by John Marsh, of Chichester.

---

* Edited by Highmore Skeats, Senr., in 1805.
* Published in 1825 in Dublin.

TAYLOR, RICHARD. B. 1758 ; D. 1813.

Composer and writer upon poetry and musical subjects at Chelmsford.

1. Hear my crying   *Cath. Mag.*
2. Hear, O Lord, and consider ,,
3. I will give thanks   *Cath. Mag.*

TOPLIFF, ROBERT. B. 1793 ; D. 1868.

Blind. Org. Holy Trinity Church, Southwark. Edited "Popular Melodies of the Wear and Tyne," and "Sabbath melodies."

1. Enter not into judgment.
2. O Lord, correct me.
3. The Lord is in His holy temple.
4. There were shepherds.

All published in Topliff's "Praise Offering," in 1857.

TRAVERS, JOHN. B. *c.* 1706 ; D. 1758.

Pupil of Greene and Pepusch. Org. St. Paul's, Covent Garden, 1725, Fulham Parish Church, and Chapel Royal, 1737.

1. Ascribe unto the Lord   *Arnold*
2. *Blessed is he that considereth *Hereford*
3. Grant, we beseech Thee   *Chap. Roy.*, 1749
4. *Hear my crying, O God *Hereford*
5. Hear my prayer, O Lord *Chap. Roy.*
6. If the Lord Himself   ,,
7. It is a good thing   ,,
8. I will magnify Thee   ,,
9. Keep, we beseech Thee   *Page*
10. Lord, be merciful to us sinners   *Hereford*
11. *O be joyful   ,,
12. *O come, let us sing   ,,
13. *O give thanks   ,,
14. *O God, forasmuch as   *Hereford*
15. O Lord, how manifold *Chap. Roy.*
16. *O Lord, rebuke me not *Hereford*
17. O praise the Lord of Heaven   *Chap. Roy.*
18. *O sing unto the Lord *Hereford* (*Psalm* 96.)
19. O sing unto the Lord *Chap. Roy.* (*Psalm* 149.)
20. Ponder my words, O Lord *Arnold*
21. *Rejoice in the Lord   *Hereford*
22. *Righteous art Thou   ,,
23. The earth is the Lord's   *Dublin*
24. This is the day   *Chap. Roy.*
25. Unto Thee, O Lord, do I lift ,,

WAINWRIGHT, JOHN. B. 1723 ; D. 1768.

Wrote the tune "Yorkshire." Org. Manchester Collegiate Church, 1767-8.

1. The Lord is ris'n. *C. & S. Thompson* |

WALMISLEY, THOMAS FORBES. B. 1783 ; D. 1866.

Son of Wm. Walmisley, Clerk of the Papers to the House of Lords. Pupil of Attwood. Org. St. Martin's-in-the Fields, 1814 (after Robert Cooke).

1. Hear me, O Lord   *Novello*
2. Hosanna to the Son of David   *Hullah's Part-Music*
3. I will praise the Name of God (*Canon 4 in 2*), *Hullah's Vocal Scores*
4. Lord of all Lords   *Hullah's Vocal Scores*
5. My soul, wait thou still   *Novello*
6. O come, let us sing   ,,
7. O God, the Protector   *Pettet*
8. O Lord, how manifold   *Novello*
9. The earth is the Lord's   ,,
10. When I was in trouble   ,,

---

* In the autograph of the Composer at Hereford Cath.

WEBBE, SAMUEL, Senr. B. 1740 (in Minorca) ; D. 1816.
Pupil of Ch. Barbandt; Chapel-Master, Portuguese Chapel, London ;
Secretary to Noblemen and Gentlemen's Catch Club, 1794.

1. All Thy works praise Thee *Joule*
2.†Almighty God, we beseech *Novello*
3. Awake, awake, put on *Husk*
4.†Christ being raised *Novello*
5.*How excellent is Thy mercy ,,
6.†How lovely are Thy dwellings ,,
7.†Let the heavens rejoice ,,
8.†O Lord, my King ,,
9. O praise the Lord with me *Joule*
10. O that men would therefore *Beverley*
11. Our Father (*Lord's Prayer*) *King's*
12. Praise the Lord, all ye angels.
13. Praise the Lord, O my soul, and all.
14.†Salvation belongeth *Novello*
15.*Save us, O God ,,
16.†Shew me Thy ways ,,
17.†Sing unto the Lord ,,
18. Sit Trinitati sempiterna gloria.
19.*Teach me, O Lord, and lead me (*Psalm* 27) *Novello*
20. Teach me, O Lord, the way (*Psalm* 119) *Joule*
21.†The day is Thine *Novello*
22.†The eyes of all wait ,,
23.*The heavens declare ,,
24.*The Lord is the portion of the just ,,
25.†The soul that sinneth ,,
26. Thou hast been my refuge *Beverley*
27. Thou, God, art *Rochester*
28.*Thou, Lord, in the beginning *Novello*
29.*Unto Thee, O Lord ,,
30.*When the fulness of time ,,
31.†When the Lord shall build up ,,

WELSH, THOMAS. B. 1770 ; D. 1848.
Pupil of Cramer and Baumgarten; Bass Singer; Gent. of the Chapel Royal.
1. Awake up, my glory.
(*Sung at Chap. Roy. on the 1st Sunday in Lent,* 1834.)
2. I will praise the Name of God.
(*Sung at Chap. Roy. on the 2nd Sunday in Lent,* 1834.)
3. Out of the deep *Joule*

WESLEY, CHARLES. B. 1757 ; D. 1834.
Son of Rev. Charles Wesley and Nephew of John Wesley ; Org. St.
George's, Hanover Square, and to King George IV.
1. Grant, we beseech Thee *Nat. Psal.*
2. Lord, remember David ,,
3. My soul hath patiently tarried *Page*
4. O worship the Lord *Weekes*
5. Thou art my King *Husk*

WESLEY, SAMUEL. B. 1766 ; D. 1837.
Younger brother of the above; Org. Camden Town. Introduced Bach's
Music to England.
1. All go to one place *Novello* (*On the death of Charles Wesley*)
2. All is vanity *Novello*
3. I said "I will take heed" *Page*
4. I will wash my hands *Joule* (*Doubtful.*)
5. Lift up your heads *Novello*
6. Might I in Thy sight *Europ. Psalm.*
7. O deliver me ,,
8. O remember not ,,
9. Sing aloud with gladness *Novello*
10. Sing we merrily ,, (*Another version of No.* 9.)
11. Thou art a priest for ever ,,
12. Thou, O God, art praised *Pettet*
13. When Israel came out *Novello*
14. Who is the trembling sinner *Europ. Psalm.*
Several of the above are Latin motets, with English words.

* Published in the Composer's "Eight Anthems" (Novello).
† Published in the Composer's "Twelve Anthems" (Novello).

WEST, Rev. LEWIS RENATUS. B. 1753 ; D. 1826.
Connected with the Moravian Brethren in Dublin, in 1784, and, subsequently, in England.

1. Have mercy, Lord   *Husk* | 2. Save me, O God   *Husk*

WESTMORELAND, JOHN FANE, D.C.L., 11th Earl of. B. 1784 ; D. 1859.
Composed when Lord Burghersh ; succeeded his father in the title, 1841). Entered Army, 1803 ; studied under foreign teachers. Founded R.A.M.

1. On the third day
   in the morning *Lonsdale*, 1841. |

WHITFELD, *see* CLARKE-WHITFELD.

WIGHT, Rev. OSBORNE.
Chaplain of New College, Oxford, *c.* 1790.

1. My God, my God   *Bumpus* |

WILLIAMS, AARON. B. 1731 ; D. 1776.
Clerk to the Scotch Church in London Wall. Publisher of Psalmody.

1. Arise, shine, O Zion.
2. Awake to celebrate.
3. Awake up, my glory.
4. Behold, the Lord is my salvation.
5. Blessed are the merciful.
6. Comfort ye, My people.
7. Hail, blest returning day.
8. House of our God.
9. How beautiful.
10. I heard a voice.
11. In guilty night.
    (*Paraphrase of 1st Book of Samuel,*
    cap. 28.)
12. I will arise.
13. Keep thy foot when thou goest.
14. Lord, make me to know.
15. O be joyful in the Lord.
16. O clap your hands.
17. O praise the Lord with me.
18. Sing unto God.
19. The Lord reigns.

All published in "Harmonia Cœlestis" by Thomas Williams, 1780, except Nos. 3, 4, and 10, published by Longman, Lukey and Broderip, and No. 8, composed for and performed by a society of gentlemen in London, and published at their request.

WILTON, THOMAS EGERTON, 2nd Earl of. B. 1790 (? 1799) ; D. 1882.
Amateur composer of vocal music.

1. O praise the Lord, all ye
   heathen   *Novello* | 2. When gathering clouds
                                   Chap. Roy.

WOAKES, W. H. B. *c.* 1780 ; D. —.
Org. St. Peter's Church, Hereford. Wrote "A Catechism of Music," 1817, published in Hereford.

WOOD, DAVID. B. early in 18th century ; D. —.
Org. Ely Cath., 1768-74 ; later on, Gent. Chap. Royal and Vicar-Choral of St. Paul's Cathedral.

1. Lord of all power and might *Page* |

WOODWARD, RICHARD, Mus. Doc., Dublin. B. *c.* 1744 ; D. 1777.
Vicar-Choral, St. Patrick's, 1772; Org., &c., Christ Church Cath., Dublin, 1765 (after Walsh).

1. Behold, now, praise   *Woodward*
2. Come, Holy Ghost   ,,
   (*Veni, Creator Spiritus.*)
3. Hear, O Thou Shepherd   ,,
4. My heart sheweth me   ,,

5. O be joyful in God   *Woodward*
6. O praise God in His
   Holiness   ,,
7. Sing, O ye heavens   ,,
8. They that go down   ,,

All published in R. Woodward's Cathedral Music, 1771.

WORGAN, JOHN, Mus. Doc., Cantab. B. 1724 ; D. 1790.
Pupil of Roseingrave and Geminiani ; Org. to Vauxhall Gardens and several London Churches.

1. It is good to give thanks
   (*2 parts.*)   *Foundling Hosp. Bk.*

2. The Lord is my Shepherd *King's*
3. We will rejoice   *Bumpus*

WRENSHALL, WILLIAM, Senr. B. 1783 ; D. 1854.
Org. of the Mayor's Chapel, Liverpool.

1. As down in the sunless
   retreat   *Nat. Psal.*

2. O Lord, Who hast taught
   us   *Joule*

WYVILL, ZERUBBABEL. B. 1762 ; D. 1837.
Of Maidenhead, Berks. Composer of the tune "Eaton."

1. O give thanks (1802)
   (*Dedicated to Miss Vansittart, of
   Bisham Abbey.*)

FOREIGN COMPOSERS.

MOZART, JOHANN CHRYSOSTOM WOLFGANG AMADEUS. B. 1756; D. 1791.
Brought by his father, as an infant prodigy, to London and the English Court, 1764-5.

1. God is our refuge   *Brit. Mus. MSS.*

Composed, when only seven years old, to English words, and presented by his father to the British Museum in 1765.

SANTINI, Abbé FORTUNATO. B. 1778 ; living in 1851.
A great collector of Church music.

1. Like as the hart   *Tenbury*
   (*Composed for Ouseley.*)

2. O Saviour of the world *Tenbury*
   (*Composed for Ouseley.*)

SPOHR, LUDWIG. B. 1784 ; D. 1859.
First appeared in London, 1820. Revisited England, 1839 and 1852.

1. From the deep I called   *Novello*
2. God is my Shepherd   ,,
3. How lovely are Thy dwellings ,,

4. Jehovah, Lord God of Hosts *Novello*
5. The earth is the Lord's   ,,

ANONYMOUS ANTHEMS.
FITZWILLIAM COLLECTION.

1. Behold, O God, our Defender.
2. I am well pleased.
3. I will give thanks.

4. O be joyful.
5. We have a strong city.
6. Whoe'er is My disciple.

FOURTH PERIOD.

NINETEENTH CENTURY.

THOMAS ATTWOOD WALMISLEY.

CHAPTER XIX.

THE FOURTH (OR MODERN) PERIOD.

It is satisfactory to pass over these forty lean years, and to enter the nineteenth century, from the fortieth year of King George III.'s reign to the present year of grace, with a feeling of consolation that is so easily acquired and confirmed when things have been so bad that, at least, they cannot be *worse*. As a fact, they become better, and we may date the commencement of better times for the Anthem from Attwood onwards. And shortly after the opening of the new century an event happened which was destined to be of immense importance to this form of composition.

In 1811 Vincent Novello established the eminent firm of English music publishers now known as Novello and Co., Limited. It is impossible to be sufficiently grateful to them for their enterprise in bringing within the reach of all, no matter how slender their means, most of the works of which I have been writing and which form the library of the Anthem from its inception to our own time.

I repeat that one cannot, in regard to the subject of this essay, over-estimate the good which, in the first place, Vincent Novello, and after that the family of Littleton and those in connection with them, have done for the cause of Church music in England and English Church music in particular.

This modern or fourth period has, then, great advantages, and starts well. By this time the works of such masters as Beethoven, Mozart, Schubert, &c., belonging to the foreign schools, were becoming known and appreciated by English musicians; music was more easily obtainable and cheaper than before, though, of course, not so cheap as it is now-a-days.

An incentive to a more elaborate and independent use of the organ in accompanying anthems was the vast improvement effected in its manufacture and compass. Elliott and Hill, Bishop, Walker, Gray, and other organ-builders were already constructing fine instruments.

Of course the pedal organ was still deficient, and concerning the compass different musicians of eminence held different views ; and, besides this, modern lightness of touch and facility of registering, and so on, were merely in their infancy.

As a result, the accompaniment to the anthem, no longer a mere echo of the voice parts, began to add to the interest and assist in illustrating the sentiment of the words set to music. It will be remembered that, in the " Motet " Period, the anthems sounded as well without as with accompaniment, and the means of accompaniment being decidedly feeble, the voices were the principal consideration, and strong enough to maintain their independence.

This state of things was followed by the " Verse " Period, in which the accompaniment, not necessarily of any interest, was an indispensable adjunct on account of the number of small interludes and the solos and duets.

Being so often simply a figured bass, it would depend upon the individual accompanists as to whether the organ part became interesting or otherwise.

But now, with increased facilities, better players and instruments, and greater knowledge, the organ, as Sir John Stainer points out, is almost converted into a solo instrument; the anthems being in some cases written less for vocal than for instrumental effect, and (if I rightly interpret him) he warns us that this ultra-independent treatment of the organ will, if we are not careful, result in the anthems of the future becoming, from the vocal standpoint, as feeble and useless to future generations as those of the latter part of the eighteenth century.

CHAPTER XX.

ATTWOOD, AND THE WALMISLEY FAMILY.

Thomas Attwood was born in 1765, being the son of a most versatile father, who combined the three businesses of trumpeter, viola player, and—coal merchant !

Attwood was a Chapel Royal boy until his fourteenth year.

Two years later, whilst performing at a concert in Buckingham House, he attracted the attention of the Prince of Wales (afterwards King George IV.), who, seeing the boy's evident talent, sent him abroad to study foreign methods and gain wider experience of what the musical world was doing. In 1783 he visited Naples, and worked there with Latilla for two years ; from there he came back to Vienna, where for two more years he had the advantage of tuition from the great Mozart, who expressed a highly favourable opinion of his talent.

Attwood was assistant-organist of the Church of St. George the Martyr, Queen Square, Bloomsbury, at that time a fashionable part of London, and he became musical instructor to the then Princess of Wales and Duchess of York. In 1796 he was appointed organist of St. Paul's Cathedral and composer to the Chapel Royal.

When the Philharmonic Society was established, in 1813, he became an original member. It is gratifying to notice the prosperous condition of this old Society at the present time.

In 1836 Attwood succeeded John Stafford Smith as organist of the Chapel Royal, and two years later he died at his house in Cheyne Walk, Chelsea, being seventy years old, and was buried under the organ in the Cathedral.

Attwood is never very *great* in his compositions, and yet we must acknowledge him as the first who made a praiseworthy attempt to supersede adaptations and distortions of other men's work by original and appropriate settings of the words in his anthems, and this attempt on his part and his evidently worthy intentions, led the way to a number of followers, some of whom stand high above Attwood in power. As was the case with several anthem writers, he composed for the stage in earlier life and devoted his latter years to church composition.

The purity and clearness of part-writing and the delicate taste with which Attwood's work is identified must be attributed to the influence of Mozart's teaching and example. It is curious to note that Attwood was one of the first musicians to recognise the genius of the youthful Mendelssohn, who dedicated to him his three fine Preludes and Fugues for the organ.

As a friend of both Mozart and Mendelssohn, he seems to form a link between the old and the new schools.

Mendelssohn spent some time at Attwood's villa at Norwood, whilst recovering from an illness in 1829, and writing from there he says: " In my bedroom luckily stands old Attwood's music-cupboard, with the key in it ; so I rummage among the music books, and after finding the other day no end of Te Deums by Croft, and twenty anthems by Boyce, and Purcell's Psalms, what should meet my eyes, in three big volumes, but ' Euryanthe ' " (Weber's opera). " That was a find ! "

Mendelssohn does not, in this case, appear to have been attracted by our fine anthems, when a modern full score was obtainable. His father, Abraham Mendelssohn, when he came over with Felix, described the latter as going to the St. Paul's organ with Attwood, where, as the bellows-blowers had left the Cathedral, Klingemann, of the Hanoverian Embassy, and two other gentlemen blew the bellows, while Mendelssohn, after extemporising for some time, played one of Attwood's coronation Anthems with the composer, the two arranging it, I presume, for four hands from the full score.

His godson, Thomas Attwood Walmisley, of whom we shall write more presently, edited several of his anthems, and besides these Attwood wrote some fine Coronation anthems: "I was glad," for King George IV.; "O Lord, grant the King a long life," for King William IV., and he had commenced a third, intended for Queen Victoria, when his work was stopped by death.

These great works had full orchestral accompaniments; and, by now, a *full* orchestra, as an accompaniment to an anthem, has become an accomplished fact, being used at many of the festivals, such as the Sons of the Clergy Festival in St. Paul's Cathedral, and the gathering of the Royal Society of Musicians in the Abbey, on which occasions not only the "viols," but also "everything that hath *breath*" doth praise the Lord.

Thomas Forbes Walmisley, who was the writer of several anthems about this period, was a pupil of Attwood's, and so was his more illustrious son, Thomas Attwood Walmisley, Attwood's godchild. The latter, who succeeded Clarke-Whitfeld* as Professor of Music at Cambridge, wrote many anthems.

I might select as fine representative specimens, "If the Lord Himself," "Hear, O Thou Shepherd of Israel," and "Remember, O Lord." In Walmisley's day there did not exist the number of capable musicians hungering and thirsting for organ appointments that we find now-a-days. If to-day an organist's post becomes vacant there would be 100 applicants for it; but in his day one man had to take several appointments simultaneously!

How Walmisley could find time for either teaching or composition it is difficult to understand, for the following is a record of his Sunday work alone at Cambridge :—

Service at St. John's College at			7.15 a.m.	
"	" Trinity	"	" 8 a.m.	
"	" King's	"	" 9.30 a.m.†	
"	" St. Mary's	"	" 10.30 a.m.†	
"	" "	"	" 2 p.m.†	
"	" King's	"	" 3.15 p.m.†	
"	" St. John's	"	" 5 p.m.	
"	" Trinity	"	" 6.15 p.m.	

Rather much for one day, and that the *day of rest!*

As a member of Corpus Christi College he distinguished himself in mathematics; he also took his M.A. in 1841 and his Mus. Doc. in 1848.

Although he had scored some of his anthems for orchestra, he foolishly abandoned orchestral writing altogether, on account of

---

* His name has for some time been erroneously spelt Whitfield.

† Walmisley, it should be understood, never held these appointments; he merely officiated for John Pratt, then incapacitated.

what he considered grave discouragement on the part of Felix Mendelssohn, to whom he showed his first Symphony. Before Mendelssohn would examine it, he asked Walmisley how many Symphonies he had written. On his replying that this was his *first*, the composer of the "Italian" and "Scotch" said: "Oh ! No. 1 ! let us see what No. 12 will be first of all ! "

Thomas Attwood Walmisley's anthems fall little short of the great works in a similar style of Wesley and Goss, and this, notwithstanding that he lived entirely *out* of London, and away from a competition and rivalry which would, undoubtedly, have compelled a keener and more earnest cultivation of those great powers which he possessed to a considerable degree.

He is especially worthy of gratitude and honour for his efforts in spreading a knowledge and instituting an affection in England for the works of that mighty giant, John Sebastian Bach, and he referred to Bach's Mass in B minor as " the greatest composition in the world." In addition to all his anthems and services he wrote several Odes, the last being in honour of the Installation of H.R.H. Prince Albert, the only Royal anthem writer, as Chancellor of the University of Cambridge.

CHAPTER XXI.

THE WESLEY FAMILY.

A WONDERFUL musical family related to a marvellously religious family now claims our attention. Whether as preachers of religion or practisers of music—the handmaid of religion—we find great originality and strength and freedom in the expression of thought, which is untrammelled by any of the restrictions which a conservative orthodoxy would demand.

Charles Wesley, a son of the Rev. Charles Wesley, the writer of " Jesu, lover of my soul," and many other beautiful hymns, and a nephew of the great John Wesley, was born at Bristol in 1757, and was, like William Crotch, an infant prodigy ; for, at the age of two years and three-quarters, he is reported to have been able to play a tune on the harpsichord readily and in just time ; but more than this—and this is the astounding part of the report—he could add a true and correct *bass* to it !

Notwithstanding these marvellous signs of promise his father had no intention that he should embrace the musical profession. This, however, he did ; but, like so many wonder-children, having attained a certain degree of proficiency so very early in life, he made little, if any, further progress.

He was organist of St. George's, Hanover Square, and organist in ordinary to King George IV. He died in 1834.

His younger brother, Samuel, although *he* also was a precocious infant, did not develop his talent quite so quickly, for he was *three* years old before he played a tune, and he had learnt his notes when he added a bass to it! However, he proved to be the greater and more gifted of the two.

Born in 1766, he had the advantage of listening in his cradle to the products of what we are bound to call his brother's mature period, the latter being then about ten years old; and this may, in some degree, account for the marvellous development of his gifts.

He appears to have *taught himself* reading and writing when five years old, and between his sixth and seventh years he learnt to read music, having, before that time, composed part of an oratorio, " Ruth," the remainder of which he completed when he was eight years old!

" Before he was of age he had become," says Mr. Husk, " a good classical scholar, had acquired some knowledge of modern languages, had successfully cultivated a taste for literature, and had obtained distinction as an extemporaneous player upon the organ and pianoforte."

When he was about twenty-one years old a sad accident happened to him, which had a bad effect upon the remainder of his life. Passing along Snow Hill one evening, he fell into a deep excavation prepared for the foundation of some new building and severely injured his skull. He refused to undergo the operation of trepanning, and, as a result, suffered from time to time long periods of despondency and nervous irritability.

He did even more than T. A. Walmisley to spread a love and knowledge of Bach's immortal works over the land. He died in 1837.

It has been suggested that his religious tendency was towards Roman Catholicism, although he refrained from avowing his faith out of respect to his reverend father's feelings. He certainly wrote more for that communion than for the English Church—four Masses and over thirty motets, but for our Church only eight anthems, one of which, " All go unto one place," was composed for his brother Charles's funeral.

He left many children, but of all these his third son, Samuel Sebastian, was the one to inherit his genius.

Samuel Sebastian Wesley was born in 1810, and was educated at Christ's Hospital; he became a chorister of the Chapel Royal, and was appointed, when sixteen years of age, organist of St. James's Chapel, Hampstead Road, and, three years later, organist of

St. Giles's Church, Camberwell, and St. John's, Waterloo Road, and of the Parish Church of Hampton-on-Thames, in 1830.

Mr. F. G. Edwards, the able editor of the *Musical Times*, favours me with the following interesting letter from Wesley to W. H. Blanch, the historian of Camberwell, contradicting the statement that he held all these appointments simultaneously. He wrote, "I made a mistake when I said I held the organ posts at Camberwell, St. John's, Waterloo Road, and Hampton simultaneously. Hampstead Road Chapel was my first post, after leaving the Chapel Royal as a boy : but I held Camberwell and Hampton together for some time, having resigned St. John's, Waterloo Road, and the Hampstead Road Chapel, there being a fuss about my holding three posts together."

In 1832 he was organist of Hereford Cathedral, in 1835 of Exeter, in 1842 of Leeds Parish Church, in 1849 of Winchester, and in 1865 of Gloucester.

But it is not of his numerous migrations that I should write : it is of the astounding genius of the man.

The testimonial which the great Spohr wrote for him when he was a candidate for the musical professorship in Edinburgh University is a good criticism of his anthem writing. "His sacred music," wrote Spohr, "is chiefly distinguished by a noble, often even an antique style, and by rich harmonies as well as by surprisingly beautiful modulations."

Whilst organist at Gloucester, Wesley was granted by Mr. Gladstone's government a Civil List pension of £100 a year, in consideration of his services to Church music.

He died in 1876, after having been in Gloucester some ten years.

His last words were "Let me see the sky ! " " Words," as Sir Herbert Oakeley, his successful antagonist for the Edinburgh Chair of Music, remarks, "appropriate for one whose motto as a composer seemed ever to be ' Excelsior.' " Wesley's fame largely rests upon his glorious anthems, a complete list of which you will find at the end of this volume.

Such mighty works as "Blessed be the God and Father" and the " Wilderness," composed at Hereford, and the even grander " O Lord, Thou art my God " and "Ascribe unto the Lord," written when at Winchester, place him in the front rank of true Church composers. Then, again, what could be more dignified or yet more exquisitely touching than either of those smaller anthems, "Thou wilt keep him in perfect peace," "O Lord, my God " (Solomon's Prayer), or "Wash me throughly." The last-named was written as a thank-offering after a severe illness.

"Blessed be the God and Father" was composed to avoid an awkward crisis at Hereford, when for some cause or other only the boys and a bass were available.

Wesley was one of the greatest of organists, and has, practically, been the founder of that solid, noble style of organ playing in England which will, I trust, never be superseded either by French trickiness or by bad orchestral mimicry.

It is a curious fact that, great executant as we know him to have been, and teacher of some of our best players, he was an advocate, and a strong-headed advocate, of unequal temperament and a G or F compass, two *bêtes noirs* to both organ-builders and players of the present day. The elevation of the standard of Church music, so basely fallen at the end of the last century, is largely to be attributed to the genius of Samuel Sebastian Wesley.

CHAPTER XXII.

GOSS, SMART, AND OUSELEY.

AMONGST the greatest of the anthem writers with whom some of us still alive have had acquaintance, there stands Sir John Goss, who was born in 1800. He was admitted a Chapel Royal boy in 1811, and had as master John Stafford Smith—and a fairly hard master he appears to have been to the young gentlemen of those years.

But Goss's principal instruction in writing was gained from Attwood, whom he eventually succeeded as organist at St. Paul's Cathedral. It is interesting to know that Goss, in 1817, sang as tenor in the opera chorus, at the time when Sir Henry Bishop was conducting there.

In 1821 he was organist of Stockwell Chapel,* and, in 1824, of St. Luke's Church, Chelsea, a post which he retained until 1838.

In 1833 Goss composed his first important Anthem, "Have mercy upon me, O God," and with it gained the Gresham Prize Medal. It was dedicated to his beloved master, Attwood.

In 1838 he became vicar-choral and organist of St. Paul's, and, in this year, for the celebration of Her late Majesty's Coronation, he wrote, "O Lord, grant the Queen a long life," and, in 1840, for her marriage, he composed "The Queen shall rejoice." In 1842 he wrote "Blessed is the man," but owing, it is said, to unkind criticisms passed upon his work, he did not venture upon another anthem for nearly ten years! In 1852, for the State funeral of the great Duke of Wellington, he composed his noble dirge "And the king said to all the people," full of pure devotional feeling, and, for the same solemnity, "If we believe that Jesus

---

* Now St. Andrew's Church, Stockwell.

SAMUEL SEBASTIAN WESLEY.

died," a beautiful short anthem in D minor. Following this time, anthems by Goss frequently appeared, some of them orchestrated, notably " Praise the Lord, O my soul," which has accompaniments for wind instruments.* " Stand up and bless the Lord," " I heard a voice from heaven," that little gem, " O Saviour of the world," the brilliant harvest anthem "Fear not, O land," " The Wilderness," and many another "thing of beauty " destined, I firmly believe, to be " a joy for ever." After the Thanksgiving for the Prince of Wales's recovery in 1872, for which Goss wrote " The Lord is my strength," he received knighthood from the Queen, and, in 1876, was made Doctor of Music of Cambridge, *honoris causâ.* He died in retirement and well-earned rest in 1880, the eightieth year of his age, and was buried in Kensal Green Cemetery. A tablet is erected to his memory in the crypt of St. Paul's Cathedral.

He was a modest, almost shy man, possessed of a most affectionate nature, and imbued with a strong religious feeling, evidence of which pervades his beautiful anthems.

Henry Smart, who died before Goss did, was born thirteen years later, in 1813. He was a nephew of Sir George Smart, whose specimens of anthem writing are not so well known as the facts that he was one of the best orchestral conductors of that day and that Weber died in his house. But his nephew, Henry Smart, made contributions to the music of the Church which are both strong and popular, his Service in F perhaps more so than his anthems. The latter deserve to be better known and more often sung than they are. One of the finest of his anthems is, to my mind, " O God, the King of Glory."

One of the most industrious of anthem composers was the Rev. Sir Frederick Arthur Gore Ouseley, Baronet, born in London in 1825.

In his writing we trace a reverence for the past, skilfully blended with an appreciation of the modern schools, and he was a striking example of the power and ability of an erudite and high-minded musician to spread the best music and to propagate the most healthful influence amongst the rising generation of musical men.

Whether as the successor to Sir Henry Bishop in the Chair of Music at Oxford, or as the Founder and first Warden of St. Michael's College, Tenbury, he was ever respected and beloved, either as didactic writer, professor, composer, organist, or friend.

His extemporaneous playing will not easily be forgotten by those of us who had the privilege of hearing him.

He wrote an enormous number of anthems, in addition to oratorios and services. He was Canon and Precentor of Hereford Cathedral at the time of his death, which occurred in the year 1889.

---

* Sons of the Clergy Festival, 1854.

CHAPTER XXIII.

MACFARREN, STERNDALE BENNETT, ELVEY, AND BARNBY.

The late Principal of the Royal Academy of Music and Professor of Music at Cambridge, Sir George Alexander Macfarren, was a very prolific writer, and contributed an enormous number of anthems, amongst them being fifty-two short anthems for Holy Days and Seasons of the Church.

Sir George will ever be remembered as a prominent figure in the musical history of the last two decades.

There is no doubt that in his strict scholastic way he exerted the very best influences upon the musicians of his time. He never tired in his endeavour to raise the musicianship of the nation, and some of the present active interest in our glorious art, daily extending and developing, is due to the personality of this great scholar, theorist, and musician. He died in 1887.

His predecessor in office, both at the Royal Academy of Music and at the University of Cambridge, was Sir Sterndale Bennett.

He was born three years later than Macfarren, but died twelve years earlier.

Mr. Statham, writing in 1879, speaks of Bennett as " the only English musical composèr since Purcell who has attained a distinct style and individuality of his own, and whose works can be reckoned among the models or classics of the Art." He was born in Sheffield, both his father and his grandfather having been musicians before him.

As his father died when Sterndale was but three years old, the grandfather cared for his education, musical and otherwise. When eight years of age he entered the choir of King's College, Cambridge, and there his exceptional musical ability became so evident that, after two years, he was sent to the Royal Academy of Music, with which Institution the latter part of his life was closely connected.

The pure style and clear form of Mozart, which we first noticed in Attwood, may be traced, in a different manner, in Bennett's writing, and this may be due to his master, Cipriani Potter's teaching, for the latter was devoted to Mozart and all things Mozartian.

Although greatest in pianoforte and orchestral works, Bennett has left us some delicate and refined anthems.

All his work had that finish and delicacy which made it more an object of admiration to the musician than one of enthusiasm for the masses; so delicate and retiring in its modesty, just as its composer was.

He founded the Bach Society in 1849, and after being offered in 1853 the conductorship of the famous Gewandhaus Concerts in Germany (one of the greatest compliments ever paid a native composer), he was engaged three years later as permanent conductor of the Philharmonic Concerts, and was appointed Professor of Music at Cambridge; he remained the Philharmonic Society's conductor for ten years.

On resigning the latter post he became Principal of the Royal Academy of Music, where he came to be looked upon by us students as a kind friend rather than anyone more distant and official.

He died, deeply regretted, on February 1, 1875, and we buried him by the organ in. Westminster Abbey, near Purcell, Blow, Croft, and the other masters of the Anthem.

In the same year in which Sterndale Bennett was born, Sir George Job Elvey first saw the light in Canterbury.

He was a chorister in that Cathedral under Highmore Skeats, senior.

In 1835 Elvey was appointed organist of St. George's Chapel, Windsor, and, from that time, devoted his talents very largely to the. composition of anthems, most of which are published and well known.

The more important specimens are "The Lord is King," composed for the Gloucester Festival, and "Sing, O Heavens," for the Worcester Festival, both scored for full orchestra.

One of his best solo anthems is "Wherewithal shall a young man."

In 1871 he received the honour of knighthood.

Like Wesley and Smart, Elvey was the writer of several good popular hymn tunes. He resigned his post at Windsor in 1882, and died 1893.

"Sublime occasionally and massive in general" is one's summing up of the anthem writing of Sir George Job Elvey, and through these compositions he takes a firm and fairly high place in the ranks of the sterling writers for the Church of England.

I may be permitted to add a short account of one who has but recently gone to his long rest, taken away in the midst of the fight, and thereby leaving the services of the Church poorer by the loss of a musician whose work was always an earnest expression of devotion and affection. I refer to Sir Joseph Barnby, born in 1838 at York.

He was a chorister in the beautiful Minster there, and when his voice broke he became a student of the Royal Academy of Music, at which Institution he ran Sullivan very close for the Mendelssohn Scholarship.

For nine years he had charge of the music at St. Andrew's Church, Wells Street, and his genius made the services of that church well known for their excellence, a mission very successfully continued by Mr. F. A. W. Docker. He was precentor and choir-master of St. Anne's, Soho, conductor of the Royal Choral Society, succentor and musical director at Eton, and afterwards Principal of the Guildhall School of Music. In all these positions, and also as a talented composer of Church music, his loss is felt and deplored.

Barnby leaves behind him some forty or fifty published anthems, and hardly a Sunday passes without one or another of them being heard in our churches. He shared with Henry Leslie the honour of being the most successful cultivator of choral singing in modern years, and he brought his choir, just as Leslie did, to high perfection.

Sir Michael Costa, the reformer of the orchestra in England, was born at Naples in 1810. He came to England to conduct his master Zingarelli's sacred composition " By the waters of Babylon," at Birmingham, in 1829, and from that year, until his death in 1884, he remained with us, and exerted a great influence upon our orchestral players in this country. He became a naturalised Englishman in 1839. He conducted the Birmingham Festival from 1849. In 1869 he was knighted, and was conductor of Drury Lane Opera House from 1871. He wrote a few anthems, which are scarcely known to the present generation, and also composed two oratorios, another peculiarly English form of com-position, although originating in Italy.

CHAPTER XXIV.

FOREIGN CONTRIBUTORS.

It seems only natural that foreign composers who have spent any length of time upon our hospitable shores should have felt themselves drawn towards this thoroughly British inheritance, the Church Anthem, and several musicians whilst residing in England have written Church music of this kind.

Amongst others were Buononcini, Handel's rival, and Draghi in the seventeenth century, Spohr, Mozart, and the Abbé Santini in the eighteenth, and in the nineteenth century, Mendelssohn, Sir Julius Benedict, and Charles Gounod.

There is little evidence to prove that Sacchini or Hasse wrote anthems to English words, but amongst those who did, and who were not, like Handel, naturalised Englishmen, we can name his rival, Buononcini, or Bononcini, a member of a distinguished Italian family of musicians. Giovanni Battista Buononcini was born in 1672, at Modena, and came to England in 1720, where, in opposition to the support given to Handel by the king, he was under the patronage of the Dukes of Rutland, Queensberry, Sunderland, and Marlborough. For the funeral of the latter nobleman, in Henry VII.'s Chapel, he wrote his anthem " When Saul was king."

In the nineteenth century Mendelssohn's fine psalms and anthems were composed, and they may quite fittingly be added to our *répertoire*. The combined grandeur and emotion of his " Judge me, O God," are qualities which all good anthems should strive to possess, and in these excellent points, rather than any weaker sentiments, should Mendelssohn be the example to modern composers.

I cannot ascertain that Sir Julius Benedict was a naturalised British subject ; he is, therefore, introduced in this chapter.

He was born in Stuttgart in 1804. There is hardly any branch of musical composition that he did not essay, and amongst the rest he wrote anthems. He resided as composer, teacher, and pianist in this country from 1835 until his death in 1885. He was knighted in 1871, and was the possessor of similar honours from many European Courts.

Charles François Gounod, the composer of " Faust," wrote many anthems to English words, combining his own fervid nature, an admixture of richness and mysticism, with his early study of Palestrina, when for some years of his youth he lived in the Villa Medici at Rome. At one time he was preparing for the priesthood, but renounced that idea later. He stayed some years in London and formed a choir, which was the forerunner of the great Albert Hall choir of the present day.

CHAPTER XXV.

THE FUTURE OF THE ANTHEM.

I will, before laying down my pen, conclude this very imperfect sketch with a brief reference to the present and the immediate future. We are producing an enormous number of anthems ; let us ask ourselves how many of them are likely to live out our life-time ? One is tempted sometimes to compare some of the products of the day with the works of those grand old masters who are dead, in much the same way that a jerry-built house might be contrasted with the solid cathedral masonry of bygone years.

Why ! those grand anthems were not written to *sell*, they were composed to *endure for ever;* built, like the Church to whose services they minister, " upon the Apostles and Prophets, Jesus Christ Himself being the head corner-stone."

But I do believe that we are now awakening to the sense of grave responsibility which attaches to every Church composer, and that in this age of increased seriousness of thought, we are beginning to realise that in one sense we must all be "ministers" to the welfare of Christian congregations.

Unless we truly have something to preach, it is waste of music-paper, of talents, of time to attempt to put together a sermon, and there can be few better sermons than a well written, earnestly conceived anthem. With the example of the best of the old writers before our eyes and in our hearts, and with the warning offered to us by many modern effusions, the future anthem writers, the contributors to this form of art, should become a strong band of successors to those glorious composers whose works and whose lives we have been glancing at together upon these pages.

Seeing that we possess better trained and more intelligent choristers, superior sight-readers and interpreters of our intentions, there need be little hesitation in presenting to them works on the grandest scale, or even of returning to that antiphonal singing, the response of choir to choir, from which our Antiphon or Anthem is supposed to have originally sprung.

But whatever is done, let it be, not as men-pleasers, but as unto the Lord.

JOHN GOSS.

LIST OF ANTHEMS AND COMPOSERS OF THE 19th CENTURY.

ALBERT, ⎧ H.R.H. The Prince (Francis Albert Augustus) B. 1819 ;
⎨ Charles Emanuel, Prince Consort, Duke of
⎩ Saxony, Prince of Coburg and Gotha.)   D. 1861.
1. Out of the deep   *Lichfield* |

ALLEN, GEORGE BENJAMIN, Mus. Bac., Oxon. B. 1822 ; D. 1896
(in Brisbane).
Established "Abbey Glee Club," 1841. Org. All Saints', Kensington ; later,
Toorak, Melbourne, Victoria.

1. Almighty and everlasting	*Novello*	15. I will turn their mourning	*Curwen*
2. And lo! I beheld the dead	,,	16. I will worship	,,
3. And there was war in heaven	,,	17. Let my complaint	*Novello*
4. Awake, thou that sleepest	*Metzler*	18. Listen, O isles	,,
5. By the waters of Babylon	*Novello*	19. Lord, what love have I	,,
6. Gentle Spirit, heavenly		20. Now is Christ risen	,,
Dove	*Metzler*	21. O be joyful in God	,,
7. Have mercy upon me	*Novello*	22. O come let us	*Curwen*
8. In the beginning was the		23. O give thanks	*Novello*
Word	,,	24. O God, the Rock of Ages	*Curwen*
9. It is a good thing to give		25. O God, Who hast prepared	*Novello*
thanks	,,	26. O Lord, Thy Word	,,
10. I will alway give thanks	*Novello*	27. O worship the Lord	*Curwen*
11. I will give thanks	,,	28. Praise the Lord, call upon	,,
12. I will praise Thee	*Curwen*	29. The Lord is King	,,
13. I will sing aloud	,,	30. The Lord is my Shepherd	*Novello*
14. I will strengthen thee	,,		

ANDREWS, RICHARD HOFMANN. B. 1803 ; D. 1891.
1. O Lord, Thou art my God. | 3. Trust ye in the Lord.
2. Praise ye the Lord.

ANGEL, ALFRED. B. 1816 ; D. 1876.
Org. Exeter Cath., 1842-76 (after S. S. Wesley).
1. Blow the trumpet in Zion *Novello* |
(*Gresham prize*, 1842.)

ANSTEY, THOMAS. Flourished about 1830.

1. Awake up, my glory	*Joule*	5. O Lord God of my salvation	*Joule*
2. By the waters of Babylon	,,	6. O Lord, rebuke me not	,,
3. Great and marvellous	,,	7. The Lord is my Light	,,
4. How long wilt Thou forget?	,,	8. Why art thou so heavy?	,,

ASHLEY, The Honourable ANTHONY WILLIAM.   B. 1803 ; D. 1877.
Master of St. Katherine's Hospital, Regent's Park.

1. Haste Thee, O God	*Bumpus*	4. Lord Jesus, at Thy feet we bow	
2. Let Thy merciful ears			*Bumpus*
	Longhurst's Anthems.	5. O Lord, in Thee have I trusted	,,
(*Collect* 10*th S. after Trinity.*)		6. Say to the prisoners	,,
3. Lighten our darkness	*Bumpus*	7. Sound the deep strain	,,

ATKINSON, FREDERICK COOKE, Mus. Bac., Cantab.   B. 1841 ; D. 1897.
Pupil of Dr. Buck ; Org. Manningham Church, Bradford, and Norwich
Cath., 1881-5.

1. Hear, O Thou Shepherd   *King's* | 2. Rend your hearts   *King's*

BAGOT, Right Honourable Lady.
Wife of Dean Bagot, of Canterbury, who was afterwards Bishop of Oxford
and of Bath and Wells.

1. If we believe that Jesus
      died   *Marshall*

BAKER, A. S., B.A.   B. 1868 ; D. 1896.
Org. St. James's Church, New York, U.S.A.

1. Be ye, therefore, followers. | 2. O God, Who hast prepared.

BALFE, MICHAEL WILLIAM.   B. 1808 ; D. 1870.
Violinist, Vocalist, and eminent Composer ; Pupil of C. E. Horn, Rooke and
Lee.

1. Save me, O God   *Novello* |

BARNBY, Sir JOSEPH, Knight.   B. 1838; D. 1896.
Chorister in York Minster ; Studied at R.A.M. ; Org. St. Andrew's, Wells
Street, 1863-71 ; Precentor, St. Anne's, Soho, 1871; Org. and Precentor,
Eton College, 1875; Conductor, Royal Choral Society, and Principal,
Guildhall School of Music ; Musical Adviser to Novello, Ewer and Co.
until 1878.

1. All praise be due	*Ransford*	15. I bow my knee	*Novello*
2. As we have borne	*Novello*	16. It is a good thing to give	
3. Awake up, my glory	,,	thanks	,,
4. Behold, I bring you good		17. It is high time to awake	,,
tidings	,,	18. I will give thanks unto Thee	,,
5. Beloved, if God so loved us	,,	19. I will lift up mine eyes	,,
6. Blessed be the Lord God	,,	20. King all glorious	,,
7. Break forth into joy	,,	21. Let the words of my mouth	,,
8. Christians, awake	,,	22. Let Thy merciful kindness	*Boosey*
9. Come, ye blessed	,,	23. Let your light so shine	*Novello*
10. Drop down, ye heavens	,,	24. Lift up your hearts	,,
11. Grant to us, Lord	,,	25. Like silver lamps	,,
12. Have mercy upon me	,,	26. Lord of all power	,,
13. Holy night	,,	27. Lord of the Harvest	,,
14. Hymn of Faith	,,	28. Make me a clean heart	,,

BARNBY, Sir JOSEPH (*continued*).

29. My God, my God, look upon me
  Novello
30. Not unto us, O Lord   ,,
31. O Father blest   ,,
32. O how amiable   ,,
33. O Lamb of God   ,,
34. O Lord God, to whom
  vengeance   ,,
35. O Lord, how manifold   ,,
36. O perfect Love   ,,
37. O praise the Lord, all ye His ,,
  (*Long version.*)
38. O praise the Lord, all ye His ,,
  (*Short version.*)
39. O risen Lord   ,,

40. Our Father, which art   *Novello*
41. Sing and rejoice   ,,
42. Sing to the Lord of Harvest
  Patey & Willis
  (*Lute Series.*)
43. Sweet is Thy mercy   *Novello*
44. The Grace of God   ,,
45. The Lord bless you *Patey & Willis*
46. The Lord is King   *Novello*
47. The Lord is the true God   ,,
48. The Lord send thee help *Chester*
49. Thou visitest the earth *Novello*
50. Thy mercy, O Lord   *Boosey*
51. While shepherds   *Novello*
52. Ye shall go out with joy   ,,

BARRETT, WILLIAM ALEXANDER, Mus. Bac., Oxon. B. 1836; D. 1891.
Pupil of W. Bayley, Geo. Cooper, and Sir John Goss. Org. St. Andrew's, Wells Street; Vicar-Choral St. Paul's; Critic, Scholar, Examiner, and Alto-singer.

1. Come, and let us go up   *Novello*
2. The eyes of all   *St. Paul's*

3. They that wait upon the
  Lord   *Mag. of Music*, 1876
4. Turn ye unto Me   *St. Paul's*

BARTHOLOMEW, Mrs. ANN SHEPPARD MOUNSEY. B. 1811 ; D. 1891.
(*Née* Mounsey). Referred to as precocious in Spohr's Diary. Org. at Clapton, St. Michael's, Wood Street, and St. Vedast's, Foster Lane.

1. Holy is the Lord of Hosts. |

BARTHOLOMEW, R. D. 1891.
Organist of the Parish Church, Ludlow.

1. O that men   *Novello* |

BATES, GEORGE. B. 1802 ; D. 1881.
Org. Ripon Cath., 1829-73.

1. Come, Holy Ghost   *Bumpus* |

BATTYE, JAMES. B. 1803 ; D. 1858.
Best known as a composer of glees. Parish Clerk of Huddersfield.

1. My soul truly waiteth   *Novello* |
  (*Gresham Prize*, 1845.)

BAUMER, HENRY. B. 1835 ; D. 1888.
Director of the Watford School of Music ; sometime Org. of Dulwich Coll.

1. If ye keep My command-
  ments   *Fowle* |
2. Lord, how are they increased
  Chester, 1876

BAYLEY, WILLIAM. B. 1810 ; D. 1858.
Vicar-Choral and Master of the Boys of St. Paul's Cath. (after Hawes) ; Org.
St. John's, Horsleydown, S.E.   Master of Stainer, Gadsby, Barrett, and
Warwick Jordan.

1. Enter not into judgement.
2. The mountains shall depart
   MS. at St. Paul's
3. To the Lord our God.
   MS. at St. Paul's

BEDSMORE, THOMAS. B. 1833 ; D. 1881.
Pupil of S. Spofforth.   Org. of Lichfield Cath., 1864.

1. Awake, thou that sleepest *Lichfield*
2. Drop down, ye heavens   ,,
3. I will go forth in the
   strength   ,,
4. I will wash my hands   *Lichfield*
5. Lord, who shall dwell   ,,
6. My God, my God, look   ,,

BEECROFT, GEORGE ANDUS BEAUMONT. B. 1845 ; D. 1873.
Amateur musician.

1. Turn Thy face from my
   sins   *Metzler*

BENNETT, ALFRED WILLIAM, Mus. B., Oxon. B. 1805 ; D. 1830
(fell from a coach *en route* to Worcester Festival).
Son of Thomas Bennett.   Org. New Coll., Oxon., and University Church,
1825.

1. And very early in the
   morning   *Marshall*
2. Grant, we beseech Thee *Tenbury*
   (*21st Sunday after Trinity.*)
3. I waited patiently   *Novello*
4. My song shall be alway *Marshall*
5. O praise the Lord of
   heaven   *Novello*
6. O Zion that bringest   ,,
7. The Lord preserveth   *Marshall*

BENNETT, HENRY ROBERT. B. *c.* 1807 ; D. 1861.
Youngest son of Thomas Bennett, whom he succeeded as Org. Chichester
Cath., 1849-60.

1. Like as the hart *Chichester*, 1823 | 2. O God, the strength   *Chichester*

BENNETT, Sir WILLIAM STERNDALE, M.A., D.C.L., Mus. Doc., Cantab.
B. 1816 ; D. 1875.
Studied at R.A.M. and Leipzig Conservatoire ; Cambridge Professor of
Music and Principal, R.A.M. ; Founder (with Goldschmidt) of the Bach
Choir.

1. Cast thy bread upon the
   waters   *Novello*
   (*Duet and Trio, Female Voices.*)
2. Grant, we beseech Thee   ,,
3. Great is our Lord   ,,
4. In Thee, O Lord   ,,
5. Let Thy hand be upon
   the man   ,,
6. Lord, to Thee our songs *Novello*
7. Lord, who shall dwell ?   *Novello*
8. Now, my God, let, I
   beseech Thee   ,,
   (*For the opening of St. John's
   College Chapel.*)
9. O that I knew !   ,,
10. Remember now thy Creator ,,
11. The fool hath said   ,,

Numbers from "The Woman of Samaria" are also used as Anthems.

BENSON, GEORGE, Mus. Bac., Cantab. B. 1814 ; D. 1884.
Gent. of the Chapels Royal and Vicar-Choral, Westminster Abbey.

1. Almighty God, unto Whom	*Novello*	4. My God, my God, look upon me	*Novello*
2. Hear me, when I call	,,	5. So God loved.	
3. I will arise	*Weekes*	6. Turn us, O God	,,
		7. When I was a child	,,

BEST, WILLIAM THOMAS. B. 1826 ; D. 1897.
Pupil of Young (of Carlisle). Org. of several Liverpool churches, St. Martin's-in-the-Fields, London, and Lincoln's Inn Chapel.

1. Almighty God, give us grace	*Joule*	5. O praise the Lord, all ye heathen	*Joule*
2. Behold, I bring you glad tidings	*Novello*	6. Praise the Lord, call upon His Name	*Novello*
3. Dies iræ *Alluded to in "Musical Times," Nov.,* 1882		7. The Lord is great in Sion	,,
4. I will magnify Thee, O God	*Novello*	8. While shepherds watched	,,

BEXFIELD, WILLIAM RICHARD, Mus. Doc., Cantab. B. 1824 ; D. 1853.
Org. Boston Church and St. Helen's, Bishopsgate.

1. Blessed be God for ever	*Novello*	6.*Not unto us, O Lord.	
2. Blessed is he that waiteth	,,	7.*O Lord, Thou art my God.	
3.*Glory be to God on high.		8.*Remember, O Lord.	
4.*Hear my prayer.		9.*The Lord is my Light	
5.*Hide Thy face.			

Also numbers from "Israel Restored."

BIRCH, WILLIAM HENRY. B. 1826 ; D. 1888.
Org. St. Mary's Church, Amersham ; Chorister in St. Paul's ; Pupil of Hawes and Attwood.

1. Behold, I bring you good tidings	*Curwen*	4. I will love thee	*Curwen*
2. Enter not into judgment	,,	5. Let not your heart be troubled	,,
3. If ye then be risen	,,	6. Ponder my words	,,

BOARDMAN, JOHN GEORGE. B. 1819 ; D. 1898.
Organist of Clapham Grammar School, 1845-76. Held various other appointments at the same time, the last being the organistship of St. Mark's, Kensington, 1866-94.

1. Behold, how good and joyful	*Bumpus*	2. It is a good thing to give thanks	*Novello*
(Opening of Clapham Grammar School.)		3. Lord, let me know	*Bumpus*

BOWLES, Rev. WILLIAM LISLE. B. 1762 ; D. 1850.
Canon of Salisbury and Rector of Bremhill, Wilts. Distinguished as a poet and pamphleteer.

1. Grant, we beseech Thee	*Marshall*	2. Haste Thee, O God	*Marshall*

---

* Anthems so marked published under the title of "Seven Church Anthems" (Novello).

BRADFORD, JACOB, MUS. DOC., OXON.   B. 1842 ; D. 1898.
Principal, South London Musical College.

1. If ye love me	*Norwich*	3. Let us now go even	*Novello*
2. I was glad (*Psalm* 122)	*Novello*	4. We have seen His star	,,

And selections from his " Judith."

BROWN-BORTHWICK, REV. ROBERT.   B. 1840 ; D. 1894.
Vicar of St. John's, Clapham.

1. Blessed are the dead	*Novello*	2. Hymn for Peace.

BUCKLAND, HENRY. B.   B. — ; D. 1867.
Vicar-Choral and Master of the boys at St. Paul's, 1858.

1. Keep, we beseech Thee		Teach me, O Lord.	*Bumpus*
MS. St. Paul's		

CALDICOTT, ALFRED JAMES, MUS.B. Cantab., 1878. B. 1842 ; D. 1897.
Chorister in Worcester Cath.   Studied also in Leipsic.

1. Behold, how good and joyful		2. He is risen	*Weekes*
	Novello	3. If I go not away	*Patey & Willis*

CALLCOTT, WILLIAM HUTCHINS.   B. 1807 ; D. 1882.
Son of J. W. Callcott ; sometime Org. St. Barnabas, Kensington.

1. From whence come wars ?	*Novello*	4. In my Father's house	*Novello* ·
2. Give peace in our time	,,	5. O Lord, revive Thy work	*Addison*
3. He maketh wars to cease	*Addison & Co.*	6. Thou visitest the earth	*Novello*

CARTLEDGE, JAMES.   D. 1864.
Senior Chorister, Manchester Cathedral, his appointment dating from 1826.

1. Behold, how good and joyful	*Novello*	8. O clap your hands	*Novello*
2. Behold, now, praise	*Joule*	9. O Lord, we beseech Thee	*Joule*
3. Blessed is the people	*Novello*	10. O praise the Lord, all ye heathen	,,
4. Bow down Thine ear	,,	11. O praise the Lord, ye that fear Him	,,
5. In that day shall this song	*Joule*	12. Save me, O God	,,
6. I will give thanks unto the Lord, His praise (*Psalm* 34.)	*Novello*	13. The earth is the Lord's	*Novello*
7. I will give thanks unto the Lord with my whole (*Psalm* 111.)	*Joule*	14. We have a strong city	,,

CHAPMAN, SHADRACH.
Of Draycott, near Wells.

1. Arise, shine	*publ.* 1838	4. O God, Thou hast been displeased	*publ.* 1838
2. O come, let us sing	,,	5. This opening morn	,,
3. O God, the King of glory	,,	(*Christmas Day.*)	

CHATER, WILLIAM.
Org. Holy Trinity Church, Coventry, 1866-1880.

1. By the waters of Babylon *Novello*	

CHAWNER, REV. C. F. F.   B. *c.* 1840 ; D. 1867.
Sometime resident at St. Michael's College, Tenbury.

1. Devout men carried	*Stephen*	2. Precious in the sight	*Novello*
	Novello		

CHIPP, EDMUND THOMAS, Mus. Doc., Cantab. B. 1823 ; D. 1886 at Nice.
Son of T. P. Chipp, Player on the Tower Drums.
Vln. in H.M. Private Band, 1843 ; Org. Albany Chapel, 1843 ; St. John's Chapel, Hampstead, 1846 ; St. Olave's, Southwark, 1847 (after Gauntlett) ; Holy Trinity, Paddington, 1856 ; St. George's, Belfast ; St. Paul's, Edinburgh ; Ely Cath., 1866-86 (after R. Janes).

1. As I live, saith the Lord *Novello*
2. Lord of all power and might „
3. O tarry thou the Lord's leisure
4. Seek ye the Lord *Norwich*
5. So teach us to number *Norwich*
6. The earth shall be full *Carlisle*
7. The Lord hath been mindful *Novello*

Also numbers from "Job" and "Naomi."

CLIPPINGDALE, JOSIAH. B. 1834. D 1890.

1. If ye walk in my statutes.
2. I will lay me down.
3. Rend your heart.

COCKRAM, HENRY T. Drowned in "Princess Alice" disaster, Woolwich, Sept., 1878.
Most promising R.A.M. pupil.

1. O that men would praise *Novello* |

COLBORNE, LANGDON, Mus. Doc., Cantuar. B. 1837 ; D. 1889.
Org. St. Michael's College, Tenbury, 1860 ; Beverley Minster, 1874 ; Wigan Parish Church ; Dorking Parish Church ; Hereford Cath., 1877.

1. Adeste, fideles *Weekes*
2. Behold, I bring you „
3. If thou shalt confess with thy mouth *Fowle*
4. I will lay me down in peace *Novello*
5. O give thanks unto the Lord *Weekes*
6. O Lord our Governour *Novello*
7. Out of the deep „
8. Ponder my words „
9. Rend your heart „
10. The Lord is my Light *Weekes*
11. This is the day „

CONGREVE, BENJAMIN. B. 1836 ; D. 1871.
Composer of songs and prize part-songs.

1. I will greatly rejoice *Novello* | 2. The Lord is risen indeed *Novello*

CONINGSBY, CHARLES.
Org. of Hornsey Parish Church in 1859.

1. Try me, O God *Joule* |

COOPER, ALEXANDER SAMUEL. B. 1835. D. (in the Charterhouse), 1901.
Org. St. John's, Putney, and St. Paul's, Covent Garden. Editor of the Parochial Psalter and Parochial Chant Book.

1. Brightest and best.
2. Come unto Me *Novello.*
3. I did call upon the Lord *Novello*
4. I will lay me down „

COOPER, GEORGE. B. 1820 ; D. 1876.
Org. Chapel Royal, SS. Anne and Agnes; St. Benet's; St. Sepulchre; Christ's Hospital; Assistant-Org. St. Paul's.

1. Teach me, O Lord   *Chap. Roy.* |

CORFE, CHARLES WILLIAM, Mus. Doc., Oxon. B. 1814 ; D. 1883.
Org. Christ Christ Cath., Oxford, and Choragus to the University.

J. Thou visitest the earth   *York* |

COSTA, Sir MICHAEL, Knight. B. 1810; D. 1884.
Naturalised 1839. Eminent Conductor of English oratorios and Italian operas.

1. God, Who cannot be unjust. | 3. Suffer little children   *Novello*
2. Lord, I have loved   *Fowle* | (*The Baptism of Prince Leopold*, 1853.)
Also extracts from " Eli " and " Naaman."

COWARD, JAMES. B. 1824 ; D. 1880.
Org. to the Crystal Palace, 1857-80 ; Chorister in Westminster Abbey, and successively Org. St. Mary's, Lambeth, St. Magnus, London Bridge, and St. George's, Bloomsbury.

1. Hear my prayer. | 3. O Lord, correct me   *Novello*
2. I acknowledge my *Mus. Standard* |

CRAMPTON, THOMAS. B. 1817 ; D. 1885.
Editor and Purchaser of Music for the British Museum.

1. Lord Jesus, receive my spirit *Fowle* | 2. The sacrifices of God   *Curwen*

CUSINS, Sir WILLIAM GEORGE, Knight. B. 1833 ; D. 1893.
Studied at R.A.M. and Brussels ; Vln. Italian Opera ; Org. Queen's Private Chapel and Master of Music to Her late Majesty.

1. Grant the Queen a long life *Mann* | 2. I will receive the cup   *Novello*

DALGLISH, ROBERT. B. 1806 ; D. 1875.

1. Create in me a clean heart. | 3. Great and marvellous.
2 God is my Rock. | 4. Hearken unto My voice.

DEARLE, EDWARD, Mus. Doc., Cantab. B. 1806 ; D. 1891.
Org. at Deptford, 1827 ; Blackheath, 1830 ; Wisbech, 1832 ; Warwick, 1833 ; Newark, 1835-64 ; then resident in London.

1. Bow down Thine ear   *King's* | 8. The Lord hear thee   *King's*
2. By the waters   *Mann* | 9. Turn Thee again   *Novello*
3. God is a Spirit   ,, | (*Gresham Prize*, 1837.)
4. O Lord, we beseech Thee   *King's* | 10. With angels and archangels
5. Rend your heart   ,, | *Novello*
6. Sing unto God, O ye Kingdoms ,, | (" *Therefore with*," *Mann*.)
7. The desert shall rejoice   *Mann* |

DEARNALEY, IRVINE. B. 1839 ; D. 1894.
Org. of Ashton-under-Lyne.

1. What reward shall I give ? *Fowle* |

DENNIS, G.
1. Hosanna   *Novello's Col.*, 1852 |

DEWBERRY, WILLIAM CHARLES, Mus. B., Cantab.   B. 1843; D. 1899.
Org. Clare College and St. Edward's Church, Cambridge.
1. Behold, a Virgin   *King's* |

DISTIN, THEODORE.   B. 1823; D. 1893.
Good Horn player and Solo Bass singer, Lincoln's Inn Chapel.

1. Blessed is the man.		3. O praise God in His	
2. Hear me when I call	*Novello*	Holiness	*Novello*
		4. The Lord is King	„

DIXON, GEORGE, Mus. Doc., Oxon. 1858.   B. 1820; D. 1887.
Org. of Grantham Parish Church.

1. I heard a voice	*Southwell*	4. Unto Thee, O my Strength.	
2. O give thanks	*Novello*	5. We will rejoice	*Novello*
3. Open ye the gates.			

DONKIN, WILLIAM FISHBURN, M.A., F.R.S., &c.   B. 1815; D. 1869.
Savilian Professor of Astronomy, Oxford.
1. Justorum animæ. |

DORRELL, WILLIAM.   B. 1810; D. 1896.
Son of Edmund Dorrell, Member of the Old Water Colour Society. Pupil
of Crotch; Professor at the R.A.M.
1. Hear me when I call   *Bumpus* |

DRAKE, THOMAS.
Chorister at Bristol Cath., 1863.
1. Preserve me, O God   *Marshall* |

DUNNE, JOHN, Mus. Doc., Dublin.   B. 1834; D. 1883.
Member of Ch. Ch., St. Patrick's, and Trin. Coll., Dublin Choirs.

1. Gracious and righteous	*Metzler*	4. The Wilderness	*Dublin*
2. In Rama was there a voice	*Fowle*	5. Unto Thee, O Lord	„
3. O give thanks	*Dublin*		

DYCE, WILLIAM, R.A.   B. 1806; D. 1864.
Painter and Musician; one of the Founders of the Old Motet Society.

1. In Thee, O Lord, have I trusted	2. O God, Thou art my God	*Burns*
(*Burns' Anthems*, 1846.)		

DYKE, Rev. WILLIAM.
Curate of Winster, Derbyshire.
1. Come, Holy Ghost   *Joule* |

DYKES, Rev. JOHN BACCHUS, M.A., Cantab.; Mus. Doc., Durham.
B. 1823; D. 1876.
Pupil of Skelton and T. A. Walmisley; Minor Canon and Precentor of
Durham; Vicar of St. Oswald, Durham.

1. At the Name of Jesus	*Durham*	5. O God, forasmuch as	*Durham*
2. Blessing and honour	„	6. The Lord is my Shepherd	*Novello*
3. Come, Holy Ghost	„	7. These are they which	„
4. Lay not up for yourselves	*Metzler*	8. The Spirit and the Bride	*Durham*

ELLERTON, JOHN LODGE.   B. 1807 ; D. 1873.

Composer and *Minor* Poet; gained prizes at Catch Club, 1836, 1838.

1. I am well pleased	*Bumpus*	4. The Lord is King	*Bumpus*
2. Let all those that seek	*Joule*	5. Thou art my King	,,
3. O do well	*Bumpus*		

ELVEY, Sir GEORGE JOB, Knight, Mus. Doc., Oxon.   B. 1816 ; D. 1893.

Pupil of Highmore Skeats, Senr., and of his brother, Stephen Elvey; Lay-Clerk, Christ Church, Oxford, 1833 ; Org. (succeeding Highmore Skeats, Junr.) St. George's Chapel, Windsor, 1835-82.

1. Almighty and everlasting.		24. O Lord, from Whom all	
2. And it was the third hour	*Novello*	good.	
3. Arise, shine	,,	25. O praise the Lord of	
(Full.)		heaven	*Novello*
4. Arise, shine	*Elvey's Suppl.*	26. O worship the Lord	*Curwen*
(Solo.)		27. O ye that love the Lord	*Novello*
5. Behold, O God	,,	28. Praise the Lord, and call	,,
(For Queen Victoria's Birthday.)		29. Praise the Lord, ye servants	*Elvey*
6. Blessed are the dead	,,	30. Rejoice in the Lord, O ye	*Novello*
7. Blessed are they that fear	*Novello*	31. Sing, O heavens	*Joule*
8. Bow down Thine ear	,,	32. Sing unto God, ye kingdoms	*Elvey*
(Gresham Prize.)		33. Teach me, O Lord	*Novello*
9. Christ being raised	,,	34. The eyes of all	,,
10. Christ is risen	,,	35. The Lord is in His holy temple.	
11. Come, Holy Ghost	,,	36. The Lord is King.	
12. Come unto Me	,,	37. The souls of the righteous	*Novello*
13. Daughters of Jerusalem	,,	38. They that go down to	
14. Hear, O heavens	*Elvey's Suppl.*	the sea	,,
15. Hide not Thy Face	,,	39. They that wait	*Curwen*
16. I beheld, and lo!	*Novello*	40. This is the day	*Elvey*
17. If we believe that Jesus		*(General Thanksgiving, May* 1, 1859.)	
died	*Patey & Willis*	41. Unto Thee have I cried	*Novello*
18. In that day	,,	42. When Israel came out	*Elvey*
19. I was glad	,,	43. Wherewithal shall a young	*Novello*
20. I will alway give thanks	*Elvey*	*(Confirmation of Prince George of*	
21. O be joyful in God	*Novello*	*Cambridge.*	
(Choir Benevolent Fund.)		44. While shepherds watched	*Novello*
22. O do well unto Thy servant	*Fowle*	45. Whom have I in heaven	,,
23. O give thanks unto the			
Lord	*Novello*		

ELVEY, STEPHEN, Mus. Doc. Oxon.   B. 1805 ; D. 1860.

Pointed a Psalter upon a new principle; Lay-Clerk, Canterbury Cath.; Org. New Coll. and St. Mary's (University) Church, Oxford, 1830 ; Choragus, 1840.

1. Almighty and everlasting	*Joule*	4. The tempter to my soul	
2. Grant, we beseech Thee	*Marshall*	hath said	
3. O Lord, Thy heavenly		*Metcalf's " Metrical Anthems."*	
grace impart		5. Wherewithal shall a young man.	
Maurice's " Choral Harmony."			

HENRY SMART.

EYLAND, H.
1. Behold the eye of the Lord |
   Novello's Catalogue, 1851

FAREBROTHER, BERNARD.   D. 1888.
Pupil of Dr. Buck, of Norwich.   Org. St. Paul's Church, Birmingham.
1. Lo, the winter is past   *Novello* | 2   O give thanks unto the Lord
                                                              Novello

FAWCETT, JOHN, Junr., Mus. Bac., Oxon.   B. 1824; D. 1857.
Son of J. Fawcett, shoemaker; Composer of the tune "Bolton-le-Moors";
Student, R.A.M.; Org. Farnworth and Bolton.
1. All they that hope   *Joule* | 4. Save me, O God, for Thy
2. But Thou, O Lord   " | Name's sake   *Joule*
3. Our fathers hoped in Thee " | 5. When the wicked man   "

FEARNSIDE, FREDERICK.   B. *c.* 1836; D. 1888.
Chorister of Norwich Cath., 1848; Didactic writer.
1. The Lord is gracious   *Mann* |

FISHER, ARTHUR COLBORNE.   B. 1864; D. 1896.
Org. St. George's Church, Cannes.
1. Blessed City | 2. God that madest.

FLOWERS, GEORGE FRENCH, Mus. Doc., Oxon.   B. 1811; D. 1872.
Org. English Church, Paris; and St. Mark's, Myddelton Square, London.
1. To God ascribe the power |
   Choral Fugue |

FORSTER, J. F.
Org. Queen Camel, Somerset   *c.* 1850.
1. Give peace in our time   *Wells* | 2. If we say we have no sin
                                                       Parochial Choir Book

FREDERICKTON, Lord Bishop of (Most Rev. JOHN MEDLEY).   B. 1804;
   D. 1892.
Consecrated Bishop of Frederickton, 1845; elected Metropolitan of Canada,
   1879.
1. Blessed are the dead   *Novello* | 4. O praise the Lord of heaven *Novello*
2. Grant, we beseech Thee   " | 5. Show me Thy ways   "
3. Like as the hart   " | 6. Why art thou so heavy?   "

GABRIEL, Miss MARY ANN VIRGINIA.   B. 1825; D. 1877 (effects of a
   carriage accident).
Best known as a Composer of Ballads.
1. The Lord is my portion |
   Chester, 1858 |

GARRETT, GEORGE MURSELL, M.A. (*propter meritis*), Mus. Doc., Cantab. B. 1834 ; D. 1896.
Pupil and Assistant of S. S. Wesley, 1850 ; Org. Madras Cath., 1856 ; St. John's College, Cambridge, 1857 ; and the University Org. 1873.

1. Blessed is the man	*Garrett's list*	13. Praise ye the Lord	*Novello*
2. Come and let us return	,,	14. Prepare ye the way	,,
3. Give alms of thy goods.		(*Same as* 18.)	
4. God, Who is rich in mercy	*Novello*	15. The Lord is full of compassion	
5. I heard a voice	*Garrett*		*St. John's Appendix*
6. In humble faith	*Novello*	16. The Lord is loving	*Novello*
7. It shall come to pass	,,	17. The Lord is risen	,,
8. I will call upon God		18. The voice of one crying	,,
St. John's Coll. Appendix		(*Same as* 14.)	
9. Just Judge of heaven	*Novello*	19. The voice of the Lord	,,
10. Lay not up for yourselves	*Garrett*	20. They that put their trust	,,
11. Our soul on God	*Novello*	21. Thou, O God, art praised	,,
12. Praise the Lord	,,	22. Thus saith the Lord	,,

GAUNTLETT, HENRY JOHN, Mus. Doc., Cantuar. B. 1806 ; D. 1876.
Solicitor, 1831 ; Org. St. Olave's, Southwark ; Christ Church, Newgate Street, &c. ; laboured for the establishment of the C *v.* the old G (or F) Organ.

1. Blessed are those servants	*Joule*	6. O Saviour of the world	*Curwen*
2. I am the Resurrection		7. O tarry thou the Lord's	
	From Farrant	leisure	*Joule*
3. If ye love Me	*H. King*	8. This is the day	*Novello*
4. I will go unto the altar	*Novello*	9. Thou wilt keep him (in D)	,,
5. Joy and gladness shall		10. Thou wilt keep him (in E♭)	,,
be found	*Joule*		

GEAR, HENRY HANDEL. B. 1805 ; D. 1884.
Tenor Vocalist and Composer in London.

1. Christ our Passover. |

GILBERT, ERNEST BENNETT. B. 1833 (? 1835) ; D. 1884.
Pupil of R.A.M. and at Leipzig ; French Horn player and Org. in Isle of Man, South Wales, and London.

1. Come unto Me   *Mann* |

GLADSTONE, WILLIAM HENRY, M.A., Oxon. ; M.P. B. 1840 ; D. 1891.
Amateur Musician and son of the eminent Statesman.

1. Almighty God, give us		6. Lighten our darkness	*Novello*
grace	*Mann*	7. Our conversation is in	
2. Behold, how good	*Novello*	heaven	,,
3. Christ our Passover.		8. Teach me Thy way	,,
(*Chant form.*)		9. These are Thy glorious	
4. Gracious and righteous	*Novello*	works	,,
5. I will wash my hands	*Mann*	10. Withdraw not Thou	*Mann*

GODDARD, JOSEPH. B. 1833; D.—.
Writer and Composer.

1. I do set my bow   *Fowle* | 2. These things I command.

GOSS, Sir JOHN, Knight, Mus. Doc., Cantab. (*honoris causâ*).
B. 1800; D. 1880.
Pupil of J. S. Smith and Attwood; Org. St. Luke's, Chelsea; St. Paul's
Cath. (1838-72); Composer to the Chapel Royal, 1856.

1.‡Almighty and everlasting
    God.
2. Almighty and merciful
    God   *Novello*
3. And the King said   ”
    (*For the State Funeral of
    the Duke of Wellington,
    1852.*)
4. Behold, I bring you good
    tidings   ”
5. Blessed is he that con-
    sidereth   *Hereford*
6. Blessed is the man   *Novello*
7.*Brother, thou art gone
    before us   ”
    (*Part 2 of No. 27, Festival of
    Sons of the Clergy, 1865.*)
8.‡Christ is risen.
9. Christ our Passover   *Novello*
10. Come, and let us return   ”
11. Enter not into judgment.   ”
12. Fear not, O land   ”
13. Forsake me not   ”
14. God so loved the world   ”
15. Have mercy upon me   ”
    (*Gresham Prize.*)
16. Hear, O Lord   *Novello*
17.‡Hosanna! for unto us.
18. I am the Resurrection   ”
19. If we believe   ”
    (*First performed at the
    Duke of Wellington's
    Funeral, 1852.*)
20. I heard a voice   ”
21. In Christ dwelleth   ”
22. I will magnify Thee   ”
23. Let the wicked   *Tenbury*
24.‡Let Thy merciful ear.
25. Lift up Thine eyes   *Novello*
26. Lord, let me know mine
    end   ”

27.‡My voice shalt Thou hear.
28. O give thanks unto the
    Lord   *Novello*
29. O Lord God, Thou
    Strength   ”
    (*Public Funeral of the Earl
    of Dundonald, 1860.*)
30. O Lord, grant the Queen   *Cramer*
    (*For Queen Victoria's Corona-
    tion, 1838.*)
31. O praise the Lord, laud
    ye   *Novello*
    (*Enthronement of Dr. Tait
    as Bishop of London,
    1856.*)
32. O praise the Lord of
    heaven   ”
33. O Saviour of the world   ”
34. O taste and see   ”
35. Praise the Lord, O my soul   ”
    (*Festival of the Sons of the Clergy,
    1854, with orchestra.*)
36.‡Praise waiteth for thee.
37. Stand up and bless   *Novello*
    (*Re-opening of Hereford
    Cath., 1863.*)
38. The glory of the Lord   ”
39.†The God of Jeshurun   ”
    (*Incomplete.*)
40. The Lord is my strength   ”
    (*For the Prince of Wales's
    recovery, 1872.*)
41. The Queen shall rejoice   *Cramer*
    (*In honour of Queen Victoria's
    Marriage.*)
42. These are they which
    follow   ”
43. The Wilderness   ”
44.‡Wherewithal shall a young ”
    man.
45. Will God in very deed?

---

* Part I. (No. 24) added later.
† Completed by Sir A. Sullivan. It commences, "There is none like unto the God of Jeshurun."
‡ All these are in "Congregational Church Music," 1871.

GREATHEED, Rev. SAMUEL STEPHENSON, M.A.   B. 1813 ; D. 1887.
Rector of Corringham, Essex, 1862.

1. Blessed art Thou	*Hereford*		6. O Lord Almighty, God	*Novello*
2. Blessed is the man	*Norwich*		7. O Saviour of the world	,,
3. Hail, gladdening Light	*Novello*		8. The harvest truly is great	*Fowle*
4. Let my soul bless God	,,		9. The Son of Man	*Novello*
5. O God, Thou art worthy	,,		10. Ye that fear the Lord	,,

GREATOREX, Rev. EDWARD.   B. *c.* 1820 ; D. 1899.
Minor Canon of Durham, 1849; Precentor, 1862-72; Rector of Croxdale, 1872, retaining his minor canonry.

1. O Saviour of the world   *Novello* |

GREENWOOD, JAMES.   B. 1837 ; D. 1894.
Author of Lancashire " Sol-fa " system ; Voice-trainer and Composer.

1. Lord, we pray Thee   *Novello* |

HACKETT, CHARLES DANVERS.   Mus. B., Oxon.   B. 1812 ; D. 1858.
Org. Rotherham Parish Church.

1. I will arise	*Nat. Psal.*		3. The Lord is my strength	*Joule*
2. Sing we merrily	*Joule*		4. The Lord shall comfort Zion	,,

HAKING, Rev. RICHARD (RANULF ?), Mus. Doc. Oxon., 1864.   B. 1830 ; D. 1896.
Rector of Easton Grey, Malmesbury, 1873 ; Congham, Norfolk, 1882.

1. Doth not wisdom cry ? | 2. Lord, let me know mine end.

HALL, CHARLES KING.   B. 1845 ; D. 1895.
Composer and Musical Reader to Messrs. Chappell ; Org. Brondesbury Church.

1. And the angel said unto her	*Novello*		4. O Lord, my trust	*Novello*
2. Hear me when I call	,,		5. To Thee do I lift up my soul	,,
3. Lord, who shall abide ?	,,			

HARRIS, JOSEPH THORNE.   B. 1828 ; D. 1869.
Son of J. J. Harris ; Org. in Edinburgh.

1. Blessed be the Lord God   *Joule* | 2. By the waters of Babylon   *Joule*

HATTON, JOHN LIPTROT.   B. 1809 ; D. 1886.
Chiefly self-taught ; Pianist at Drury Lane and Director of Music to the eminent actor Charles Kean.

1. All the ends of the world	*Metzler*		8. Hosanna to the son of	
2. And at that time	,,		David	*Metzler*
3. Blessed be the Lord God	*Novello*		9. In the beginning	,,
4. Blessed be the Lord my strength	,,		10. In the days of Herod	,,
5. Blessed is He that cometh	*Metzler*		11. I will extol Thee	*Novello*
6. Come, Holy Ghost	*Mann*		12. I will praise Thee	,,
7. Come unto Me	*Curwen*		13. Know, therefore, that the Lord	*Curwen*

HATTON, JOHN LIPTROT (*continued*).

14. Let us now go even   *Metzler*
15. Like as a Father   *Boosey*
16. Now when Jesus was born   *Metzler*
17. Out of the deep   *Novello*
18. Pastor holy   *Metzler*
19. The Lord preserveth His
     saints   *Boosey*
20. The Lord preserveth the
     souls   *Novello*

21. The Lord waked as one out
     of sleep.
22. The morning stars   *Augener*
23. There was a man sent from
     God   *Metzler*
24. Thou art gone up   *Novello*
25. Thou art my God   *Metzler*
26. While the bridegroom
     tarried   ,,

HAVERGAL, Rev. HENRY EAST, M.A. B. 1820 (? 1821) ; D. 1875.
Son of Rev. W. H. Havergal. Org. and Rector of Cople, Beds.

1. Hosanna to the Son of
     David   *Novello* |

HAWES, Rev. THOMAS HENRY, B.D. B. 1806 ; D. 1888.
Chaplain of New Coll., Oxon.; successively Minor Canon of Wells and
Vicar of Burgh Castle, Suffolk.

1. Blessed are the people   *Marshall*
2. How doth the city sit   *Parker*

3. Remember, O Lord, what is
     come   *Parker*

HAYCRAFT, H. J., A.R.A.M.
1. Blessed be the Lord *Haycraft*, 1837 | 2. The sorrows of death *Haycraft*, 1851

HAYNE, Rev. LEIGHTON GEORGE, Mus. Doc., Oxon. B. 1836 ; D. 1882.
Precentor of Eton College.

1. Haste Thee, O God. | 2. Ponder my words   *Novello*

HAYNES, WALTER BATTISON. B. 1859 ; D. 1900.
Studied at Leipzig; Org. St. Philip's, Sydenham, 1884, and Chapel Royal,
Savoy, 1891-1900.

1. Awake up, my glory. | 2. Lo! God, our God.

HAYTER, AARON UPJOHN. B. 1799 ; D. 1873 (in America).
Org. Hereford Cath., 1818-20, and Collegiate Church, Brecon, 1820. Went to
America, 1835.

1. Withdraw not Thou   *Marshall* |

HEAP, CHARLES SWINNERTON, Mus.D., Cantab., 1872. B. 1847 ;
D. 1900.
Studied in Leipzig ; Conductor of several Musical Festivals in the Midlands.

1. Blessed be the Lord God   *Novello*
2. I cried unto the Lord   ,,
3. If ye love Me   ,,

4. I will not be afraid   *Lichfield*
5. The earth is the Lord's   *Novello*
6. While the earth remaineth   ,,

HELMORE, Rev. THOMAS, M.A. B. 1811 ; D. 1890.
Master of Choristers, Chapel Royal ; Precentor of St. Mark's College, Chelsea.

1. Jesus said, " Let the
     little children "   *Chap. Roy.* |

HEMPEL, CHARLES FREDERICK, Mus. Doc., Oxon.   B. 1811; D. 1867.
Son of C. W. Hempel.   Org. of Truro Parish Church.

1. Almighty and everlasting God	3. Awake ! put on thy strength *Joule*
Joule	4. Let God arise ,,
(*Collect for 2nd after Epiphany.*)	5. The Lord is King ,,
2. Almighty and everlasting God	
Joule	
(*Collect for Ash Wednesday.*)	

HERBERT, EDWARD, Mus. Bac., Oxon.   B. 1830 ; D. 1872.
Org. in Perth, N.B., Sherborne Abbey, and Wimborne Minster.

1. I saw also the Lord *Novello*	3. Thou art gone up *Novello*
2. Now it is high time to awake	
Salisbury	

HEWITT, JOHN.   D. 1848.
Org. St. Michael's, Lichfield.
1. O praise the Lord of Heaven *Joule*

HEWLETT, THOMAS, Mus. Bac., Oxon.   B. 1845 ; D. 1874.
Organist and Composer in Dalkeith and Edinburgh.
1. I am the Resurrection   *Fowle* |

HILES, JOHN.   B. 1810 ; D. 1882.
Org. in Shrewsbury, Portsmouth, Brighton, and London.
1. Therefore with angels   *Novello* |

HIRD, FREDERICK WILLIAM.   B. 1826 ; D. 1887.

1. Behold, O God our Defender	4. Bread of Heaven, on Thee *Lichfield*
Novello	5. Let your light so shine ,,
2. Be not Thou far *Lichfield*	6. O ye priests of the Lord ,,
3. Blessed be the man ,,	7. Whoso hath this world's goods ,,

HOOPER, Rev. W. Nixon.
Precentor of Winchester, 1848.
1. Teach me, O Lord
  Binfield's Choral Service, 1849 |

HOPKINS, EDWARD JOHN.   Mus. Doc., Cantuar, 1882.   B. 1818 ;
D. 1901.
Brother of J. and cousin of J. L. Hopkins ; Pupil of T. F. Walmisley ;
Chorister in Chapel Royal ; Org. Mitcham Parish Church, 1834 ; St. Peter's,
Islington, 1838 ; St. Luke's, Berwick Street, 1841 ; Temple Church, 1843-98.

1. Acquaint thyself with God *Curwen*	11. I will wash my hands *Novello*
2. Arise, shine *Weekes*	12. Let us now go ,,
3. Blessed are the poor in spirit ,,	13. O praise the Lord, all ye nations
4. Bless the Lord, O my soul ,,	*Hopkins*
5. For God is the King *Novello*	14. O sing unto the Lord *Mann*
6. God is gone up *Husk*	15. Out of the deep *Husk*
(*Gresham Prize*, 1860).	(*Gresham Prize*, 1838).
7. God, Who commanded the light	16. The King shall rejoice *Novello*
Novello	17. The Lord is my portion *Mann*
8. He was despised *Weekes*	18. Thou shalt cause the trumpet
9. In my distress I cried *Novello*	*Weekes*
10. I will give thanks ,,	19. Thy mercy, O Lord *Novello*
(*London Church Choir Association*,	20. Try me, O God ,,
1875.)	21. Why seek ye the living ,,

HOPKINS, JOHN LARKIN, Mus. Doc., Cantab.   B. 1820 ; D. 1873.
Pupil of Turle at the Abbey.   He succeeded Ralph Banks as Organist of
Rochester Cath., 1841, and T. A. Walmisley, at Trinity College,
Cambridge, 1856.

1. Be merciful	*Rochester*	15.*O sing unto the Lord with thanks-	
2. Blessed is he that con-		giving.	
sidereth	*Joule*	16.*Ponder my words, O Lord.	
3. Bow down Thine ear	*Rochester*	17.*Rejoice in the Lord, O ye.	
4. Hear my cry, O God	*Rochester*	18.*Save me, O God.	
5. Hear the voice and		19. The eyes of the Lord	*Rochester*
prayer	*Novello*	20. The fostering earth	*Novello*
6.*I heard a voice.		21. The Lord hear thee	
7. I was glad.	*Rochester*	22. The Lord is my Light	*Rochester*
8.*Let Thy merciful ears.		23.*The Lord shall comfort Zion.	
9. Lift up your heads	*Novello*	24.*Turn Thee unto me.	
10.*My God, my God.		25. We give Thee thanks	*Lichfield*
11. O clap your hands	*Lichfield*	26. When Jesus was born	*Novello*
12. O Lord, grant the King	*Carlisle*	27. With angels and arch-	
13.*O Lord, we beseech Thee.		angels	,,
14. O sing unto the Lord a			
new	*Novello*		

HOPKINS, JOHN.   B. 1822 ; D. 1900.
Chorister of St. Paul's ; Org. Mitcham Parish Church, 1838; St. Stephen's,
Islington, 1839; Holy Trinity, Islington, 1843; St. Mark's, Jersey, 1845 ;
St. Michael's, Chester Square, 1846; Parish Church, Epsom, until 1856;
Rochester Cath., 1856, until his death.

1. The earth is the Lord's	*Joule*	2. The Lord is full of compassion
		Novello

HORAN, GEORGE FREDERICK.   B. 1858 ; D. 1898.
Org. of St. Thomas', Dublin, 1876; of St. Mary's, Dublin, 1877 ; again of
St. Thomas', 1881; of Rathmines Parish Church, 1886-95.

1. A King shall reign and prosper	4. Hallelujah! Christ is risen *Pigott*
Pigott (Dublin).	5.†Remember now thy Creator ,,
2. Awake up, my glory	6. Surely the Lord is in this place
Bristol Anthem Book	*Pigott*
3. God said, Behold, I have given	7. Thou shalt bless the Lord
you *Pigott*	*Bristol Anthem Book*

HORSLEY, CHARLES EDWARD.   B. 1821 ; D. 1876 (in New York).
Org. St. John's, Notting Hill.   Visited Australia, 1868.   Settled in U.S.A.

1. I was glad *Novello*	2. The sacrifices of God.
(*Consecration of Fairfield Church,*	*Hullah's Singer's Library.*
Liverpool.)	3. Thou art my portion. *Tenbury*

HOUGHTON, WILLIAM.   B. 1844 ; D. 1871.
Deputy Org. Christ Church Cath., Dublin, and St. Ann's, Dublin.

1. Lord, we pray Thee (Collect)
Dublin

---

* These published in a collection of " Ten Anthems " (Surman).
† Feis Ceoil Prize Anthem, awarded by Sir Walter Parratt in 1898, after the
composer's death.

HOWELL, FRANCIS. B. 1834 ; D. 1882.
Son of James Howell, the double-bass player. Composed two Oratorios.
Organist of Penkridge, Staffs.

1. By the Word of the Lord *Novello*
2. He maketh the storm to
   cease *Fowle*

3. Many there are that trouble me
   Novello
4. We have heard with our
   ears „

HUDSON, CHARLES M. D. 1896.
1. I will extol Thee.

HULLAH, JOHN PYKE, LL.D., Edin. B. 1812 ; D. 1884.
Org. of Charterhouse ; Musical Inspector of Training Schools, 1872-83 ;
Lecturer, &c., on Wilhelm's vocal method.

1. I will magnify Thee *Lichfield*
2. O most merciful God *Novello*

3. The day is past *Novello*

INGHAM, RICHARD. B. 1804 ; D. 1841.
Org. St. Mary's, Gateshead, and Carlisle Cath., 1833-41.
1. O clap your hands together *Joule*

INGRAM, THOMAS.
Some time Secretary of the Motett Society ; Org. of All Souls', Langham Place.
1. Rend your heart *Winchester*
Numerous *adaptations* from works of the old Italian masters.

IONS, THOMAS, Mus. Doc., Oxon. B. 1817 ; D. 1857.
Org. St. Nicholas' Church, Newcastle-on-Tyne. Editor of "Cantica
Ecclesiastica."
1. By the waters of Babylon *Novello*

ISHERWOOD, JAMES WRIGHT. B. 1812 ; D. 1854.
Organist of St. Anne's, Manchester.

1. As the hart desireth *Joule*
2. How long wilt Thou forget? „

3. The Lord is my Shepherd *Joule*
4. Wherewithal? „

JACKSON, THOMAS. B. 1806 ; D. 1868.

1. In Thee, O Lord *Novello*
2. O clap your hands „
3. O God, Thou art my God „

4. O praise the Lord, all ye heathen
   Novello

JACKSON, WILLIAM (of Masham). B. 1816 ; D. 1866.
Org. and Tallow Chandler at Masham ; Org. St. John's Church and Horton
Chapel, Bradford.

1. Awake, awake, put on *Joule*
2. Blessed be the Lord God *Novello*
3. Blessed is he that considereth „
4. Christ our Passover „
5. *Come and let us return „
6. For joy let fertile valleys.
7. *Hear, O Thou Shepherd *Durham*
8. *Holy, Holy, Holy *Chester*
9. Not unto us *Novello*
10. *O Lord, Thou hast been *Durham*
11. O come hither and behold *Novello*
12. O Lord, there is none like „

13. O Zion, that bringest
    good tidings *Novello*
14. *Praise the Lord, all ye
    people *Exeter*
15. Praise the Lord, O my
    soul (*Psalm* 103.) *Novello*
16. †Praise ye the Lord „
17. Sing, O heavens „
18. †The Lord hear thee „
19. †We have heard with our
    ears „

---

* Attributed by Dr. Mann to W. Jackson, of Exeter.
† For men's voices.

JACKSON, WILLIAM, Junr. B. 1853 ; D. 1877.
Org. Morningside Parish Church, Edinburgh.
1. O give thanks   *Nov. Cat.* |

JONES, JOHN JEREMIAH, Mus. Bac., Oxon.   B. — ; D. 1856.
Org. St. Paul's Church, Manchester.
1. When the wicked man   *Joule* |

JONES, THOMAS EVANCE. B. 1805 ; D. 1873.
Pupil of Skeats; Org. Canterbury Cath., 1831-72.
1. Arise, O Lord, into Thy   2. Blessed is he that con-
    resting-place   *Joule*   sidereth   *Joule*
                                   3. Unto Him that loved us   *Metzler*

JOULE, BENJAMIN ST. JOHN BAPTIST. B. 1817 ; D. 1895.
Hon. Org. St. Peter's, Manchester. Collector of Words of 2,270 Anthems.
1. The Lord is my Shepherd   *Joule*   3. Vital spark   *Joule*
2. They that wait upon the
    Lord   ,,

KERBUSCH, LEO, Mus. Doc., Dublin.   B. 1828 ; D.—.
Pupil of Spohr. Writer and Composer.
1. Rise up, my love   *Novello* |

KEY, JOSEPH.
Composer, of Nuneaton, Warwickshire, in early part of the century.

1. Almighty God unto Whom.	17. Lord, let me know.
2.*Arise, shine.	18. Man that is born.
3. Behold, how good and joyful.	19.*Not unto us.
4.*Blessed are all they that fear.	20.*O clap your hands.
5. Blessed Lord, Who hast caused.	21. O God the Author of peace.
6.*Blow ye the trumpet.	22.*O God the King of glory.
7. Christ our Passover.	23. O God Who hast prepared.
8.*Come unto Me, all ye.	24.*O how amiable.
9. God be merciful.	25. O Lord, Thou hast searched me.
10. I am the Resurrection.	26. O praise the Lord of Heaven.
11. I heard a great voice.	27.*The King shall rejoice.
12. I was glad when they said.	28. The Lord hath prepared.
13. I will sing unto the Lord.	29. The Lord is my Shepherd.
14.*Let God arise.	30. The Lord is risen indeed.
15.*Let not your heart.	31. There were shepherds.
16. Lift up your heads.	32. We will go into the House.

All published by Thompson, 75, St. Paul's Churchyard.
The Eleven marked with a * have Symphonies and Thorough Basses for two
hautboys and a bassoon, particularly designed for Parochial Choirs.

KILNER, THOMAS. B. 18— ; D. 1876.
Author of Books on Psalmody, &c., published about 1850. Org. of Christ
    Church, Highbury, 1848-68.
1. My voice shalt Thou hear   *Fowle* |

LAKE, GEORGE ERNEST. B. 1854 ; D. 1893.
Org. St. John's (Episcopal), Edinburgh, and, subsequently, All Saints', Kensington Park, and Weybridge.
1. O Lamb of God   *Novello* |

LAVINGTON, CHARLES WILLIAMS. B. 1819 ; D. 1895.
Pupil of Perkins and Turle; Org. Wells Cath., 1860-95.
1. Fear thou not   *Wells* | 3. O Almighty God   *Wells*
2. How excellent   ,, |

LEFFLER, ADAM. B. 1808 ; D. 1857.
Chorister in Westminster Abbey.
1. Try me, O God   *King's* |

LE JEUNE, G. F.
1. To God, our never failing |
   strength   *Novello* |

LESLIE, HENRY DAVID. B. 1822 ; D. 1896.
Pupil of Lucas. Founder and Conductor, 1855-80, of Leslie's Choir, which gained the prize at the Paris Exhibition, 1878.
1. Blow ye the trumpet   *Novello* | 5. Let God arise   *Husk*
2. Fear not, we bring you   ,, | 6. O have mercy upon me   *Novello*
3. Great is the Lord   ,, | 7. Sing unto the Lord   *Salisbury*
4. I will extol Thee, O God   ,, | 8. Take heed, watch and pray
                                                 Norwich
And selections from his "Immanuel."

LIMPUS, Rev. HENRY F. B. — ; D. 1893.
Minor Canon of St. George's, Windsor ; Vicar of Twickenham.
1. Bring unto the Lord   *Novello* | 2. The Lord is my Shepherd *Novello*
And selections from his " Prodigal Son."

LIVINGSTONE, JAMES R.
Author of the " Organ Defended." Resided in Glasgow from 1844.
1. Turn ye even unto Me |

LOCKETT, WILLIAM H. B. 1835 ; D. 1893.
Org. in Manchester churches, 1855-77, and Deputy-Assistant-Org. Manchester Cath.
1. Praised be the Lord | 2. Watch and pray   *Novello*
   (*Psalm* 68)   *Novello* |

LOHR, FREDERICK N. B. 1844 ; D. 1888.
Org. at Plymouth.
1. The Lord is my Shepherd *Novello* |

LOMAS, GEORGE, Mus. Bac., Oxon. B. 1834 ; D. 1884.
1. Praised be the Lord daily *Novello* | 2. Whoso dwelleth   *Novello*

FREDERICK ARTHUR GORE OUSELEY.

LOWE, ALBERT. B. — ; D. 1886.

1. Hosanna   *Novello*   3. The Lord is my Strength   *Novello*
2. The earth is the Lord's   ,,

LUCAS, CHARLES. B. 1808 ; D. 1869.

Pupil of A. T. Corfe; Studied R.A.M.; Violoncello in the Opera and in Queen Adelaide's Private Band; Principal R.A.M., 1859, after C. Potter; Org. Hanover Chapel, 1839.

1. Blessed be the Lord   *Addison*   5. O God, the Strength
2. Blessed is He   ,,   *Hullah's " Singer's Library "*
3. Bow down Thine ear   6. O Lord, open Thou   *Addison*
    Haycraft's " Sacred Music "   7. O Thou that dwellest   *Salisbury*
4. Hosanna!   *Addison*   8. Sing, O heavens   *Addison*

MACFARREN, Sir GEORGE ALEXANDER, Knight, Mus. Doc., Cantab. B. 1813 ; D. 1887.

Studied under his father, George Macfarren, and C. Lucas and Cipriani Potter at R.A.M.; Professor, 1834; Professor of Music, Cambridge University, 1875; Principal R.A.M., 1876.

1. A day in Thy Courts *Novello*	28. Hosanna to the Son of David.	
2. As Christ was raised ,,	29. If we believe.	
3. As He which hath called	30. I know whom I have believed.	
you ,,	31. In Christ ye are circumcised.	
4. Behold! the Tabernacle ,,	32. I was exalted.	
(*2-part.*)	33. I will look unto the Lord.	
5. Behold, to obey is better ,,	(*2-part.*)	
6. Be strong.	34. I will love Thee.	
7. Be thou faithful *Novello*	35. Keep innocency.	
8. Blessed are the dead.	36. Let the brother.	
9. Blessed are the poor in spirit.	37. Let us not be weary.	
10. Blessed are the pure.	38. Lord! when saw we Thee?	
11. Blessed are they.	*Curwen*	
12. Blessed be the name *Novello*	39. Love your enemies.	
(*2-part.*)	40. Not unto us.	
13. Blessed is the man ,,	41. Now, saith the Lord.	
14. Blessed is the soul ,,	42. O Holy Ghost *Novello*	
(*2-part.*)	43. O how amiable ,,	
15. Blest are the departed *Winchester*	44. O Lord, how manifold ,,	
16. Christ our passover *Novello*	45. O magnify the Lord ,,	
17. Come, and let us return ,,	46. One thing have I desired ,,	
(*2-part.*)	47. O praise the Lord ,,	
18. Come ye and let us go up ,,	48. O Saviour of the world ,,	
(*2-part.*)	49. O send out Thy light ,,	
19. Drop down, ye heavens.	50. O sing unto the Lord ,,	
20. For unto us was born.	51. O taste and see ,,	
21. God said, " Behold, I have."	52. Our Lord Jesus Christ ,,	
22. Great and marvellous *Curwen*	53. O worship the Lord ,,	
23. Have mercy upon me *Novello*	54. Praised be the Lord *Curwen*	
24. Hear me when I call *Metzler*	55. Rejoice with them that do	
25. He cometh forth *Novello*	*Novello*	
26. Holy, Holy, Holy.	56. Remember me, O Lord ,,	
27. Hosanna! blessed is He.	57. Remember, O Lord *Curwen*	

MACFARREN, Sir GEORGE ALEXANDER (*continued*).

58. Sing unto the Lord, O ye saints	*Novello*	71. This day is born	*Metzler*
59. The law of the Lord is perfect	*Curwen*	72. This is the day	*Novello*
60. The Lord hath been mindful	*Novello*	73. Unto us was born (2-*part*.)	,,
61. The Lord is King	*Metzler*	74. We are no more strangers	,,
62. The Lord is my Light	*Novello*	75. We give Thee thanks	,,
63. The Lord is my Shepherd	,,	76. We have heard with our ears.	
64. The Lord redeemeth	,,	77. We wait for Thy loving-kindness	*Novello*
65. The Lord reigneth	,,	78. What shall it profit	,,
66. These were redeemed	,,	79. Wherewithal shall a young man?	,,
67. The souls of the righteous	,,	80. While all things	,,
68. The Spirit of the Lord	,,	81. Why stand ye gazing	,,
69. They that put their trust	,,	82. Work your work betimes	,,
70. They that wait	,,	83. Ye men of Galilee	,,

Also selections from his " King David," " St. John Baptist," &c.

MANN, RICHARD. B. 1837 ; D. 1869.
Member of the choir at St. Michael's Coll., Tenbury, and subsequently Org. at Cirencester. Author of a Manual of Singing, London, 1866.

1. Grant, we beseech Thee *Novello* |

MARTIN, GEORGE WILLIAM. B. 1827 ; D. 1881.
Chorister of St. Paul's under Hawes. Conductor of the National Choral Society, &c. Editor of musical journals and composer of prize glees, &c.

1. Forsake me not	*Novello*	3. O sing unto God.	
2. O Israel, trust thou in the Lord	*Joule*	4. Teach me, O Lord.	

MAURICE, Rev. PETER, D.D. B. 1804 ; D. 1878.
Vicar of Yarnton, Woodstock, and Chaplain, New College, Oxon. Writer on Music.

1. With Angels and Archangels *The Sacred Melodist*, 1836 |

MILLER, WILLIAM F. B. — ; D. 1863.

1. O Lord, rebuke me not. | 2. O pray for the peace.

MONK, EDWIN GEORGE, Mus. Doc., Oxon., F.R.A.S. B. 1819 ; D. 1900.
Org. York Minster, 1859-83.

1. Blessed are all they (*Holy Matrimony*.)	*Novello*	3. Great and marvellous	*Novello*
2. God so loved the world	,,	4. My God truly waiteth	,,
		5. The pains of hell	,,

MONK, JAMES J. B. 1846; D. 1890.
Musical critic in Liverpool.

1. And very early in the morning	*Mann*	2. Let your light	*Metzler*
		3. O be joyful in God	*Mann*

MONK, WILLIAM HENRY. B. 1823; D. 1889.
Pupil of T. Adams, J. A. Hamilton, and G. A. Griesbach. Org. Eaton Chapel,
Pimlico; St. George's Chapel, Albemarle Street; Portman Chapel; Org.
(1849) and Professor of Vocal Music, King's College, 1874; Org. St.
Mathias, Stoke Newington, 1852. Musical Editor of " Hymns Ancient and
Modern," &c.

1. And the Angel Gabriel	*Novello*	6. Like as the hart	*Novello*
2. Blessed are they that		7. Now upon the first day	,,
alway keep judgment	,,	8. O Lamb of God	,,
3. Hallelujah ! for unto us a		9. The earth is the Lord's	*Morley*
Child	,,	10. The Lord is my strength	*Novello*
4. If ye love Me, keep	,,	11. They shall come and sing	,,
5. In God's Word will I re-			
joice	,,		

MORGAN, GEORGE WASHBOURNE. B. 1823 ; D. 1892 (at Tacoma,
Washington, U.S.A.).
Org. Christ Church and St. James's, Gloucester; South Hackney; and St.
Olave's, Southwark, &c. After this he settled in U.S.A., 1853, where he was
Org. St. Thomas's Episcopal Church, New York, Grace Church, St.
Anne's, and Brooklyn Tabernacle.

1. Ponder my words	*Joule*	2. There were shepherds	*Joule*

MUDIE, THOMAS MOLLESON. B. 1809; D. 1876.
Pupil of Crotch, Potter, &c., at the R.A.M., 1823-32. Pianoforte Professor
at the R.A.M. 1832-44; Org. of Gatton, Surrey, 1834-44. Taught in
Edinburgh for a time and returned to London, 1863.

1. Blessed be Thy Name for ever. |

MULLEN, JOSEPH. B. 1826; D. 1896.
Org. of Tuam Cath.; Org. and Succentor of Limerick Cath.; Org. St.
Mary's Church, St. Catherine's Church, and Christ Church, Leeson Park,
Dublin.

1. O give thanks unto the Lord |
   (*Psalm* 118) *Dublin* |

MUNDELLA, MISS EMMA. B. 1858; D. 1896.
Director of Music at Wimbledon High School.

1. Blessed be the Lord God	*Weekes*	3. Thro' wisdom is an house builded.
2. Our God is Lord of the		(*2-part.*)
harvest	*Novello*	

NAYLOR, JOHN, MUS. DOC., OXON. B. 1838; D. 1897.
Pupil of R. S. Burton (Leeds). Org. Parish Church, Scarborough, 1856
All Saints' Church, Scarborough, 1873; Org. York Minster, 1883.

1. Christ our Passover	*Novello*	5. O praise the Lord with me	*Novello*
2. If ye then be risen	,,	6. Out of the deep	,,
3. My soul truly waiteth	,,	7. O ye that love the Lord	,,
4. O Almighty God	*Joule*	8. Sing, O daughter of Zion	,,
(*St. Peter's Day.*)			

NAYLOR, SYDNEY. B. 1841 ; D. 1893.

Pianist, Conductor, and Composer. Temple Choir boy under Dr. Hopkins; Org. St. George's, Bloomsbury; St. Michael's, Bassishaw ; St. Mary's, Newington. Well known as an accompanist.

1. Blessed are all they that fear   *Novello*

OBERTHUR, CHARLES. B. 1819 ; D. 1895.

Pupil of G. V. Röder. Harpist at Zurich Theatre, Weisbaden Court Theatre and Mannheim. Settled in London, 1844. Harpist to Italian Theatre London. Teacher and Composer.

1. Give ear, O Lord   *Novello* |

OSBORNE, GEORGE ALEXANDER. B. 1806 ; D. 1893.

Irish Pianist and Composer. Pupil of Fetis and Kalkbrenner in Paris. Settled in London, 1843.

1. Hail! thou that art highly favoured | 2. The Lord is my Shepherd
(The Lord is with thee) *Novello* | *Chappel*

OUSELEY, Rev. Sir FREDERICK ARTHUR GORE (Bart.), M.A., LL.D., Mus. Doc., &c. B. 1825 ; D. 1889.

Educated at Christ Church, Oxford. Curate of St. Paul's, Knightsbridge, and St. Barnabas, Pimlico, 1849-51. Founder and first Warden of St. Michael's College, Tenbury, 1856 ; Professor of Music, Oxford, 1855 ; Precentor, 1855, and Canon, 1886, of Hereford.

1. All the Kings of the earth *Novello*
2. And there was a pure river ,,
3. Ascribe ye greatness ,,
4. Awake, thou that sleepest ,,
5. Behold how good and joyful ,,
6. Behold now, praise the Lord ,,
(*Double Choir and extra Chorus.*)
7. Be merciful unto me ,,
8. Blessed be the Lord God of Israel ,,
9. Blessed be Thou, Lord God ,,
(*Double Choir, re-opening Hereford Cath., 1863.*)
10. Blessed is he whose ,,
11. Blessed is the man that feareth ,,
12. Christ is risen ,,
13. Drop down, ye heavens *Chester*
14. Except the Lord build *Novello*
15. Fear not, I am thy shield *Carlisle*
16. Forsake me not   *Tenbury MSS.*
17. From the rising of the sun *Novello*
18. Give thanks, O Israel ,,
19. Great is the Lord ,,
20. Happy is the man ,,
21. Haste Thee, O God ,,
22. Hear my cry, O God ,,
23. Hear my voice, O Lord *Chichester*

24. Hear, O Lord, and have mercy   *Novello*
25. Help us, O God of our salvation ,,
26. His seed shall endure for ever   *Carlisle*
27. How goodly are thy tents *Novello*
(*On seeing Milan Cath. by moonlight.*)
28. How long wilt Thou forget? ,,
29. I know that the Lord is great ,,
30. In God's word ,,
31. In Jewry is God known   *Lithographed*
32. In the sight of the unwise
33. I saw the souls *Novello*
34. Is it nothing to you? ,,
35. It came even to pass ,,
36. I waited patiently ,,
37. I will give thanks ,,
38. I will love Thee ,,
39. I will magnify Thee ,,
40. Judge me, O God ,,
41. Let all the world *Lithographed*
42. Let Thy priests be clothed   *Salisbury*
43. Like as the hart   *Novello*
44. Lord, be merciful   *Morley*

OUSELEY, Rev. Sir FREDERICK ARTHUR GORE (*continued*).

45. Lord, I call upon Thee	*Novello*	67. Rend your heart (G	
46. Love not the world	,,	minor)	*Tenbury MSS.*
47. My song shall be alway	,,	68. Righteous art Thou, O	
48. Now, therefore, ye are no		Lord	*Novello*
more strangers	*Norwich*	69. Save me, O God	,,
49. O Almighty and most		70. Sing, O daughter of Zion	,,
merciful	*Novello*	71. Sing unto the Lord, all	,,
50. O God, wherefore art Thou	,,	72. The Lord is King	,,
51. O how plentiful	,,	73. The Lord is my Shepherd	,,
52. O Lord, Thou art my God	,,	74. The Lord shall roar out	
53. O Lord, we beseech Thee	,,	of Zion	,,
54. O love the Lord	,,	75. There was war in heaven	*Fowle*
55. One thing have I desired		76. The salvation of the	
	Lithographed	righteous	*Novello*
56. O praise our God, ye people	*Novello*	77. They that wait	,,
57. O praise the Lord, all ye		78. Thou art my Portion	,,
heathen	,,	79. Thus saith the Lord	,,
58. O praise the Lord with me	,,	80. Thy mercy, O Lord	,,
59. O Saviour of the world	,,	81. To the Lord our God	,,
60.*O send out Thy light.		82. Trust ye in the Lord	*Carlisle*
61. O sing unto God, and sing		83. Unto Thee, O Lord	*Novello*
praises	*Novello*	84. Unto Thee will I cry	,,
62.*O ye that love the Lord.		85. Walk before Me	*Carlisle*
63. Plead Thou my cause	*Metzler*	86. Whom have I in heaven?	*Novello*
64. Praise the Lord, O my soul	*York*	87. Who shall ascend?	,,
65. Rejoice with Jerusalem	*Lichfield*	88. Why standest Thou?	,,
66. Rend your heart (A minor)	*Novello*		

Some numbers from his oratorios " St. Polycarp " and " Hagar " are used as Anthems.

PALMER, JOHN. B. 1804 ; D. 1863.

Org. at Godalming, Surrey.

1. Lord, what is man? |

PARSONS, CHARLES.

Sometime chorister in Wells Cathedral.

1. Blessed is the man	*Bumpus*	5. Hear my prayer	*Wells*
2. Grant to us, Lord	,,	6. I will give thanks	,,
3. Great and marvellous	,,	7. O love the Lord	*Bumpus*
4. Hearken unto my voice	,,	8. Remove far from me	*Wells*

PATTEN, WILLIAM. B. 1803 ; D. 1863.

Organist of St. Cross, Winchester.

1. Awake up, my glory	*Addison*	6. The Lord is in His Holy	
2. Blessed is the man	*Novello*	temple	*Addison*
3. O sing unto the Lord	*Addison*	7. The Lord is my Shepherd	,,
4 .Praise the Lord	,,	8. Thou shalt open my lips	,,
5. Sing unto God	,,		

PEARSON, GEORGE.

1. Bear ye one another's burdens *Fowle* |

---

* In MS., the property of the Rev. John Hampton, at Tenbury

PITTMAN, JOSIAH. B. 1816 ; D. 1886.

Pupil of S. S. Wesley, Moscheles, and Schnyder von Wartensee. Org. at Sydenham, 1831 ; Spitalfields, 1835-47 ; Lincoln's Inn, 1852-64 ; H.M. Theatre, 1865-8 ; Covent Garden, 1868-80.

1. The Lord is King   *Novello* |

POLE, WILLIAM, Mus. Doc., Oxon., F.R.S., C.E. B. 1814 ; D. 1901.

Examiner for Musical Degrees in London University.

1. All people that on earth   *Novello* |

PRENTICE, THOMAS RIDLEY. B. 1842 ; D. 1895.

Student, Medalist, and Associate R.A.M. Org. Christ Church, Lee ; Pianoforte Professor Guildhall School of Music, 1880.

1. Break forth into joy   *Novello* | 3. I love the Lord   *Novello*
2. Hear our prayer   ,, | 4. Thou shalt guide me   *Metzler*

PYNE, JAMES KENDRICK. B. 1810 ; D. 1893.

Org. of Bath Abbey. Son of the celebrated tenor who for a long time sang at the Foundling Hospital. Father of the Organist of Manchester Cathedral.

1. Proclaim ye this   *Milsom (Bath)* |
   (*Gresham Prize*, 1839.)

RICHARDSON, JOHN. B. 1816 ; D. 1879.

Org. St. Mary's Catholic Ch., Liverpool, 1835 ; St. Nicholas Ch., Liverpool, 1837-57.

1. The Lord reigneth   *King's* |

RICHARDSON, THOMAS BENTICK. B. 1831 ; D. 1893.

Chorister, and Assistant-Org. Salisbury Cath., and Org. Bury St. Edmunds for thirty years.

1. Thou, O God, art praised   *Mann* |

RIMBAULT, EDWARD FRANCIS, LL.D. (of Göttingen), F.S.A. B. 1816 ; D. 1875.

Pupil of S. Wesley and Crotch. Org. of the Swiss Church, Soho, Curzon Chapel, and St. Peter's, Vere Street, 1866-71 ; Founder of Musical Antiquarian Society and Editor of the earlier Anthems.

1. In God the Lord   *Novello* | 3. The Lord is righteous   *Metzler*
2. O Lord, Thou art my God   ,, |

ROBINSON, JOSEPH. B. 1815 ; D. 1898.

Established Antient Society, 1834 ; Professor of Irish Academy of Music, 1856 ; Vicar-Choral of St. Patrick's Cath.

1. Bow down Thine ear *Dublin*, 1881 | 3. I am well pleased   *Dublin*
2. Glory to God on high   ,, | (*With Sir John Stevenson.*)
                                      | 4. Not unto us, O Lord   *Novello*

ROCKSTRO, WILLIAM SMYTH.   B. 1823 ; D. 1895.
Pupil of Mendelssohn.   Precentor of All Saints', Babbacombe, Devon.
Eminent Author and Antiquary.
1. O Lord, rebuke me not *Salisbury* | 2. Woe unto us   *Salisbury*

ROWDEN, Rev. GEORGE CROKE.   B. 1820 ; D. 1863.
Precentor of Chichester Cath.   Chaplain to the Royal Society of Musicians.
1. Come unto Me   *Chichester*, 1868 |

SANGSTER, WALTER HAY, MUS. DOC., OXON.   B. 1837 ; D. 1899.
Org. Christ Church, Ealing ; Embassy Chapel in Berlin ; St. Michael's,
Chester Square ; All Saints', St. John's Wood ; St. James's, Weybridge ;
St. Michael's, Paddington ; and (since 1879) St. Saviour's, Eastbourne.

1. Blessed is the man	*Weekes*	4 O praise the Lord	*Novello*
2. Except the Lord build	,,	5. Suffer little children	*Fowle*
(2-*part.*)		6. There were shepherds	*Novello*
3. Lo ! star-led chiefs	,,		

SCARISBRICK, THOMAS.   B. 1805 ; D. 1869.
Org. Kendal Parish Church.

1. O Lord my God	*Bumpus*	4. Sing and rejoice	*Curwen*
2.*Praise our God, all ye His		5. Tell ye the daughter	*Bumpus*
servants	,,		
3. Praise our God, all ye people	,,		

SEYMOUR, CHARLES A.   B. 1810 ; D. 1875.
Violinist and Leader at the Gentlemen's Concerts, Manchester, 1845-75.
1. Fret not thyself   *Joule* |

SHEPHERD, CHARLES H.   B. 1847 ; D. 1886.
Org. St. Thomas's Church, Newcastle-on-Tyne.
1. Hallelujah ! what are | 2. House of Israel   *Novello*
   these   *Anthem*, 1878 | 3. O praise the Lord   ,,

SHOUBRIDGE, JAMES.   B. 1804 ; D. 1872.
Lay-Clerk of Canterbury Cath., and subsequently (1847) Vicar-Choral of St.
Paul's.   Conductor of the Cecilian Society, London, 1852.
1. He comes, He comes ! |
   Clark's " Seraphim," 1834 |

SIMPSON, JAMES F.   B. 1845 ; D. 1882.
1. Evening song of praise   *Weekes* |

SMALLWOOD, WILLIAM.   B. 1831 ; D. —.
Org. St. George's Parish Ch., Kendal, 1847.

1. All Thy works praise Thee.	8. O clap your hands.
2. Awake, awake !	9. O pray for the peace.
3. Hear my prayer.	10. Praised be the Lord daily.
4. In the beginning.	11. The Lord hath prepared.
5. I will give thanks.	12. The Lord reigneth.
6. I will magnify Thee.	13. The Lord whom ye seek *Fowle*
7. Lift up your heads.	14. Thus saith the Lord.

---

* Inauguration of monument to Crimean Heroes of Westmoreland Regiment.

SMART, HENRY THOMAS.   Born 1813 : D. 1879.
Pupil of W. H. Kearns. Org. Blackburn Parish Church, 1831-38; St. Philip's,
Regent Street, 1839; St. Luke's, Old Street, 1844; and St. Pancras,
Euston Road, 1865.   Became blind.

1. All creatures serve	Novello	11. Lord, Thou hast been	Metzler
(Part of No. 16.)		(L.C.C. Assoc., 1878.)	
2. Angels holy	Weekes	12. Now, unto Him	Curwen
3. Be glad, O ye righteous	Novello	13. O be joyful in God	Boosey
4. Behold, how good and		14. O God, the King of Glory	Novello
joyful	Carlisle	15. Oh, praise the Lord	J. Williams
5. Behold, O Lord		16. Sing, O Heavens	Novello
Organist and Choirmaster		(Part of No. 11.)	
6. Blessed is the man	Carlisle	17. Sing to the Lord	,,
7. God be merciful	Norwich	(L.C.C. Assoc., 1876.)	
8. Gracious is the Lord, and		18. The Angel Gabriel	,,
righteous	J. Williams	19. The Lord hath done	,,
9. Grant, we beseech Thee		20. The Lord is my Shepherd	Weekes
" Choralist,"	Boosey	21. The Lord is my strength	Novello
10. I saw an angel fly	Chappell	22. Unto Him that loved	Curwen
(Tercentenary of the Reformation, 1835.)		23. What are these ?	,,

SMEE, FREDERICK.   B. 18—; D. 1879.
Of the Bank of England.

1. I will magnify Thee	Novello	3. O Lord, we beseech Thee	Novello
2. Lord of all power	,,		

SMITH, ALFRED MONTEM.   B. May 13 ("Montem" Day), 1828;
D. 1891.
Tenor Vocalist and Composer. Chorister of Windsor Chapel Royal; Lay-Vicar
Westminster Abbey and Gent. of Chapel Royal, 1858; Professor of Singing
R.A.M. and Guildhall School.

1. Be ye kind one to another	Novello	4. The eyes of all wait	Chester
2. Fret not thyself	,,	5. The night is far spent	Novello
3. Lord, how long wilt Thou ?	,,		

SMITH, GEORGE TOWNSEND.   B. 1813 ; D. 1877.
Pupil of Highmore Skeats and S. Wesley. Org. Old Parish Church,
Eastbourne; St. Margaret's, Lynn; Hereford Cathedral, 1843; Conductor
and Hon. Sec. of Three Choirs Festival.

1. Behold, God is mighty	Hereford	6. O how amiable	Novello
2. Do well, O Lord	Novello	(Re-opening of Hereford	
3. Hearken unto My voice	Joule	Cathedral, 1863.)	
4. If ye then be risen	Mann	7. The souls of the righteous	Norwich
5. Lord, I call upon Thee	Novello		

SMITH, SIDNEY.   B. 1839 ; D. 1889.
Pupil at Leipzig Conservatoire of Moscheles, Plaidy, Hauptmann, and Richter,
from 1855. Settled in London as pianist and composer, 1859.
1. The Lord is great   Curwen |

SMITH, WILLIAM.   B. 1803 ; D. 1878.
1. Praise the Lord, O my
   soul   Novello |

SNEYD, Lady CHARLOTTE.

1. O God the Protector   *Marshall* |

SPARK, WILLIAM, Mus. Doc., Dublin. B. 1825 ; D. 1897.

Articled to Dr. S. S. Wesley, 1834. Org. St. Lawrence, Exeter, 1840 ; also at Tiverton, Daventry, Northampton, and St. George's Church, Leeds, 1850 ; Leeds Town Hall, 1859.

1. Abraham foresaw the Gospel day	*Wells*	6. Holy, Holy, Holy (*Male voices.*)	*Novello*
2. All we like sheep	*Novello*	7. Hosanna	*L. Mus. Publ. Co.*
3. And Thou, Child, shalt be	*Spark's List*	8. I shall see Him	*Novello*
4. Behold, O God our Defender	,,	9. Now, let us join	,,
5. Christ being raised	*Novello*	10. O God, have mercy	,,
		11. The Lord is my Shepherd	,,

SPINNEY, WALTER. B. 1852 ; D. 1894.

Pupil of J. E. Richardson and Org. of Leamington Parish Church.

1. Come up hither	*Weekes*	10. O Death, where is thy sting	*Weekes*
2. Emmanuel, Emmanuel	,,	11. Rejoice ye with Jerusalem	,,
3. God is gone up	,,	12. The Glory of the Lord	,,
4. He watereth the hills	,,	13. The Harvest is the end of the world	,,
5. How beautiful upon the mountains	,,	14. Thou shalt shew us	,,
6. I will lift up	,,	15. Thou visitest the earth	,,
7. Lead us, Heavenly Father	,,	16. Unto us a Child is born	,,
8. Lord, Thou hast been our dwelling-place	,,	17. Ye choirs of new Jerusalem	,,
9. My righteousness is near	,,	18. Ye that stand in the House of the Lord	,,

STAINER, Sir JOHN, Knight, M.A., D.C.L., Mus.D., Oxon., 1865. B. 1840 ; D. 1901.

Org. Magdalen Coll., Oxford, 1860-72; St. Paul's Cath., 1872-88. Musical Inspector to the Education Department, 1882. Professor of Music in Oxford University, 1889-99.

1. Alleluia ! O Zion that bringest.	15. Honour the Lord with thy substance.
2. Alleluia ! the hallowed day.	16. Hosanna in the highest.
3. And all the people saw.	17. I am Alpha and Omega.
4. And Jacob was left alone.	18. I desired wisdom.
5. Awake, awake, put on.	19. I saw the Lord.
6. Behold, God is my helper.	(*Double Choir.*)
7. Behold, two blind men.	20. It came upon the midnight clear.
8. Blessed is the man.	21. Jesus said unto the people.
9. Deliver me, O Lord.	22. Lead, kindly Light.
10. Drop down, ye heavens.	23. Leave us not.
11. For a small moment.	24. Let every soul be subject.
12. Grieve not the Holy Spirit.	(*For Queen Victoria's Jubilee*, 1887.)
13. Hallelujah ! what are these ?	25. Let not thine hand be stretched out.
(*Dedication Festival of All Saints' Church, Lathbury*, 1871.)	
14. Have mercy upon me (*Ps.* 51).	26. Let the peace of God.

STAINER, Sir JOHN (*continued*).

27.*Lord, Thou art God.
    (*Festival of the Sons of the Clergy.*)
28.*Lo, Summer comes again.
29. Mercy and truth are met.
30. My Maker and my King.
31.*O clap your hands.
    (*For Richmond and Kingston Church
    Choral Association*, 1873.)
32. O saving Victim.
33. O Zion, that bringest.
34. Rogate quæ ad pacem.
35. Seven of the Great Antiphons :—
(α) O Dayspring.
(β) O Emmanuel.
(γ) O Key of David.
(δ)O King and Desire.
(ε) O Lord and
        Ruler.
(ζ) O Root of Jesse.
(η) O Wisdom.

36. Sing a song of praise.
37. The Lord is in His Holy Temple.
38. The morning stars.
39. There was a marriage.
40. There was silence.
41. The righteous live.
42. The Story of the Cross.
43. They have taken away my Lord.
44. They were lovely.
45. Thou, Lord, in the beginning.
46. Thus speaketh the Lord of Hosts.
47. Ye shall dwell in the land.

All published by Novello and Co.

STANISTREET, HENRY DAWSON, Mus. Bac., Oxon., 1862 ; Mus. Doc.,
    Dublin, 1878.   B. — ; D. 1883.
Chorister of York Minster ; Org. in Bandon, Cork, and Tuam Cath., 1873.

1. How beautiful are the feet   *Fowle*
2. O how amiable   ,,
3. Thou, Lord, art my hope   *Fowle*

STEED, ALBERT ORLANDO.   B. 1839 ; D. 1881.
Composer and author of works on music.
1. Sing unto the Lord   *Novello* |

STEPHENS, CHARLES EDWARD, Hon. R.A.M.   B. 1821 ; D. 1892.
Nephew of the Countess of Essex. Pupil of C. Potter, J. A. Hamilton, and
    Henry Blagrove. Org. St. Mark's, Myddelton Square, 1843 ; Trinity Church,
    Paddington, 1846 ; St. John's, Hampstead, 1856 ; St. Mark's, Hamilton
    Terrace, 1862-63 ; St. Clement Danes, 1864-69 ; St. Saviour's, Paddington,
    1872-75.

1. O praise the Lord, all ye nations   2. We have seen His star   *Fowle*
        Novello |

STEWART, Sir ROBERT PRESCOTT, Knight, Mus. Doc., Dublin.
    B. 1825 ; D. 1894.
Org. Christ Church Cath., Dublin, 1844 ; Trinity College, 1844 ; Org.
    St. Patrick's Cath., 1852, and Vicar-Choral, 1861 ; Professor of Music,
    Dublin, 1861. Knighted 1872.

1. Blessed is He that considereth
        Mann
2. If ye love Me   *Novello*
3. In the Lord put I   ,,
4. Let your light   *Metzler*
5. Lord, who shall dwell?   *Dublin*
6. O Lord my God   ,,
7. Plead Thou my cause   ,,

8. St. Patrick's Breastplate
        Cramer & Wood
9. The King shall rejoice   *Novello*
    (*Jubilee of Queen Victoria*, 1887.)
10. Thou, O God, art praised in
        Zion   *Novello*
11. Veni Creator Spiritus   *Metzler*

* These have Orchestral Accompaniments.

STIMPSON, JAMES. B. 1820 ; D. 1886.
Chorister of Durham, 1827. Articled to R. Ingham (Carlisle), 1834. Org. St. Andrew's, Newcastle, 1836; Carlisle Cath., 1841; Town Hall, Birmingham, 1842; St. Paul's, Birmingham. Founded the Birmingham Festival Choral Society, 1843, and was its Conductor until 1855.

1. O Lord, rebuke me not   *Novello* |

Adapted "As pants the hart" to the music of "Though all thy friends prove faithless," in Spohr's "Crucifixion."

STURGES, EDWARD. B. 1808 ; D. 1848.
Chorister in St. Paul's; Org. of the Foundling Hospital.

1. I know their sorrows   *Rochester* |
                          And several "arrangements."

SULLIVAN, Sir ARTHUR SEYMOUR, Knight. Mus.D., Cantab. et Oxon.
B. 1842 ; D. 1900.
Chorister of Chapel Royal. First Mendelssohn Scholar at the R.A.M. Org. St. Michael's, Chester Square, 1867, and St. Peter's, Cranley Gardens. The most popular composer of the century.

1. Hearken unto me	*Novello*	12. The righteous live	*Norwich*
2. I will mention the loving-kindness	,,	13. The Son of God goes forth	*Novello*
3. I will worship	*Boosey*	(*Hymn Anthem, on St. Anne's Tune.*)	
4. Lord, who hath believed?	*Carlisle*	14. The strain upraise	,,
5.*Mercy and truth	*Novello*	15.*Turn Thee again	,,
6. O God, Thou art worthy	,,	16. Turn Thy face from my sins	,,
7. O love the Lord	,,	17. We have heard with our ears	,,
8. O taste and see	,,	18. Who is like unto Thee?	,,
9. Rejoice in the Lord	*Boosey*		
10. Sing, O heavens	,,		
11. Sing unto the Lord	*MSS.*		

(*His first composition, in possession of C. V. Bridgman.*)

Numbers from his oratorios are also used as Anthems.

SYDENHAM, EDWARD AUGUSTUS. B. 1847 ; D. 1891.
Org. All Saints', Scarborough, 1882.

1. Be merciful unto me	*Novello*	6. Sing unto the Lord (*Psalm* 147)	*Novello*
2. Christ is risen	,,		
3. Great is the Lord	,,	7. Spare us, Lord, most Holy	,,
4. Hearken unto my voice	,,	8. The Lord is my Light	,,
5. O give thanks	,,	9. There were shepherds	,,

TILLEARD, JAMES. B. 1827 ; D. 1876.
Composer and Musical Editor.

1. Church bells softly pealing	*Weekes*	3. Star of morn and even	*Weekes*
2. Lost and found	,,	4. Tho' Nature's strength decay	,,

TOLHURST, GEORGE. B. 1827 ; D. 1877.
Composed "Ruth," an Oratorio.

1. I will lay me down   *Fowle* |

---

* From the Music of the Russian Church.

TOURS, BERTHOLD. B. 1838 ; D. 1897.

Born in Rotterdam, but settled in London after 1861.   Student in Brussels and Leipzig Conservatoriums.   Musical Editor to Novello, Ewer & Co., 1878.

1. Behold, the Angel of the Lord	*Novello*	10. O come, let us sing	*Novello*
2. Blessed are they that dwell	,,	11. O praise the Lord, laud ye	*Mann*
3. Blessing, glory, wisdom	,	12. O saving Victim (*Motet*)	*Novello*
4. Christ our Passover	,,	13. Praise God in His Holiness	,,
5. God be merciful	,,	14. Rejoice in the Lord	,,
6. God hath appointed a day	,,	15. Sing, O Heavens	,,
7. In Thee, O Lord	,,	16. The pillars of the earth are the Lord's	,,
8. It shall come to pass	,,	17. There were shepherds	,,
9. I waited patiently	*Mann*	18. While the earth remaineth	,,

TRIMNELL, THOMAS TALLIS, Mus. Bac., Oxon.   B. 1827 ; D. 1897.

From 1886, Org. and Conductor in Wellington, N.Z., where he died.

1. A fruitful land maketh He barren	*Fowle*	7. Sing, O Heavens	*Novello*
2. I have surely built Thee	*Novello*	8. The earth is the Lord's (*Opening of Wellington (N.Z.) Exhibition*, 1896.)	,,
3. I was glad	,,		
4. Let God arise	,,	9. The Lord is King	,,
5. O clap your hands	,,	10. Thou wilt keep him	,,
6. O praise God in His Holiness	,,		

TUCKERMAN, SAMUEL PARKMAN, Mus. Doc., Cantuar.   B. 1819 ; D. 1890.

American Composer and Org.   Born in Boston, U.S.A.   Pupil of C. Zeuner.   Org. St. Paul's Church, Boston, 1841.   In England, until 1860 ; then lived in Switzerland.

1.*†And they rest not	*Novello*	8.*Lighten our darkness	*Novello*
2.*Come unto Him	,,	9.*†Their sun shall no more go down	,,
3. Come unto Me.			
4.*God so loved the world	,,	10.*Thou shalt shew me the path	,,
5. Hear my prayer.		11. Turn Thy Face from my sins	*Chester*
6. I looked, and behold a door	,,		
7. I was glad when they said	,,		

TURLE, JAMES. B. 1802 ; D. 1882.

Org. Christ Church, Blackfriars, 1819-29 ; St. James's, Bermondsey, 1829-31 ; Westminster Abbey, 1831-75.

1. Almighty and most merciful	*Novello*	4. Teach me, O Lord.	
2. Father of Life, confessing	,,	5. The Lord that made	*Novello*
3. Hear my crying, O God	,,	6. This is the day	,,

And an adaptation from Marcello ("Arise, and help us").

---

* Six Short Anthems.
† From the Anthem "I looked, and behold."

TURNER, BRADBURY, Mus. Bac., Cantab. B. 18— ; D. 1898.
Pupil at R.A.M., of Sterndale Bennett. Org. St. Mary-the-Virgin, Primrose Hill. Connected with Trinity College, London, from its foundation.

1. But my trust is in Thy mercy	*Weekes*	2. Consider and hear me	*Weekes*
		3. How long wilt Thou forget me	,,

WALKER, R. H. B. 1839 ; D. 1876.
Youngest son of J. H. Walker, Music Master at Rugby School.

1. Jerusalem is built as a city	*Lichfield*	2. Open ye the gates	*Lichfield*
		3. The ways of Zion	,,

WALLIS, EBENEZER JOHN. B. 1831 ; D. 1879.

1. Glad tidings	*Weekes*	3. Rend your heart	*Weekes*
2. If we say that we have	,,	4. The Lord is in His holy temple	,,

WALMISLEY, THOMAS ATTWOOD, M.A., Mus. Doc., Cantab. B. 1814 ; D. 1856.
Son of T. F. Walmisley and godson and pupil of Attwood. Org. Croydon Parish Church, 1830 ; Trinity and St. John's, Cambridge (following Samuel Matthews), 1833. Professor of Music in the University, 1836.

1.*Behold, O God our Defender	*Novello*	12.*O give thanks unto the Lord (*Psalm* 106)	*Novello*
2. Blessed is He that cometh	,,	13.*O God, the King of Glory	,,
3.*Blessed is he that considereth	,,	14. O Lord, we beseech Thee	(?) *St. Paul's*
4.*Father of Heaven	,,	15. Out of the deep	*King's*
5. From all that dwell	*Nat. Psal.*	16.*Ponder my words	*Novello*
6. Hail, gladdening Light	*Hullah's Vocal Scores*	17. Praise the Lord	*Hullah*
		(*Canon, 4 in 2.*)	
7.*Hear, O Thou Shepherd	*Novello*	18. Remember, O Lord	*Novello*
8.*If the Lord Himself	,,	(*Dublin prize*, 1838.)	
9. Let God arise	*Lichfield*	19.*The Lord shall comfort Zion	,,
10.*Not unto us, O Lord	*Novello*	20. The Lord shall endure	*King's*
11. O give thanks unto the Lord, and call (*Ps.* 105)	,,	21. Who can express !	*Marshall*

WATSON, WILLIAM MICHAEL. B. 1840 ; D. 1889.
Successful song-writer.

1. Come near, ye nations	*Mann*	3. Praise the Lord	*Patey & Willis*
2. Hear, O Lord	*Patey & Willis*		(*Lute series.*)
	(*Lute series.*)		

---

* Published in the volume of his Cathedral music, edited by his father, Thos. Forbes Walmisley, 1857.

WESLEY, SAMUEL SEBASTIAN, Mus. Doc., Oxon. B. 1810 ; D. 1876.
Son of Samuel Wesley. Org. St. James's, Hampstead Road, 1819 ; St. Giles's,
Camberwell ; St. John's, Waterloo Road, 1828 ; Hampton Parish Church,
1831 ; Org. Hereford, 1833, after Clarke-Whitfeld ; Exeter, 1835, after
James Paddon ; Parish Church, Leeds, 1842 ; Winchester Cath. and
College, 1849, after Dr. Chard ; and Gloucester, 1865, after John Amott.

1. All go to one place	*Novello*	18. Lord of all power and	
(*On the death of the Prince*		might	*Metzler*
Consort.)		19.*Man that is born	*Novello*
3. Almighty God, give us grace	,,	20.*O give thanks unto the	
2.*Ascribe unto the Lord	,,	Lord	,,
4.*Blessed be the God and		21.*O God, whose nature	,,
Father	,,	22. O how amiable	*Weekes*
5. Blessed be the Lord God		23. O Lord Jesus Christ	*Chap. Roy.*
of Israel	,,	24.*O Lord my God (*Solomon's*	
6. Blessed is the man	*Durham*	*Prayer*)	*Novello*
7. Blessed Lord, Who hast		25.*O Lord, Thou art my God	,,
caused	*Novello*	(*Degree Exercise*, 1839)	
8. By the Word of God.		26. O remember not	,,
(*Opening of Winchester Cath.*		27. Praise the Lord, O my soul	,,
Organ.)		28. The bruised reed	*Nat. Psal.*
9.*Cast me not away	,,	29. The Face of the Lord	*Novello*
10. Give the King	,,	30. The Lord is my Shepherd	*Weekes*
11. Glory be to God on high	,,	31.*The wilderness	*Novello*
12. God be merciful	,,	32.*Thou Judge of quick and	
13. I am Thine, O save	,,	dead	,,
14. I will arise	,,	(*Part of No. 16.*)	
15. I will magnify Thee	*Chester*	33.*Thou wilt keep him	,,
16.*Let us lift up our heart	*Novello*	34. Trust ye in the Lord *MSS., Exeter*	
17. Let us now praise famous		35.*Wash me throughly	*Novello*
men	*Weekes*	36. Wherewithal shall a young	
		man ?	*Weekes*

WESTBROOK, WILLIAM JOSEPH, Mus. Doc., Cantab. B. 1831 ; D. 1894.
Org., Composer, and Arranger for the organ. Org. St. Bartholomew,
Bethnal Green, 1849 ; St. Bartholomew, Sydenham, 1851-84. Established
(with A. W. Hammond and John Crowdy) the *Musical Standard*, 1862.

1. God be merciful unto us	*Novello*	7. O God, Thou art my God.	
2. Holy, Holy, Holy.		8. O God, Who by the leading	
3. If ye love me.	"*Lute*"	of a star.	
4. I saw the Lord.		9. Rejoice in the Lord (1865).	
5. Let them give thanks.		10. Set up Thyself, O God.	
6. Now is Christ risen.		11. With hearts renewed.	

WESTROP, HENRY. B. 1812 ; D. 1879.
Org. St. Stephen's, Norwich; Little Stanmore, 1831; Fitzroy Chapel, 1833;
St. Edmund, King and Martyr, 1834. Violinist and Conductor.
1. O taste and see. |

WILKINS, GEORGE. B. 1806 ; D. 1897.
Org. Ilfracombe Parish Church, 1828 ; St. Nicholas, Guildford, 1837 ; Stoke
Parish Church, 1871 ; Christ Church, Stoke, 1878.
1. Christ our Passover   *Novello* | 2. The Lord is King *Salisbury*, 1852

---

* These were also printed collectively by Hall and Virtue, 1853, in *score*.

WILKINSON, GEORGE. B. 1808 ; D. 1857.
Of Huddersfield.
1. The Lord is full of compassion *Joule* |

WINTERBOTTOM, JOSEPH. B. 1815 ; D. 1859.
Org. St. James's Church, East Crompton, Lancashire.
1. Thou wilt keep him   *Joule* |

WINTLE, Rev. OGLE RICHARD, M.A. B. — ; D. *c.* 1860.
Master at Uppingham School, and afterwards Head Master of Bridgwater
Grammar School.
1. Come, My people   *Novello* | 2. O praise the Lord with me *Novello*

WOOD, WILLIAM G. B. 1859 ; D. 1895.
Educated at the R.A.M. Org. St. Mary's, Hornsey Rise, and Highgate
School.
1. O praise the Lord   *Novello* | 2. Praise the Lord, O Jerusalem
                                     (s. *Solo and Chorus.*) *Novello*

WRAY, Rev. HENRY. B. — ; D. 1879.
Precentor of Winchester Cath. ; Vicar of Holt, Denbighshire.
1. Come unto Me   *Novello* |

YATES, CHARLES JAMES. B. 1820 ; D. 1889.
Org. St. George's Church, Preston.
1. I will magnify Thee   *Joule* | 2. Unto Thee, O Lord   *Joule*

YOUNG, JOHN MATTHEW WILSON. B. 1822 ; D. 1897.
Pupil of Henshaw. Org. Lincoln Cath., 1850.
1. Holy Eternal Spirit *Lincoln MSS.* | 5. Sing with gladness   *Novello*
2. I will extol my God   *Novello* | ("*Return of Israel to Palestine*")
3. O Lord God of my salvation ,, | 6. The wilderness   *Novello*
4. O Lord Thou art great   ,, | (*Part II. of the same work.*)

ZOELLER, CARLI. B. 1840 ; D. 1889.
Studied in Berlin, but settled in England 1873. Bandmaster of the 2nd Life
Guards and 7th Hussars, 1879. Fine player on the viola d'amore.
1. Bless the Lord, O my soul. | 3. The hosts of heaven.
2. O Lord, who dwellest on
   high o'er the Cherubim   *Klein* |

FOREIGN MUSICIANS.

BENEDICT, Sir JULIUS, Knight. B. 1804 ; D. 1885.
Pianist, Composer, and Conductor. Conducted Liverpool Festival, 1874.
1. God is our hope   *Novello* | 4. Praise the Lord, call   *Novello*
2. Like to the grass that's | 5. Tremble, thou earth   ,,
   newly sprung   ,, | 6. Try me, O God   ,,
3. Not unto us, O Lord   *Metzler* |

Numbers from " St. Peter " are used as Anthems.

GOUNOD, CHARLES FRANÇOIS. B. 1818; D. 1893.

1. All ye who weep.
2. As the hart pants.
3. Blessed is He.
4. By Babylon's wave.
5. Come unto Him.
6. Daughter of Jerusalem.
7. Jesu, blessed word.
8. Jesu our Lord.
9. O come near to the Cross.
10. O Day of Penitence.
11. O saving Victim.
12. O sing to God (Noël).
13. Out of darkness.
14. Send out Thy light *Metzler*
15. Sing praises unto the Lord.
16. The seven last words.
17. While my watch I am keeping.
18. Word of God incarnate.

All published by Novello. Several numbers from " Redemption," " Gallia," " Mors et Vita," &c., are used as Anthems.

MAINZER, Abbé JOSEPH. B. 1801 (1807); D. 1851.

Studied (Trèves Coll.) under Kinck, Seyfried, and Stadler. Ordained Priest, 1826. Came to England 1839. Resided at Manchester as teacher of the Wilhelm method, and writer.

1. Entreat me not to leave thee
   Novello |

MENDELSSOHN-BARTHOLDY, JAKOB LUDWIG FELIX. B. 1809; D. 1847.

1. Above all praise.
2. As the hart pants.
3. Come, let us sing.
4. For ever blessed.
5. For our offences.
6. Grant us Thy peace.
7. Hear my prayer.
8. In deep distress.
9. Judge me, O God.
   (*Double Choir*.)
10. Let our hearts be joyful.
11. Lord, bow down Thine ear.
12. Lord, how long wilt Thou forget?
13. Man is mortal.
14. My God, O why hast Thou?
    (*Double Choir*.)
15. Not unto us, O Lord.
16. Rejoice, O ye people.
17. Saviour of sinners.
18. Saw ye not the pallid angel.
19. Sing to the Lord.
    (*Double Choir*.)
20. The righteous living for ever.
21. The word went forth.
22. Thou, Lord, our refuge.
23. When Israel out of Egypt.
24. Why rage fiercely the heathen?
    (*Double Choir*.)

Excerpts from his Oratorios are employed as Anthems.

ANONYMOUS.

NOVELLO'S WORDS OF ANTHEMS.

1. O Rex Gloriæ. |

COLLECTION OF ANTHEMS, 1878.

1. Awake, thou that sleepest. |

THE END.

JOSEPH BARNBY.

INDEX OF COMPOSERS.

SIXTEENTH CENTURY.

SEVENTEENTH CENTURY.

EIGHTEENTH CENTURY.

NINETEENTH CENTURY.

INDEX OF ANTHEMS.

JOHN STAINER.

* Handel, with imperfect knowledge of our language, entitled his Anthem on p. 72, "Blessed are they that considereth."